D0837022

Norwegian
phrase book

Easy to use features
- Handy thematic colour coding
- Quick Reference Section—opposite page
- Tipping Guide—inside back cover
- Quick reply panels throughout

Berlitz Publishing Company, Inc.

Princeton   Mexico City   London   Eschborn   Singapore

How best to use this phrase book

● We suggest that you start with the **Guide to pronunciation** (pp. 6–9), then go on to **Some basic expressions** (pp. 10–15). This gives you not only a minimum vocabulary, but also helps you get used to pronouncing the language. The phonetic transcription throughout the book enables you to pronounce every word correctly.

● Consult the **Contents** pages (3–5) for the section you need. In each chapter you'll find travel facts, hints and useful information. Simple phrases are followed by a list of words applicable to the situation.

● Separate, detailed contents lists are included at the beginning of the extensive **Eating out** and **Shopping guide** sections (Menus, p. 39, Shops and services, p. 97).

● If you want to find out how to say something in Norwegian, your fastest look-up is via the **Dictionary** section (pp. 164–189). This not only gives you the word, but is also cross-referenced to its use in a phrase on a specific page.

● If you wish to learn more about constructing sentences, check the **Basic grammar** (pp. 159–163).

● Note the **colour margins** are indexed in Norwegian and English to help both listener and speaker. Additionally, there is an **index in Norwegian** for the use of your listener.

● Throughout the book, this symbol ☞ suggests phrases your listener can use to answer you. If you still can't understand, hand this phrase book to the Norwegian-speaker to encourage pointing to an appropriate answer. The English translation for you is just alongside the Norwegian.

Second Revised edition-Twelfth printing-August 2001
Printed in Spain

Contents

Acknowledgments
We are particularly grateful to Dr. T.J.A. Bennett who devised the phonetic transcription of this book.

Guide to pronunciation

You'll find the pronunciation of Norwegian letters and sounds—based on the Oslo accent—explained below, as well as the symbols we use in the transcriptions. The imitated pronunciation should be read as if it were English, with exceptions as indicated below. It is based on Standard British pronunciation, though we have tried to take into account General American pronunciation as well. If you follow the instructions carefully, you'll have no difficulty in reading our transcriptions so as to make yourself understood.

In the phonetic transcription, some letters are placed in parentheses, e.g. meh(d). In daily conversation, these are rarely pronounced, although it is certainly not incorrect to do so. A bar over a vowel symbol indicates a long sound, usually a pure vowel, not a diphthong (see explanations below). Syllables printed in **bold type** should be stressed.

Consonants

Letter	Approximate pronunciation	Symbol	Example	
b, c, d, f, h, l, m, n, p, q, t, v, x	as in English			
g	1) before **ei, i** and **y**, generally like **y** in yes	y	**gi**	yee
	2) before **e** and **i** in some words of French origin, like **sh** in shut	sh	**geni**	sheh**nee**
	3) elsewhere, like **g** in go	g	**gått**	got
gj	like **y** in yes	y	**gjest**	yehst
j	like **y** in yes	y	**ja**	yaa
k	1) before **i,** and **y,** generally like **ch** in German ich (quite like **h** in huge, but with the tongue raised a little higher)	kh	**kino**	**khee**noo
	2) elsewhere, like **k** in kit	k	**kaffe**	**kah**fer

kj	like **ch** in German i**ch** (quite like **h** in huge, but with the tongue raised a little higher)	kh	**kjøre**	kh$\overline{u}$rrer
r	rolled near the front of the mouth (except in south-western Norway, where it's pronounced in the back of the mouth, like in French)	r	**rare**	raarer
rs	like **sh** in shut	sh	**norsk**	noshk
s	like **s** in sit	s/ss	**spise**	speesser
sj	generally like **sh** in shut	sh	**stasjon**	stahsh$\overline{oo}$n
sk	1) before **i**, **y** and **ø**, gene-rally like **sh** in shut	sh	**ski**	shee
	2) elsewhere, like **sk** in skate	sk	**skole**	sk$\overline{oo}$ler
skj	like **sh** in shut	sh	**skje**	sh$\overline{ay}$
w	like **v** in vice	v	**whisky**	viski
z	like **s** in sit	s	**zoom**	s$\overline{oo}$m

If preceded by **r**, the consonants **l**, **n** and **t** (and sometimes **d**) are pronounced with the tip of the tongue turned up well behind the front teeth. The **r** then ceases to be pronounced, but influences the tone of the following consonant. We indicate this pronunciation by printing a small **r** above the line (e.g. pah^{r}t). (This "retroflex" pronunciation also occurs in words ending with an **r** if the following word begins with a **d**, **l**, **n**, **s** or **t**.)

Silent consonants

1. The letter **d** is generally silent after **l**, **n** or **r** (e.g. ho**ld**e, la**nd**, gå**rd**).
2. The letter **g** is silent in the endings -**lig** and -**ig**.
3. The letter **h** is silent when followed by a consonant (e.g. **hj**em, **hv**a).
4. The letter **t** is silent in the definite form ("the") of neuter nouns (e.g. eple**t**) and in the pronoun de**t**.
5. The letter **v** is silent in certain words (e.g. sel**v**, tol**v**, hal**v**).

Vowels

In Norwegian, a vowel is generally long in stressed syllables when it's the final letter or followed by one consonant only, and short if followed by two or more consonants.

a	1) when long, like **a** in car	aa	**dag** daag
	2) when short, between **a** in cat and **u** in cut	ah	**takk** tahk
e	1) when long, like **ay** in say, but a pure vowel, not a diphthong	a̅y	**sent** sa̅ynt
	2) when followed by **r**, often like **a** in a man (long or short)	æ̅	**her** hæ̅r
	3) when short, like **e** in get	eh	**herre** hæ̅rer
			penn pehn
	4) when unstressed, like **a** in about	er *	**betale** bertaaler
i	1) when long, like **ee** in bee	ee	**hit** heet
	2) when short, like **i** in sit	i	**sitt** sit
o	1) when long, often like **oo** in soon, but with the lips more tightly rounded	o̅o̅	**ord** o̅or
	2) the same sound can be short, like **oo** in foot	oo	**ost** oost
	3) when long, sometimes like **aw** in saw	aw	**·tog** tawg
	4) when short, sometimes like **o** in got (British pronunciation)	o	**stoppe** stopper
u	1) something like **ew** in few, or Scottish **oo** in good (long or short); since it is very close to the Norwegian **y**-sound, we use the same symbol for both	e̅w	**mur** me̅wr
		ew	**busk** bewsk
	2) occasionally like **oo** in foot	oo	**nummer** noommerr
y	very much like the sound described under **u** (1) above (long or short); put your tongue in the position for the **ee** in bee, and then round your lips as for the **oo** in pool	e̅w	**by** be̅w
		ew	**bygge** bewger

---

* The **r** should not be pronounced when reading this transcription.

æ	like a in act (long or short)	ǣ æ	lære færre	lǣrer færer
ø	like ur in fur, but with the lips rounded (long or short)	ūr * ur *	dør sønn	dūrr surn
å	1) when long, like aw in saw 2) when short, like o in got (British pronunciation)	aw o	såpe sånn	sawper son

Diphthongs

au	rather like ou in loud, though the first part is the Norwegian æ-sound	ou	sau	sou
ei, eg, egn	like ai in wait, though the first part is the Norwegian æ-sound	æi	geit jeg tegne	yæit yæi tæiner
øy	rather like oy in boy, though the first part is the Norwegian ø-sound	oy	gøy	goy

Intonation

Norwegian uses intonation (tones) to distinguish between certain words. Since no one expects a foreigner to master such subtleties, these tones are not shown in our transcriptions.

Pronunciation of the Norwegian alphabet							
A	aa	I	ee	Q	kew̄	X	ehkss
B	bāy	J	yod	R	ær	Y	ēw
C	sāy	K	kaw	S	ehss	Z	seht
D	dāy	L	ehl	T	tāy	Æ	ǣ
E	āy	M	ehm	U	ēw	Ø	ūr
F	ehf	N	ehn	V	vāy	Å	aw
G	gāy	O	ōo	W	dobberlt-		
H	haw	P	pāy		vāy		

---

* The r should not be pronounced when reading this transcription.

Some basic expressions

Yes.	**Ja.**	yaa
No.	**Nei.**	næi
Please.	**Vær (så) snill å ... /** **..., takk.**	vǣr (saw) snil aw / ... tahk
Thank you.	**Takk.**	tahk
Thank you very much.	**Mange takk.**	**mahng**er tahk
That's all right / You're welcome.	**Ingen årsak.**	**ing**ern **aw**shaak

Greetings *Hilsning*

Good morning.	**God morgen.**	goo**maw**er'n
Good afternoon.	**God dag.**	goo**daag**
Good evening.	**God aften / God** **kveld.**	goo(d)**ahf**tern / goo**kvehl**
Good night.	**God natt.**	goo**naht**
Goodbye.	**Adjø.**	ah**dyūr**
See you later.	**På gjensyn / Vi ses.**	paw **yehns**ēwn / vee **sāyss**
Hello / Hi!	**Hallo / Hei!**	hah**lōō** / **hæi**
How do you do? (Pleased to meet you.)	**God dag.**	goo**daag**
How are you?	**Hvordan står det** **til?**	**voo**'dahn stawr deh til
Very well, thanks. And you?	**Bare bra, takk.** **Og med deg?**	**baa**rer braa tahk. o(g) meh(d) dæi
Fine.	**Bra, takk.**	braa tahk
I beg your pardon?	**Unnskyld?**	**ewn**shewl
Excuse me. (May I get past?)	**Unnskyld.**	**ewn**shewl
Sorry!	**Beklager!**	ber**klaag**err

INTRODUCTIONS, see page 92

Questions *Spørsmål*

Where?	**Hvor?**	voor
How?	**Hvordan/Hvor?**	voo^rdahn/voor
When?	**Når?**	nor
What?	**Hva?**	vaa
Why?	**Hvorfor?**	voorfor
Who?	**Hvem?**	vehm
Which?	**Hvilken*?**	vilkern
Where is ...?	**Hvor er ...?**	voor ær
Where are ...?	**Hvor er ...?**	voor ær
Where can I find ...?	**Hvor finner jeg ...?**	voor finnerr yæi
Where can I get ...?	**Hvor kan jeg få tak i ...?**	voor kahn yæi faw taak ee
How far?	**Hvor langt?**	voor lahngt
How long?	**Hvor lenge?**	voor lehnger
How much?	**Hvor mye?**	voor mēwer
How many?	**Hvor mange?**	voor mahnger
How much does this cost?	**Hvor mye koster dette**?**	voor mēwer kosterr dehter
How do I get to ...?	**Hvordan kommer jeg til ...?**	voo^rdahn kommerr yæi til
When does ... open/close?	**Når åpner/ stenger ...?**	nor awpnerr/ stehngerr
What do you call this/that in Norwegian?	**Hva heter dette/ det på norsk?**	vaa hāyterr dehter/ deh paw noshk
What does this/ that mean?	**Hva betyr dette/ det?**	vaa bertēwr dehter/deh
Who's that?	**Hvem er det?**	vehm ær deh
Which bus goes to ...?	**Hvilken buss går til ...?**	vilkern bewss gawr til

---

* Common gender; neuter = *hvilket*; plural = *hvilke*.
** Neuter; common gender = *denne*; plural = *disse* (see also grammar section, page 161).

Do you speak ...? *Snakker du ...?*

Do you speak English?	**Snakker du engelsk?**	snahkerr dew ehngerlsk
Does anyone here speak English?	**Er det noen her som snakker engelsk?**	ær deh nooern hær som snahkerr ehngerlsk
I don't speak (much) Norwegian.	**Jeg snakker ikke (så bra) norsk.**	yæi snahkerr ikker (saw braa) noshk
Could you speak more slowly?	**Kan du snakke litt langsommere?**	kahn dew snahker lit lahngsommerrer
Could you repeat that?	**Kan du gjenta det?**	kahn dew yehntah deh
Could you spell it?	**Kan du stave det?**	kahn dew staaver deh
How do you pronounce this?	**Hvordan uttaler du dette?**	voo^rdahn ēwtahlerr dew dehter
Could you write it down, please?	**Kan du skrive det ned, er du snill?**	kahn dew skreever deh nāy(d) ær dew snil
Can you translate this for me/us?	**Kan du oversette dette for meg/oss?**	kahn dew awvershehter dehter for mæi/oss
Could you point to the ... in the book?	**Kan du peke på ... i boken?**	kahn dew pāyker paw ... ee bookern
phrase	**uttrykket ***	ēwtrewker
sentence	**setningen**	sehtningern
word	**ordet**	oorer
Just a moment.	**Et øyeblikk.**	eht oyerblik
I'll see if I can find it in this book.	**Jeg skal se om jeg kan finne det i denne boken.**	yæi skahl sāy om yæi kahn finner deh ee dehner bookern
I understand.	**Jeg forstår.**	yæi foshtawr
I don't understand.	**Jeg forstår ikke.**	yæi foshtawr ikker
Do you understand?	**Forstår du?**	foshtawr dew

Can/May ...? *Kan ...?*

Can I have ...?	**Kan jeg få ...?**	kahn yæi faw
Can we have ...?	**Kan vi få ...?**	kahn vee faw

---

* For information on the definite article, see grammar section, page 159.

Can you show me ...?	**Kan du vise meg ...?**	kahn dew **vee**sser mæi
I can't.	**Jeg kan ikke.**	yæi kahn **ik**ker
Can you tell me ...?	**Kan du si meg ...?**	kahn dew see mæi
Can you help me?	**Kan du hjelpe meg?**	kahn dew **yehl**per mæi
Can I help you?	**Kan jeg hjelpe deg?**	kahn yæi **yehl**per dæi
Can you direct me to ...?	**Kan du vise meg veien til ...?**	kahn dew **vee**sser mæi **væi**ern til

Do you want ...? *Ønsker du ...?*

I'd like to ...	**Jeg vil gjerne ...**	yæi vil y**ǣ**ʳner
We'd like to ...	**Vi vil gjerne ...**	vee vil y**ǣ**ʳner
I'd like a ...	**Jeg vil gjerne ha en/et ...**	yæi vil y**ǣ**ʳner haa ehn/eht
Could you bring/ give me ...?	**Kan du gi meg ...?**	kahn dew yee mæi
Could you show me ...?	**Kan du vise meg ...?**	kahn dew **vee**sser mæi
I'm looking for ...	**Jeg ser etter ...**	yæi s**āy**r ehterr
I'm searching for ...	**Jeg leter etter ...**	yæi l**āy**terr ehterr
I'm hungry.	**Jeg er sulten.**	yæi ær **sewl**tern
I'm thirsty.	**Jeg er tørst.**	yæi ær tursht
I'm tired.	**Jeg er trett.**	yæi ær treht
I'm lost.	**Jeg hat gått meg bort.**	yæi haar got mæi boo**ʳ**t
It's important.	**Det er viktig.**	deh ær **vik**ti
It's urgent.	**Det haster.**	deh **hah**sterr

It is/There is ... *Det er ...*

It is ...	**Det er ...**	deh ær
Is it ...?	**Er det ...?**	ær deh
It isn't ...	**Det er ikke ...**	deh ær **ik**ker
Here it is.	**Her er det/den.**	hǣr ær deh/dehn
Here they are.	**Her er de.**	hǣr ær dee

There it is.	**Der er det.**	dǣr ær deh
There they are.	**Der er de.**	dǣr ær dee
There is/are ...	**Det er ...**	deh ær
Is/Are there ...?	**Er det ...?**	ær deh
There isn't/aren't ...	**Det er ikke ...**	deh ær ikker
There isn't any.	**Det er ikke noe.**	deh ær ikker nōōer
There aren't any.	**Det er ikke noen.**	deh ær ikker nōōern

Opposites *Motsetninger*

beautiful/ugly	**pen/stygg***	pāyn/stewg
better/worse	**bedre/verre**	bāydrer/værer
big/small	**stor/liten**	stōōr/leetern
cheap/expensive	**billig/dyr**	billi/dēwr
early/late	**tidlig/sen**	teeli/sāyn
easy/difficult	**lett/vanskelig**	leht/vahnskerli
free (vacant)/ occupied	**ledig/opptatt**	lāydi/optaht
full/empty	**full/tom**	fewl/tom
good/bad	**bra/dårlig**	braa/dāw^rli
heavy/light	**tung/lett**	toong/leht
here/there	**her/der**	hǣr/dǣr
hot/cold	**varm/kald**	vahrm/kahl
near/far	**nær/fjern**	nǣr/fyǣ^rn
next/last	**neste/siste**	nehster/sister
old/new	**gammel/ny**	gahmerl/nēw
old/young	**gammel/ung**	gahmerl/oong
open/shut	**åpen/stengt**	awpern/stehngt
quick/slow	**rask/sakte**	rahsk/sahkter
right/wrong	**riktig/feil**	rikti/fæil

Quantities *Mengde*

a little/a lot	**lite/mye**	leeter/mēwer
few/a few	**få/noen (få)**	faw/nōōern (faw)
much/many	**mye/mange**	mēwer/mahnger
more/less	**mer/mindre**	māyr/mindrer
more than/less than	**mer enn/mindre enn**	māyr ehn/mindrer ehn

---

* For neuter and plural forms, see grammar section, page 160 (adjectives).

| enough/too much | **nok/for mye** | nok/for mēwer |
| some/any | **litt, noe(n)/noe(n)** | lit, nōōer(n)/nōōer(n) |

A few more useful words   *Noen flere nyttige ord*

above	**over**	awverr
after	**etter**	ehterr
and	**og**	o(g)
at	**ved**	veh(d)
before	**før**	fūrr
behind	**bak**	baak
below	**under**	ewnerr
between	**mellom**	mehlom
but	**men**	mehn
down/downstairs	**ned/nede**	nāy(d)/nāyder
during	**i løpet av**	ee lūrper(t) ahv
for	**for**	for
from	**fra**	fraa
in	**i**	ee
inside	**inne**	inner
never	**aldri**	ahldri
next to	**ved siden av**	veh(d) seedern ahv
none	**ingen**	ingern
not	**ikke**	ikker
nothing	**ingenting, ikke noe**	ingernting, ikker nōōer
now	**nå**	naw
on	**på**	paw
only	**bare**	baarer
or	**eller**	ehlerr
outside	**ute**	ēwter
perhaps	**kanskje**	kahnsher
since	**siden**	seedern
soon	**snart**	snaaʳt
then	**da**	dah/daa
through	**gjennom**	yehnom
to	**til**	til
too (also)	**også**	osso
towards	**mot**	mōot
under	**under**	ewnerr
until	**til**	til
up/upstairs	**opp/oppe**	op/opper
very	**meget**	māygert
with	**med**	meh(d)
without	**uten**	ēwtern
yet	**ennå**	ehnaw

Arrival

Passport control   *Passkontroll*

Here's my passport.	**Her er passet mitt.**	hǣr ær **pah**sser mit
I'll be staying ...	**Jeg kommer til å bli ...**	yæi **kom**merr til aw blee
a few days	**noen dager**	nōōern **daa**gerr
a week	**en uke**	ehn **ēw**ker
a month	**en måned**	ehn **maw**nerd
I don't know yet.	**Jeg vet ikke ennå.**	yæi vāyt **ik**ker eh**naw**
I'm here on holiday (vacation).	**Jeg er her på ferie.**	yæi ær hǣr paw **fāy**ryer
I'm here on business.	**Jeg er her i forretninger.**	yæi ær hǣr ee for**reht**ningerr
I'm just passing through.	**Jeg er bare på gjennomreise.**	yæi ær **baa**rer paw **yehn**nomrǣisser

If things become difficult:

| I'm sorry, I don't understand. | **Jeg beklager, men jeg forstår ikke.** | yæi ber**klaa**gerr mehn yæi fosh**tawr ik**ker |
| Does anyone here speak English? | **Er det noen her som snakker engelsk?** | ær deh nōōern hǣr som **snah**kerr **ehn**gerlsk |

> **TOLL**
> CUSTOMS

After collecting your baggage at the airport (*flyplassen*— flēw plahssern), you have a choice: use the green exit if you have nothing to declare, or leave via the red exit if you have items to declare.

> **varer å fortolle**
> goods to declare

> **ingenting å fortolle**
> nothing to declare

The chart below shows what you can bring in duty (tax) free (the allowances in parentheses are for non-European residents).*

Cigarettes	Cigars	Tobacco	Spirits	Wine
200 (400)	or 250 g. (500 g.)	or 250 g. (500 g.)	1 l. (1 l.	and 1 l. and 1 l.)

I have nothing to declare.	**Jeg har ikke noe å fortolle.**	yæi haar **ikker** nōōer aw fo**r**toller
I have ...	**Jeg har ...**	yæi haar
a carton of cigarettes	**en kartong sigaretter**	ehn kah**r**tong siggah**reh**terr
a bottle of whisky	**en flaske whisky**	ehn **flah**sker viski
That's for my personal use.	**Det er til personlig bruk.**	deh ær til pæ**shōō**nli brēwk
This is a gift.	**Dette er en gave.**	**deh**ter ær ehn **gaa**ver

Passet, takk.	Your passport, please.
Har du noe å fortolle?	Do you have anything to declare?
Vær snill å åpne denne bagen.	Please open this bag.
Du må betale toll for dette.	You'll have to pay duty (tax) on this.
Har du mer bagasje?	Do you have any more luggage?

---

* All allowances are subject to change.

Baggage—Porter *Bagasje – Bærer*

Where are the luggage trolleys (carts)?	**Hvor er bagasje-trallene?**	voor ær bahgaasher-trahlerner
Porter!	**Bærer!**	bǣrerr
Please take this luggage.	**Vær så snill å ta denne bagasjen.**	vær saw snil aw taa dehner bahgaashern
That's my suitcase/bag.	**Det er min koffert/bag.**	deh ær meen koofferᵣt/''bag''
That one is mine.	**Den der er min.**	dehn dǟr ær meen
Please take this to the ...	**Vær så snill å ta dette til ...**	vær saw snil aw taa dehter til
bus	**bussen**	bewssern
information desk	**informasjons-skranken**	informahshōōns-skrahngkern
luggage lockers	**oppbevarings-boksene**	opbervaaringsbokserner
taxi	**drosjen**	droshern
How much is that?	**Hvor mye blir det?**	voor mēwer bleer deh
There's one suitcase missing.	**Det mangler en koffert.**	deh mahnglerr ehn koofferᵣt

Changing money *Valutaveksling*

Where's the currency exchange office?	**Hvor er vekslings-kontoret?**	voor ær vehkshlings-koontōōrer
Can you change these traveller's cheques (checks)?	**Kan du veksle disse reisesjekkene?**	kahn dew vehkshler disser ræissershehkerner
I'd like to change some ...	**Jeg vil gjerne veksle noen ...**	yæi vil yǣᵣner vehkshler nōōern
dollars	**dollar**	dollahr
pounds	**pund**	pewn
Can you change this into Norwegian kroner?	**Kan du veksle dette til norske kroner?**	kahn dew vehkshler dehter til noshker krōōnerr
What's the exchange rate?	**Hva er vekslings-kursen?**	vaa ær vehkshlings-kewshern

BANK—CURRENCY, see page 129

Where ...?   *Hvor ...?*

Where is the ...?	**Hvor er ...?**	voor ær
booking office	**billettkontoret**	bill**eh**tkoont**ōō**rer
duty (tax)-free shop	**tax-free-butikken**	t**ah**ks-free-bewtikkern
newsstand	**aviskiosken**	ahv**ee**skhyoskern
restaurant	**restauranten**	rehstewr**ah**ngern
Where can I hire (rent) a car?	**Hvor kan jeg leie en bil?**	voor kahn yæi l**æ**ier ehn beel
Where can I get a taxi?	**Hvor kan jeg få tak i en drosje?**	voor kahn yæi faw taak ee ehn drosher
How do I get to ...?	**Hvordan kommer jeg til ...?**	voo^rdahn **kom**merr yæi til
Is there a bus into town?	**Går det en buss inn til byen?**	gawr deh ehn bewss in til b**ēw**ern

Hotel reservation   *Værelsesbestilling*

Do you have a hotel guide (directory)?	**Har du en hotell-fortegnelse?**	haar dew ehn hoot**eh**l-fo^rtæinerlser
Could you reserve a room for me?	**Kan du bestille et rom til meg?**	kahn dew berstiller eht room til mæi
in the centre	**i sentrum**	ee **seh**ntrewm
near the airport	**i nærheten av flyplassen**	ee n**æ**rhehtern ahv fl**ew**plahssern
near the railway station	**i nærheten av jernbanestasjonen**	ee n**æ**rhehtern ahv yæ^rnbaanerstah-sh**ōō**nern
a single room	**et enkeltrom**	eht **eh**ngkerltroom
a double room	**et dobbeltrom**	eht **dob**berltroom
not too expensive	**ikke for dyrt**	**ik**ker for d**ēw**^rt
I'll be staying from ... to ...	**Jeg kommer til å bli fra ... til ...**	yæi **kom**merr til aw blee fraa ... til
Where is the hotel?	**Hvor er hotellet?**	voor ær hoot**eh**ler
Can you recommend a guesthouse?	**Kan du anbefale et pensjonat?**	kahn dew **ah**nberfahler eht pahngshoon**aa**t
Are there any flats (apartments) vacant?	**Fins det noen ledige leiligheter?**	finss deh n**ōō**ern l**ay**-deeyer læilihehterr
Do you have a street map?	**Har du et kart over byen?**	haar dew eht kah^rt **aw**verr b**ēw**ern

HOTEL/ACCOMMODATION, see page 22

Car hire (rental) *Bilutleie*

To hire a car you must produce a valid driving licence, that you have held for at least one year, and your passport. Some firms set a minimum age of 21, others 23, 25 or 30 depending on the vehicle's engine size. Most companies require a deposit, but this is waived if you present a recognized credit card.

I'd like to hire (rent) a car.	**Jeg vil gjerne leie en bil.**	yæi vil yǣ'ner læier ehn beel
small	**liten**	leetern
medium-sized	**mellomstor**	mehlomstōōr
large	**stor**	stōōr
automatic	**med automatgir**	meh(d) outoomaatgeer
I'd like it for ...	**Jeg vil ha den ...**	yæi vil haa dehn
a day	**en dag**	ehn daag
a week	**en uke**	ehn ēwker
Are there any weekend arrangements?	**Fins det noen weekend-tilbud?**	finss deh nōōern veekehnd-tilbēwd
Do you have any special rates?	**Har dere noen spesialpriser?**	haar dāyrer nōōern spehsseeaalpreesserr
What's the charge ...?	**Hvor mye koster det ...?**	voor mēwer kosterr deh
per day	**pr. dag**	pær daag
per week	**pr. uke**	pær ēwker
Is mileage included?	**Er kjørelengden inkludert?**	ær khūrrerlehngdern inklewdāy't
What's the charge per kilometre?	**Hvor mye koster det pr. kilometer?**	voor mēwer kosterr deh pær khilloomayterr
I'd like to leave the car in ...	**Jeg vil gjerne levere bilen tilbake i ...**	yæi vil yǣ'rer lehvāyrer beelern tilbaaker ee
I'd like full insurance.	**Jeg vil ha full forsikring.**	yæi vil haa fewl foshikring
How much is the deposit?	**Hvor mye må jeg betale i depositum?**	voor mēwer maw yæi bertaaler ee dehpōōssitewm
I have a credit card.	**Jeg har kredittkort.**	yæi haar krehditko't
Here's my driving licence.	**Her er førerkortet mitt.**	hǣr ær fūrrerko'ter mit

CAR, see page 75

Taxi *Drosje/Taxi*

All taxis are metered. When they are free, the "Taxi" sign on the roof is illuminated. Drivers rarely cruise for passengers and are not allowed to pick up customers within 100 metres of a taxi rank (those waiting at the rank have priority).

Where can I get a taxi?	**Hvor kan jeg få tak i en drosje?**	voor kahn yæi faw taak ee ehn drosher
Where is the taxi rank (stand)?	**Hvor er drosje-holdeplassen?**	voor ær drosher-hollerplahssern
Could you get me a taxi?	**Kan du skaffe meg en drosje?**	kahn dew skahfer mæi ehn drosher
What's the fare to ...?	**Hva koster det til ...?**	vaa kosterr deh til
How far is it to ...?	**Hvor langt er det til ...?**	voor lahngt ær deh til
Take me to ...	**Kjør meg til ...**	khūrr mæi til
this address	**denne adressen**	dehner ahdrehssern
the airport	**flyplassen**	flewplahssern
the town centre	**sentrum**	sehntrewm
the ... Hotel	**... hotell**	... hootehl
the railway station	**jernbanestasjonen**	yærⁿnbaanerstahshoonern
Turn ... at the next corner.	**Sving til ... ved neste gatehjørne.**	sving til ... veh(d) nehster gaateyūrⁿner
right/left	**høyre/venstre**	hoyrer/vehnstrer
Go straight ahead.	**Kjør rett frem.**	khūrr reht frehm
Please stop here.	**Stans her.**	stahnss hær
I'm in a hurry.	**Jeg har det travelt.**	yæi haar deh traaverlt
Could you drive more slowly?	**Kan du kjøre litt saktere?**	kahn dew khūrrer lit sahkterrer
Could you help me carry my luggage?	**Kan du hjelpe meg å bære bagasjen?**	kahn dew yehlper mæi aw bærrer bahgaashern
Could you wait for me?	**Kan du vente på meg?**	kahn dew vehnter paw mæi
I'll be back in 10 minutes.	**Jeg er tilbake om 10 minutter.**	yæi ær tilbaaker om 10 minnewter
How much do I owe you?	**Hvor mye skylder jeg?**	voor mēwer shewlerr yæi?

TIPPING, see inside back cover

Hotel—Other accommodation

Early reservation and confirmation are essential in most major tourist centres during high season. Most towns and arrival points have a tourist information office (*turist-kontor*—tew**rist**koontoōr) with an accommodation service (*innkvarterings-service*—**in**kvah^rtāyrings-sūrrviss); that's the place to go to if you're stuck for a room.

Although there is no official rating system, there are different classes of accommodation.

Hotell (hoo**teh**l)	Hotel; simple or deluxe, your room will be spotless. Facilities—and prices—vary across a wide range. Breakfast is usually included; half- and full-board accommodation is also available.
Turisthotell (tew**rist**hootehl)	Tourist hotel; high-standard resort establishments mostly located in the fjord country. Most offer only half- or full-board accommodation.
Hytte (**hew**ter)	Hut/Chalet; self-catering accommodation that can be hired by the week.
Høyfjellshotell (**hoyf**yehls-hootehl)	Mountain hotel; first-class or deluxe establishments in winter-sports resorts. Most offer only full-board accommodation.
Fjellstue (**fyehl**stēwer)	Mountain inn; unpretentious but scrupulously clean establishments. Most offer only full-board accommodation, serving wholesome food.
Pensjonat (pahngshoo**naat**)	Guesthouse; offers full- or half-board accommodation.
Turisthytte (tew**rist**hewter)	Tourist hut; simple hostels, some with a café in the grounds. Most bedrooms are for four to six people.
Vandrerhjem (**vahn**drerryehm)	Youth and family hostel; for the backpack brigade. Sleeping arrangements may be in dormitories.

Checking in—Reception *Ankomst – Resepsjon*

My name is ...	**Mitt navn er ...**	mit nahvn ær
I have a reservation.	**Jeg har bestilt rom.**	yæi haar berstilt room
We've reserved 2 rooms.	**Vi har bestilt 2 rom.**	vee haar berstilt 2 room
Here's the confirmation.	**Her er bekreftelsen.**	hær ær berkrehfterlsern
Do you have any vacancies?	**Har dere noen ledige rom?**	haar dāȳrer nōōern lāȳdeeyer room
I'd like a ...	**Jeg vil gjerne ha et ...**	yæi vil yǣʳner haa eht
single room	**enkeltrom**	ehngkerltroom
double room	**dobbeltrom**	dobberltroom
We'd like a room ...	**Vi vil gjerne ha et rom ...**	vee vil yǣʳner haa eht room
with twin beds	**med to senger**	meh(d) tōō sehngerr
with a double bed	**med dobbeltseng**	meh(d) dobberltsehng
with a bath	**med bad**	meh(d) baad
with a shower	**med dusj**	meh(d) dewsh
with a balcony	**med balkong**	meh(d) bahlkong
with a view	**med utsikt**	meh(d) ēwtsikt
at the front	**på forsiden**	paw fosheedern
at the back	**på baksiden**	paw baakseedern
It must be quiet.	**Det må være rolig.**	deh maw vǣrer rōōli
What floor is it on?	**I hvilken etasje er det?**	ee vilkern ehtaasher ær deh
Is there ...?	**Fins det ...?**	finss deh
air conditioning	**air-conditioning**	āȳr-kondisherning
a conference room	**konferanserom**	koonferrahngserroom
a gymnasium	**trimrom**	trimroom
heating	**varme**	vahrmer
hot water	**varmt vann**	vahrmt vahn
a laundry service	**vaskeri-service**	vahskerree-sūrrviss
a radio/television in the room	**radio/TV på rommet**	raadyoo/tāȳveh paw roommer
running water	**rennende vann**	rehnerner vahn
a sauna	**badstue/sauna**	bahstew/sounah
a swimming pool	**badebasseng**	baaderbahssehng
a private toilet	**toalett på rommet**	tooahleht paw roommer

CHECKING OUT, see page 31

| Could you put an extra bed/a cot in the room? | **Kan du sette inn en ekstra seng/barne-seng på rommet?** | kahn dew sehter in ehn ehkstrah sehng/baaˈner-sehng paw roommer |

How much? *Hvor mye?*

How much does it cost ...?	**Hvor mye koster det ...?**	voor mēwer kosterr deh
per night	**pr. natt**	pær naht
per week	**pr. uke**	pær ēwker
for bed and break-fast	**for rom med frokost**	for room meh(d) frōokost
excluding meals	**uten måltider**	ēwtern mawlteederr
for full board (A.P.)	**for helpensjon**	for haylpahngshōōn
for half board (M.A.P.)	**for halvpensjon**	for hahlpahngshōōn
Is ... included?	**Er ... inkludert?**	ær ... inklewdāyˈt
breakfast	**frokost**	frōokost
value-added tax (sales tax)	**moms**	moomss
Do you have reduced rates for the weekend?	**Er det lavere pris i helgen?**	ær deh laaverer preess ee hehlgern
Is there any reduc-tion for children?	**Er det reduksjon for barn?**	ær deh rehdewkshōōn for baaˈn
Do you charge for the baby?	**Koster det noe for babyen?**	kosterr deh nōoer for baybyern
That's too expensive.	**Det er for dyrt.**	deh ær for dewˈt
Do you have anything cheaper?	**Har dere noe rimeligere?**	haar dayrer nōoer reemerleeyerrer

How long? *Hvor lenge?*

We'll be staying ...	**Vi blir ...**	vee bleer
overnight only	**bare natten over**	baarer nahtern awverr
a few days	**et par dager**	eht pahr daagerr
until Sunday morning	**til søndag morgen**	til surndah(g) mawerˈn
a week (at least)	**en uke (minst)**	ehn ēwker (minst)
I don't know yet.	**Jeg vet ikke ennå.**	yæi vāyt ikker ehnaw

NUMBERS, see page 147/DAYS OF THE WEEK, see page 150

Decision   *Beslutning*

May I see the room?	**Kan jeg få se rommet?**	kahn yæi faw say roommer
That's fine. I'll take it.	**Det er bra. Jeg tar det.**	deh ær braa. yæi taar deh
No. I don't like it.	**Nei. Jeg liker det ikke.**	næi. yæi leekerr deh ikker
It's too ...	**Det er for ...**	deh ær for
cold/hot	**kaldt/varmt**	kahlt/vahrmt
dark/small/noisy	**mørkt/lite/støyende**	murrkt/leeter/stoyerner
I asked for a room with a bath.	**Jeg ba om et rom med bad.**	yæi baa om eht room meh(d) baad
Do you have anything ...?	**Har dere noe ...?**	haar dayrer nooer
better	**bedre**	baydrer
bigger	**større**	sturrer
cheaper	**rimeligere**	reemerleeyerrer
quieter	**roligere**	rooleeyerrer
Do you have a room with a (better) view?	**Har dere et rom med (bedre) utsikt?**	haar dayrer eht room meh(d) (baydrer) ewtsikt

Registration   *Innskriving*

Upon arrival at a hotel or guesthouse you'll be asked to fill in a registration form (*meldeskjema*—**meh**lershaymah).

Etternavn/Fornavn	Surname/First name
Fødselsdato/Fødested	Date of birth/Place of birth
Yrke	Occupation
Hjemsted	Home town
Nasjonalitet	Nationality
Passnummer	Passport No.
Passutstedende myndighet	Issuing passport authority
Dato for ankomst til Skandinavia/Norge	Date of arrival in Scandinavia/Norway
Hensikt med oppholdet	Reason for visit
Underskrift	Signature

| What does this mean? | **Hva betyr dette?** | vaa bertewr dehter |

Kan jeg få se passet, takk?	May I see your passport, please?
Kan du fylle ut dette skjemæt?	Would you mind filling in this form?
Undertegn her.	Please sign here.
Hvor lenge kommer du til å bli?	How long will you be staying?

What's my room number?	**Hvilket romnummer har jeg?**	vilkert roomnoommerr haar yæi
Will you have our luggage sent up?	**Kan jeg få brakt opp bagasjen?**	kahn yæi faw brahkt op bahgaashern
Where can I park my car?	**Hvor kan jeg parkere bilen?**	voor kahn yæi pahrkayrer beelern
Does the hotel have a garage?	**Har hotellet egen garasje?**	haar hootehlert aygern gahraasher
I'd like to leave this in the hotel safe.	**Jeg vil gjerne deponere dette i hotellets safe.**	yæi vil yæ^rner dehpoonayrer dehter ee hootehlerss ''safe''

Hotel staff *Hotellpersonale*

hall porter (bell captain)	**portier**	poo^rtyay
maid	**værelsespike**	værerlserspeeker
manager	**direktør**	dirrehkturr
porter (bellman)	**bærer**	bærerr
receptionist	**resepsjonist**	rehsehpshoonist
switchboard operator	**sentralbord- betjent**	sehntraalboor- bertyaynt
waiter	**kelner/servitør**	kehlner/særveeturr
waitress	**serveringsdame/ servitør**	særvayringsdaamer/ særveeturr

To attract the attention of staff members say "Excuse me" —*Unnskyld* (**ewn**shewl).

TELLING THE TIME, see page 153

General requirements   *Allmenne forespørsler*

The key to room ..., please.	**Nøkkelen til rom ..., takk.**	nurkerlern til room ... tahk
Could you wake me at ..., please?	**Kan du vekke meg kl. ...?**	kahn dew vehker mæi klokkern
When is breakfast/lunch/dinner served?	**Når serveres det frokost/lunsj/middag?**	nor særvayrerss deh frookost/lurnsh/middah(g)
May we have breakfast in our room, please?	**Kan vi få frokosten servert på rommet?**	kahn vee faw frookostern særvay't paw roommer
Is there a bath on this floor?	**Fins det bad i denne etasjen?**	finss deh baad ee dehner ehtaashern
Where's the shaver socket (outlet)?	**Hvor er stikkontakten for barbermaskinen?**	voor ær stikkoontahktern for bahrbayrmahsheenern

Can you find me a ...?	**Kan du skaffe meg en ...?**	kahn dew skahfer mæi ehn
babysitter	**barnevakt**	baa'nervahkt
secretary	**sekretær**	sehkrertær
typewriter	**skrivemaskin**	skreevermahsheen

May I have a/an/some ...?	**Kan jeg få ...?**	kahn yæi faw
bath towel	**et badehåndkle**	eht baaderhongkler
(extra) blanket	**et (ekstra) ullteppe**	eht (ehkstrah) ewltehper
hangers	**noen hengere**	nooern hengerrer
hot-water bottle	**en varmeflaske**	ehn vahrmerflahsker
ice cubes	**noen isbiter**	nooern eesbeeterr
needle and thread	**nål og tråd**	nawl o(g) traw
(extra) pillow	**en (ekstra) pute**	ehn (ehkstrah) pewter
(extra) quilt	**en (ekstra) dyne**	ehn (ehkstrah) dewner
reading lamp	**en leselampe**	ehn laysserlahmper
soap	**en såpe**	ehn sawper

Where's the ...?	**Hvor er ...?**	voor ær
bathroom	**badet**	baader
dining room	**spisesalen**	speessersssaalern
emergency exit	**nødutgangen**	nurdewtgahngern
hairdresser	**frisørsalongen**	frissurshahlongern
lift (elevator)	**heisen**	hæissern
telephone	**telefonen**	tehlerfoonern

| Where are the toilets? | **Hvor er toalettet?** | voor ær tooahlehtern |

BREAKFAST, see page 38

Telephone—Post (Mail) *Telefon – Post*

Can you get me Tromsø 12 34 56?	**Kan jeg få Tromsø 12 34 56?**	kahn yæi faw **troom**sur 12 34 56
Do you have any stamps?	**Har du frimerker?**	haar dew **free**mærkerr
Would you post (mail) this for me, please?	**Kan du poste dette for meg?**	kahn dew **poster dehter** for mæi
Are there any letters for me?	**Er det noen brev til meg?**	ær deh $\overline{noo}$ern br$\overline{ay}$v til mæi
Are there any messages for me?	**Er det noen beskjed til meg?**	ær deh $\overline{noo}$ern bersh$\overline{ay}$ til mæi
How much is my telephone bill?	**Hvor stor er telefon-regningen min?**	voor st$\overline{oo}$r ær tehler**f$\overline{oo}$n**-ræiningern meen

Difficulties *Vanskeligheter*

The ... doesn't work.	**... virker ikke.**	... **virk**err **ikk**er
air conditioning	**air-conditioningen**	$\overline{ay}$r-kondisherningern
bidet	**bidetet**	bee**day**er
heating	**varmen**	**vahr**mern
light	**lyset**	**lew**sser
radio	**radioen**	**raad**yooern
refrigerator	**kjøleskapet**	kh$\overline{u}$r**ler**skaaper
television	**TV'en**	**tay**vehern
The tap (faucet) is dripping.	**Kranen drypper.**	**kraan**ern **drew**perr
There's no hot water.	**Det er ikke noe varmt vann.**	deh ær **ikk**er n$\overline{oo}$er vahrmt vahn
The washbasin (sink) is blocked.	**Vasken er tett.**	**vahsk**ern ær teht
The window is jammed.	**Vinduet sitter fast.**	**vind**ewer **sitt**err fahst
The curtains are stuck.	**Gardinene henger fast.**	gah^r**dee**nener **hehng**err fahst
The bulb is burned out.	**Lyspæren har gått.**	**lew**sp$\overline{æ}$rern haar got
My bed hasn't been made up.	**Sengen min er ikke blitt redd opp.**	**sehng**ern meen ær **ikk**er blit rehd op

POST OFFICE AND TELEPHONE, see page 132

The ... is/are broken.	... er i stykker.	... ær ee stewkerr
blind	rullegardinen	rewlergah'deenern
lamp	lampen	lahmpern
plug	støpslet	sturpshler
switch	bryteren	brēwterrern
venetian blinds	persiennen	pæshyehnern
Can you get it repaired?	Kan du få det reparert?	kahn dew faw deh rehpahrāy'rt

Laundry—Dry cleaner's *Vask – Rens*

I'd like these clothes ...	Jeg vil gjerne ha disse klærne ...	yæi vil yǣ'rner haa disser klǣ'rner
dry-cleaned	renset	rehnsert
ironed	strøket	strürkert
pressed	presset	prehssert
washed	vasket	vahskert

I need them ...	Jeg trenger dem ...	yæi trehngerr dehm
today	i dag	ee daag
tonight	i kveld	ee kvehl
tomorrow	i morgen	ee mawer'n
before Friday	før fredag	fürr frāydah(g)

Can you ... this?	Kan du ... dette?	kahn dew ... dehter
mend/stitch	lappe/sy sammen	lahper/sēw sahmern

Can you sew on this button?	Kan du sy i denne knappen?	kahn dew sēw ee dehner knahpern
Can this be invisibly mended?	Kan du kunststoppe dette?	kahn dew kewnststopper dehter
Can you get this stain out?	Kan du få bort denne flekken?	kahn dew faw boo'rt dehner flehkern
Is my laundry ready?	Er vasken min klar?	ær vahskern meen klaar
This isn't mine.	Dette er ikke mitt.	dehter ær ikker mit
There's something missing.	Det er noe som mangler.	deh ær nōōer som mahnglerr
There's one item missing.	Det mangler et plagg.	deh mahnglerr eht plahg
There's a hole in this.	Det er gått hull i dette.	deh ær got hewl ee dehter

Hairdresser—Barber *Damefrisør – Herrefrisør*

Is there a ... in the hotel?	**Fins det en ... på hotellet?**	finss deh ehn ... paw hootehler
hairdresser	**frisørsalong**	frissūrshahlong
beauty salon	**skjønnhetssalong**	shurnhehtssahlong
Can I make an appointment for Thursday?	**Kan jeg få time på torsdag?**	kahn yæi faw teemer paw tawshdah(g)
Could you ... my hair, please?	**Kan du ... håret mitt?**	kah dew ... hawrer mit
blow-dry	**føne**	fūrner
cut	**klippe**	klipper
dye	**farge**	fahrgger
tint	**tone**	tōoner
with a fringe (bangs)	**med lugg**	meh(d) lewg
I'd like a/some ...	**Jeg vil gjerne ha ...**	yæi vil yǣ^rner haa
colour rinse	**fargeskylling**	fahrggershewling
face massage	**ansiktsmassasje**	ahnsiktsmahsaasher
face pack	**ansiktsmaske**	ahnsiktsmahsker
manicure	**manikyr**	mahnikēwr
perm(anent wave)	**permanent**	pærmahnehnt
setting lotion	**leggevann**	lehgervahn
shampoo and set	**vask og legg**	vahsk o(g) lehg
I'd like a shampoo for ... hair.	**Jeg vil ha en sjampo for ... hår.**	yæi vil haa en shampoo for ... hawr
normal	**normalt**	noormaalt
dry	**tørt**	tur^rt
greasy (oily)	**fett**	feht
Do you have a colour chart?	**Har du et farge-kart?**	haar dew eht fahrgger-kah^rt
I don't want any hair spray.	**Jeg vil ikke ha hårlakk.**	yæi vil ikker haa haw^rlahk
I'd like a haircut. please.	**Klipping, takk.**	klipping tahk
Don't cut it too short.	**Klipp det ikke for kort.**	klip deh ikker for ko^rt
A little more off the ...	**Ta litt mer ...**	taa lit māyr
back	**bak**	baak

DAYS OF THE WEEK, see page 150

top	på issen	paw issern
neck	i nakken	ee nahkern
sides	på sidene	paw seederner
I'd like a shave.	Barbering, takk.	bahrbāyring tahk
Would you trim my ..., please?	Kan du stusse ...?	kahn dew stewsser
beard	skjegget	shehger
moustache	barten	bahᵣtern
sideboards (sideburns)	kinnskjegget	khinshehger

Checking out   Avreise

May I have my bill, please?	Kan jeg få regningen?	kahn yæi faw ræiningern
I'm leaving early in the morning.	Jeg reiser i morgen tidlig.	yæi ræisserr ee mawerᵣn teeli
Please have my bill ready.	Kan du ha regningen klar?	kahn dew haa ræiningern klaar
We'll be checking out around noon.	Vi reiser ved tolv-tiden.	vee ræisserr veh(d) tolteedern
I must leave at once.	Jeg må reise med én gang.	yæi maw ræisser meh(d) āyn gahng
Can I pay by credit card?	Kan jeg betale med kredittkort?	kahn yæi bertaaler meh(d) krehditkoᵣt
I think there's a mistake in the bill.	Jeg tror det er en feil på regningen.	yæi trōōr deh ær ehn fæil paw ræiningern
Can you get us a taxi?	Kan du skaffe oss en drosje?	kahn dew skahfer oss ehn drosher
Could you have our luggage brought down?	Kan vi få båret ned bagasjen?	kahn vee faw bawrert nāy(d) bahgaashern
Here's the forwarding address.	Her er etter-sendingsadressen.	hāᵣ ær ehterr-sehningsahdrehssern
You have my home address.	Du har min hjem-stedsadresse.	dew haar meen yehm-stāydsahdrehsser
It's been a very enjoyable stay.	Det har vært et meget hyggelig opphold.	deh haar væᵣt eht māygert hewgerli ophol

TIPPING, see inside back cover

Camping *Camping*

Norway has some 1,500 registered camp sites, classified by one, two or three stars according to facilities offered. Many have cabins for rent. The camping season is normally from mid-May or early June to the end of August. Camping outside organized sites is permitted, but you will have to ask permission from the landowner or tenant.

Is there a camp site nearby?	**Er det en camping-plass i nærheten?**	ær deh ehn **kæmping**-plahss ee **næ**rhehtern
Can we camp here?	**Kan vi campe her?**	kahn vee **kæmp**er hær
Do you have room for a ...?	**Har dere plass til ...?**	haar **dāy**rer plahss til
tent	**et telt**	eht tehlt
caravan (trailer)	**en campingvogn**	ehn **kæm**pingvongn
What's the charge ...?	**Hva koster det ...?**	vaa **kost**err deh
per day	**pr. dag**	pær daag
per person	**pr. person**	pær pæsh**ōōn**
for a car	**for en bil**	for ehn beel
for a tent	**for et telt**	for eht tehlt
for a caravan	**for en campingvogn**	for ehn **kæm**pingvongn
Is there/Are there (a) ...?	**Fins det ...?**	finss deh
cabins	**hytter**	**hew**terr
cafeteria	**kafeteria**	kahfertā**y**reeah
cooking facilities	**kokemuligheter**	**kōō**kermewlihehterr
drinking water	**drikkevann**	**drikk**ervahn
electricity	**elektrisitet**	ehlehktrissit**ā**yt
playground	**lekeplass**	**lāy**kerplahss
restaurant	**restaurant**	rehstew**rahng**
shopping facilities	**shoppingmuligheter**	**shopp**ingmewlihehterr
sauna	**badstue/sauna**	**bahs**tew/**sou**nah
swimming pool	**badebasseng**	**baa**derbahssehng
Where are the showers/toilets?	**Hvor er dusjene/toalettet?**	voor ær **dew**sherner/tooah**leh**ter
Where can I get butane gas?	**Hvor kan jeg få tak i butangass?**	voor kahn yæi faw taak ee bewt**aang**ahss
Is there a youth hostel nearby?	**Er det et vandrer-hjem i nærheten?**	ær deh eht **vahn**drerr-yehm ee **næ**rhehtern

CAMPING EQUIPMENT, see page 106

Eating out

The following rundown of places to eat will help you decide what to look for.

Bar (baar)	Only found in hotels in large towns.
Bistro (bistroo)	Small, informal restaurant.
Brasserie (brahsserree)	Normally a simple but welcoming medium-priced establishment.
Fiskerestaurant (fiskerrehstewrahng)	Fish and seafood specialities.
Gatekjøkken (gaaterkhurkern)	"Kitchen on the street". Serves fast food like sausages and hamburgers with mashed potatoes or chips (French fries); *pølse med lompe*, frankfurter (wienerwurst) in a small potato pancake; ice cream and soft drinks.
Kafé (kahfāy)	Café, also called *kaffebar* (**kah**ferbaar); serves pastries and open sandwiches, coffee, tea and soft drinks.
Kafeteria (kahfertāyreeah)	Cafeteria.
Konditori (koondittooree)	Teashop (coffee shop); often a bakery, serving pastries, ice cream and sandwiches.
Kro (krōō)	Usually a road-side diner; mostly self service.
Lunsjbar (lurnshbaar)	Lunch bar; usually self service.
Pizzapub/-bar (pitsah"pub"/-baar)	Pizzas in different sizes or by the slice.
Pølsebod (purlserbood)	Hot-dog stand.
Restaurant (rehstewrahng)	Up-market establishment serving Norwegian and international food with all the trimmings.
Rotisserie (rotisserree)	Specializes in grilled meat; can be expensive.

Salatbar (sahlaatbaar)	Salad bar.
Vertshus (væ^rtshewss)	Normally a small and informal neighbourhood restaurant.

Eating habits *Spisevaner*

Most Norwegians start the day with a meal that is somewhat more substantial than the typical continental breakfast—coffee or tea and open sandwiches (*smørbrød*). Country hotels and some places in the city offer breakfast buffets. Lunch is usually a fast-food snack, but many hotels and restaurants serve hot meals, and some feature a smorgasbord (*koldtbord*). Dinner is the main meal of the day.

Norwegians often drink plain tap water with their meals. Most restaurants are licensed to serve beer, and many offer wine, too; only the more elegant ones have a licence to serve spirits (liquor).

Meal times *Spisetider*

Breakfast (*frokost*—**froo**kost) is usually served from 7 or 8 to 10 a.m. and is often included in the hotel arrangement.

Lunch (*lunsj*—lurnsh) is normally served from 11 a.m. and dinner (*middag*—**mid**dah[g]) from around 6 p.m. (much earlier in smaller establishments).

Norwegian cuisine *Det norske kjøkken*

Some of the best food in Norway comes from the sea, which is to be expected in one of the world's leading fishing nations. You can dine on lobster or salmon in elegant surroundings, or go down to the waterfront and buy a picnic lunch of prawns (shrimp) right off the trawler. But you'll also find beef, pork, mutton and game dishes.

Norwegians go berserk over berries. They love scouring the countryside in search of wild berries, to eat them fresh or in jams. The supreme delicacy is *multer med krem*, arctic cloud-berries with cream.

For those who enjoy a slice of bread with their meal, Norway offers a wide variety ranging from white, black, unleavened and wholemeal to crispy crackers and delicate wafers in all shapes and sizes. You'll probably see the full range at break-fast or when having *koldtbord*—the traditional self-service buffet.

Hva skal det være?	What would you like?
Jeg kan anbefale dette.	I recommend this.
Hva vil du/dere* ha å drikke?	What would you like to drink?
Vi har ikke ...	We don't have ...
Vil du ha ...?	Would you like ...?

Hungry? *Sulten?*

I'm hungry/I'm thirsty.	Jeg er sulten/ Jeg er tørst.	yæi ær **sewltern**/ yæi ær tur* rsht
Can you recommend a good restaurant?	Kan du anbefale en bra restaurant?	kahn dew **ahn**berfaaler ehn braa rehstew**rahng**
Are there any inexpensive restaurants around here?	Fins det noen rimelige restauranter i nærheten?	finss deh **noo**ern reemerleeyer rehstew-**rahng**err ee **nær**hehtern

If you want to be sure of getting a table in a popular restau-rant, it's better to book in advance.

I'd like to reserve a table for 4.	Jeg vil gjerne bestille et bord til 4.	yæi vil yææ**r**ner berstiller eht boor til 4
We'll come at 8.	Vi kommer kl. 8.	vee **kom**merr **klok**kern 8

* *du* = singular, *dere* = plural

Could we have a ...?	**Kan vi få et ...?**	kahn vee faw eht
table in the corner	**hjørnebord**	yur'nerbōōr
table by the window	**vindusbord**	vindewsbōōr
table outside	**bord ute**	bōōr ēwter
Could we have a table in a ...?	**Kan vi få et bord ...?**	kahn vee faw eht bōōr
non-smoking area	**for ikke-røykere**	for ikker-roykerrer
smoking area	**for røykere**	for roykerrer

Asking and ordering *Spørsmål og bestilling*

Waiter/Waitress!	**Unnskyld!** *	ewnshewl
We'd like to eat.	**Vi vil gjerne spise.**	vee vil yǣr'ner speesser
I'd like something to eat/drink.	**Jeg vil gjerne ha noe å spise/drikke.**	yæi vil yǣr'ner haa nōōer aw speesser/drikker
May I have the menu, please?	**Kan jeg få se spisekartet?**	kahn yæi faw sāy speesserkah'ter
Do you have a ...?	**Har dere en ...?**	haar dāyrer ehn
set menu	**meny**	mehnēw
children's menu	**barnemeny**	baa'nermehnēw
local speciality	**lokal spesialitet**	lookaal spehsseeahlitāyt
What do you recommend?	**Hva kan du anbefale?**	vaa kahn dew ahnberfaaler
Could we have a/ an ..., please?	**Kan vi få ...?**	kahn vee faw
ashtray	**et askebeger**	eht ahskerbāygerr
cup	**en kopp**	ehn kop
extra chair	**en stol til**	ehn stōōl til
fork	**en gaffel**	ehn gahferl
glass	**et glass**	eht glass
knife	**en kniv**	ehn kneev
napkin (serviette)	**en serviett**	ehn sehrvyeht
plate	**en tallerken**	ehn tahlærkern
spoon	**en skje**	ehn shāy
May I have some ...?	**Kan jeg få litt ...?**	kahn yæi faw lit
bread	**brød**	brūr
butter	**smør**	smurr

---

* *Unnskyld*: Excuse me

NUMBERS, see page 147

oil/vinegar	olje/eddik	olyer/ehdik
salt/pepper	salt/pepper	sahlt/pehperr
seasoning	krydder	krewderr
sugar	sukker	sookkerr

Some useful expressions for those with special requirements:

I'm on a special diet.	Jeg holder diett.	yæi hollerr deeyeht
I mustn't eat food containing ...	Jeg kan ikke spise mat som inneholder ...	yæi kahn ikker speesser maat som innerhollerr
fat/flour	fett/mel	feht/māyl
salt/sugar	salt/sukker	sahlt/sookkerr
Do you have any ... dishes?	Har dere retter med ...?	haar dāyrer rehterr meh(d)
low-fat	lavt fettinnhold	laavt fehtinhol
low-cholesterol	lavt kolesterolinnhold	laavt koolehsterrōōlinhol
Is there alcohol in it?	Er det alkohol i det?	ær deh ahlkoohōōl ee deh
Do you have ... for diabetics?	Har dere ... for diabetikere?	haar dāyrer ... for deeahbāytikkerrer
cakes	kaker	kaakerr
a fruit juice	en juice	ehn yēwss
a special menu	en spesialmeny	ehn spehsseeaalmehnēw
Do you have any vegetarian dishes?	Har dere noen vegetariske retter?	haar dāyrer nōōern vehgertaarisker rehterr
Could I have ... instead of dessert?	Kan jeg få ... i stedet for dessert?	kahn yæi faw ... ee stāyder for dehssǣr
Can I have an artificial sweetener?	Kan jeg få et søtningsmiddel?	kahn yæi faw eht sūrtningsmidderl

And ...

I'd like some more.	Jeg vil gjerne ha litt mer.	yæi vil yǣ'rner haa lit māyr
Can I have more ...?	Kan jeg få litt mer ...?	kahn yæi faw lit māyr
Just a small portion.	Bare en liten porsjon.	baarer ehn leetern pooshōōn
Nothing more, thanks.	Takk, ikke mer.	tahk ikker māyr

Breakfast *Frokost*

Most hotels offer a continental breakfast as well as a buffet, consisting of a variety of breads, butter, cheese, cold cuts, eggs, herring, jam, cereals, fruit juice, milk, coffee and tea.

I'd like breakfast, please.	**Jeg vil gjerne ha frokost.**	yæi vil yǣ^rner haa frōokost
I'll have a/an/some ...	**Jeg tar ...**	yæi taar
bacon and eggs	**egg og bacon**	ehg o(g) bæikern
boiled egg	**et kokt egg**	eht kookt ehg
soft/hard	**bløtkokt/hardkokt**	blūrtkookt/haarkookt
cereal	**frokostblanding**	frōokostblahning
cheese	**ost**	oost
eggs	**egg**	ehg
fried egg	**et speilegg**	eht spæilehg
scrambled eggs	**eggerøre**	ehgerrūrer
fruit juice	**juice**	yēwss
grapefruit	**grapefrukt-**	grāypfrewkt-
orange	**appelsin-**	ahperlseen-
ham and eggs	**egg og skinke**	ehg o(g) shingker
jam	**syltetøy**	sewltertoy
marmalade	**appelsinmarmelade**	ahperlseenmahrmerlaader
omelet	**omelett**	oomerleht
porridge	**grøt**	grūrt
roll	**et rundstykke**	eht rewnstewker
toast	**litt ristet brød**	lit ristert brūr
yoghurt	**en yoghurt**	ehn yogew^rt
May I have some ...?	**Kan jeg få ...?**	kahn yæi faw
bread	**litt brød**	lit brūr
butter	**litt smør**	lit smurr
(hot) chocolate	**(varm) sjokolade**	(vahrm) shookoolaader
coffee	**kaffe**	kahfer
decaffeinated	**koffeinfri**	koffeheenfree
black	**svart**	svah^rt
with cream	**med fløte**	meh(d) flūrter
honey	**litt honning**	lit honning
(cold/hot) milk	**litt (kald/varm) melk**	lit (kahl/vahrm) mehlk
pepper	**litt pepper**	lit pehperr
salt	**litt salt**	lit sahlt
tea	**te**	tāy
with milk/lemon	**med melk/sitron**	meh(d) mehlk/sitrōōn
(hot) water	**litt (varmt) vann**	lit (vahrmt) vahn

What's on the menu? *Hva står på menyen?*

Many restaurants display their menu (*spisekart/meny*) outside. In addition to the à la carte menu, some restaurants offer a dish of the day (*dagens rett*).

Under the headings below you'll find alphabetical lists of dishes that might be offered on a Norwegian menu, with their English equivalent. You can simply show the book to the waiter. If you want some cheese, for instance, let *him* point to what's available on the appropriate list. Use pages 36 and 37 for ordering in general.

EATING OUT

Mat og drikke

Reading the menu   Å lese spisekartet

Dagens rett/suppe/ grønnsaker	Dish/Soup/Vegetables of the day
Barnemeny	Children's menu
Vegetar ...	Vegetarian ...
Kjøkkensjefen anbefaler ...	The chef proposes ...
Som vår kjøkkensjef liker det	As our chef likes it
(Husets) Spesialiteter	Specialities (of the house)
Serveres/Servert med ...	Served with ...
Velg mellom ...	Choice of ...
Valgfritt tilbehør	Choice of side dishes
På bestilling	Made on request
... med ass. ...	... with assorted ...
... m/ ...	... with ...
... inkl.	... included

dessert	dehssǣr	dessert
drikker	drikkerr	drinks
fisk	fisk	fish
forretter	forrehterr	starters (appetizers)
frukt	frewkt	fruit
fugl	fēwl	poultry
hovedretter	hōōverdrehterr	main courses (entrees)
is(krem)	ees(krāym)	ice cream
kaker	kaakerr	pastries/cakes
kjøtt	khurt	meat
koldtbord	koltbōōr	smorgasbord
leskedrikk	lehskerdrik	soft drinks
ost	oost	cheese
pastaretter	pahstahrehterr	pasta dishes
risretter	reesrehterr	rice dishes
salatbar	sahlaatbaar	salad bar
smørbrød	smurrbrūr	open sandwiches
supper	sewperr	soups
varme smørbrød	vahrmer smurrbrūr	sandwiches with hot meat, fish, etc.
varmretter	vahrmrehterr	hot dishes
vilt	vilt	game

Open sandwiches *Smørbrød*

Smørbrød means bread and butter, which is quite an understatement when you consider Scandinavia's reputation for elaborate open sandwiches. Almost anything may turn up on one of these appetizing *smørbrød*, most of which are served cold. Two or three open sandwiches will generally satisfy most appetites. *Landgang* (**lahn**gahng), literally "gangway", is a halved French loaf with several different toppings (fish, egg, meat, cheese, etc.).

I'd like an open sandwich with ...	**Jeg vil gjerne ha et smørbrød med ...**	yæi vil yæ^rner haa eht smurrbrūr meh(d)

egg og ansjos (ehg o[g] ahngsh**ōō**ss)	sliced egg and marinated sprats
italiensk salat (eetahlee**ay**nsk sahlaat)	"Italian" salad; sliced ham, apple, potato, onion, carrot, peas in mayonnaise dressing
reker (r**ay**kerr)	prawns (shrimp) with mayonnaise
rekesalat (r**ay**kersahlaat)	prawn (shrimp) salad; prawns, apple, celery, sometimes in a tomato dressing, sometimes in a mayonnaise dressing
roastbiff (rostbif)	sliced roast beef, often served with a herb-flavoured mayonnaise sauce
røkelaks (r**ū**rkerlahkss)	sliced smoked salmon, often served with scrambled eggs
sildesalat (sillersahlaat)	herring salad; pickled herring, potato, beetroot, apple, egg, onion in cream-and-beetroot dressing

Smorgasbord *Koldtbord*

The Swedish name, *smørgåsbord* ("sandwich table"), is better known than its Norwegian equivalent, *koldtbord* ("cold table"). Some restaurants and mountain hotels specialize in this bountiful self-service buffet. A scaled-down version of the *koldtbord* is often prepared in Norwegian homes for special occasions, particularly during the Christmas season.

Dishes may vary according to season, but there is always a variety of fish (marinated and smoked herring, herring salads, cold salmon, trout or halibut in aspic) and seafood, meat (cold cuts, pâtés, hot sausages, meatballs), vegetables, egg dishes, salads, fruit, cheese and bread.

One of the mainstays of *koldtbord*, particularly in summer and early autumn, is *spekemat* (**spāy**kermaat) or cured meat. Norway has a long tradition of curing meat, originating from the time when there was no other way of conserving food. Usually *spekemat* is eaten with scrambled eggs and a crisp, paper-thin barley-and-wheat or barley-and-rye cracker called *flatbrød* (**flaht**brūr).

Another speciality that may be found among *koldtbord* dishes is *rømmegrøt* (**rur**mergrūrt), a tasty, refreshing and filling porridge made from thick sour cream, flour and milk, which is topped with butter, sugar and cinnamon.

Start with the fish dishes. Use a fresh plate for meat, salad and egg dishes, and another for cheese and fruit. Don't hurry yourself; the whole point of *koldtbord* is to enjoy a large meal with as many trips back to the buffet as desired, and all at a leisurely pace.

Aquavit and beer go particularly well with this spread. It is rare to drink wine with *koldtbord*.

I'd like to try some Norwegian specialities.	**Jeg vil gjerne prøve noen norske spesialiteter.**	yæi vil yǣᵣner prūrver nōōern noshker sehsseeahlitāyterr
What do you recommend?	**Hva anbefaler du?**	vaa ahnberfaalerr dew
fenalår (fāynahlawr)	cured leg of mutton	
spekepølse (spāykerpurlser)	slices of smoked, cured sausage made from different meats that range in colour from pinkish to black	
spekeskinke (spāykershingker)	smoked, cured ham, as a main dish often served with thick sour cream (*rømme*) and boiled potatoes	

Starters (Appetizers) *Forretter*

Except on special occasions, Norwegians are usually content with soup as a starter. In more elegant restaurants, however, there will be a choice of appetizing hors d'œuvres; maybe one of the dishes from the *koldtbord*, a mixed salad or a selection of scaled-down *smørbrød* called *snitter* (**snit**terr).

I'd like a starter (an appetizer).	**Jeg vil gjerne ha en forrett.**	yæi vil yǣ^rner haa ehn **forr**eht
blåskjell	blawshehl	mussels
froskelår	froskerlawr	frogs' legs
gåselever	gawsserlehverr	goose liver
hummer	hoommerr	lobster
kaviar	kahveeaar	caviar
krabbe	krahber	crab
laks	lahkss	salmon
gravet	graavert	cured
røkt/røkelaks	rurkt/rūrkerlahkss	smoked
rekecocktail	rāykerkoktæil	prawn (shrimp) cocktail
(speke)skinke	(spāyker)shingker	(smoked, cured) ham
skinke med melon	shingker meh(d) mehlōōn	ham with melon
snegler	snæilerr	snails
sursild	sēwshil	marinated herring
tomatjuice	toomaatyēwss	tomato juice
østers	urstersh	oysters
ål i gelé	awl ee shehlāy	jellied eel
fiskekabaret (fiskerkahbahrāy)	assorted seafood and vegetables in aspic, usually served with bread, butter and a mayonnaise sauce	
gravlaks (graavlahkss)	salt-and-sugar-cured salmon (same as *gravet laks*), often served with a sweet mustard-and-dill sauce	
rakørret (raakurreht)	specially processed, salt-cured and fermented trout, often served with small potatoes, sour cream and *flatbrød*	
(ferske) reker ([fæshker] rāykerr)	(unshelled) prawns (shrimp), usually served with lemon, toast and butter	
sildebrikke (sillerbrikker)	a variety of herring, served with bread and butter	
sjømannsskjell (shūrmahnssshehl)	mussels simmered in white wine with onion and parsley	

Soups *Supper*

I'd like some soup.	**Jeg vil gjerne ha en suppe.**	yæi vil yǣ^rner haa ehn sewper
What do you recommend?	**Hva foreslår du?**	vaa fawrershlawr dew

aspargessuppe	ah**spahr**ggerssewper	asparagus soup
betasuppe	bay̅tahsewper	thick meat-and-vegetable soup
blomkålsuppe	blomkawlsewper	cauliflower soup
buljong	bewl**yong**	consommé
fiskesuppe	fiskersewper	fish soup
fransk løksuppe	frahnsk lūrksewper	French onion soup
grønnsaksuppe	grurnsaaksewper	vegetable soup
gul ertesuppe	gewl æ^rtersewper	yellow pea soup
hummersuppe	hoommerrsewper	lobster soup
kjøttsuppe	khurtsewper	meat soup
løksuppe	lūrksewper	onion soup
neslesuppe	nehshlersewper	nettle soup
oksehalesuppe	ookserhahlersewper	oxtail soup
rekesuppe	ray̅kersewper	prawn (shrimp) soup
sellerisuppe	sehlerreesewper	celery soup
sjampinjongsuppe	shahmpin**yong**sewper	button mushroom soup
soppsuppe	sopsewper	field mushroom soup
tomatsuppe	toomaatsewper	tomato soup

Salads *Salater*

Many restaurants offer an appetizing self-service salad bar (*salatbar*—sah**laat**baar).

What salads do you have?	**Hva slags salater har dere?**	vaa shlahkss sah**laa**ter haar day̅rer

agurksalat (ah**gewrk**sahlaat)	cucumber salad, usually with a vinegar-sugar dressing
blandet salat (**blah**nert sahlaat)	mixed salad (lettuce, tomatoes, cucumber, etc., with oil-and-vinegar dressing); accompanies many main courses
størje-/tunfisksalat (**stur**ryer-/tō̅̅wnfisk-sahlaat)	tuna fish salad—Norwegian version of salad Niçoise
skalldyrsalat (**skahl**dew̅rsahlaat)	seafood salad (mostly mussels and prawns, but also lobster or crab)

Egg dishes *Eggeretter*

eggerøre	ehgerrurrer	scrambled eggs
forlorent egg	forloorernt ehg	poached egg
omelett	oomerleht	omelet
med kryddergrønt	meh(d) krewderr-grurnt	with fine herbs
med ost	meh(d) oost	with cheese
med skinke	meh(d) shingker	with ham
med sjampinjong	meh(d) shahmpinyong	with button mushrooms
med sopp	meh(d) sop	with mushrooms
med -stuing	meh(d) -stewing	with ... sauce
pannekake	pahnerkaaker	pancake
speilegg/stekt egg	spæilehg/stehkt ehg	fried egg

Fish and seafood (shellfish) *Fisk og skalldyr*

Fish plays no less an important part in the diet of Norwegians today than it did a thousand years ago. Nowadays, however, visitors will be offered a much wider choice of fish and seafood, prepared in a variety of imaginative and interesting ways.

What kind of ... do you have?	**Hva slags ... har dere?**	vaa shlahkss ... haar dayrer
fish	**fisk**	fisk
seafood (shellfish)	**skalldyr**	skahldewr

abbor	ahbor	perch
ansjos	ahngshooss	marinated sprats
blekksprut	blehksprewt	octopus
blåskjell	blawshehl	mussels
brasme	brahsmer	bream
brisling	brishling	sprat/brisling
flyndre	flewndrer	flounder
gjedde	yehder	pike
hellefisk	hehlerfisk	halibut
hummer	hoommerr	lobster
hvitting	vitting	whiting
hyse	hewsser	haddock
kamskjell	kahmshehl	scallop
karpe	kahrper	carp
klippfisk	klipfisk	salted and dried cod
knurr	knewr	gurnard

kolje	kolyer	haddock
krabbe	krahber	crab
kreps	krehpss	freshwater crayfish
kveite	kvæiter	halibut
lake	laaker	burbot
laks	lahkss	salmon
lysing	lēwssing	hake
makrell	mahkrehl	mackerel
piggvar	pigvaar	turbot
regnbueørret	ræinbēwerurreht	rainbow trout
reker	rāykerr	prawns (shrimp)
rogn	rongn	roe
rødspette	rūrspehter	plaice
røye	royer	char
sardell	sah^rdehl	anchovy
sardin	sah^rdeen	sardine
sei	sæi	coalfish (pollack)
sik	seek	whitefish
sild	sil	herring
sjøtunge	shūrtoonger	sole
sjøørret	shūrurreht	sea trout
slettvar	shlehtvaar	brill
steinbit	stæinbeet	catfish
stør	stūrr	sturgeon
størje	sturryer	tuna
torsk	toshk	cod
tunfisk	tēwnfisk	tuna
uer	ēwehr	rosefish
ørret	urreht	trout
østers	urstersh	oysters
åbor	awboor	perch
ål	awl	eel

au gratin	gratinert	grahtināy^rt
boiled	kokt	kookt
breaded	griljert/panert	grilyāy^rt/pahnāy^rt
deep fried	fritert/frityrstekt	fritāy^rt/fritēwshtehkt
fried	stekt	stehkt
grilled (broiled)	grillet/grillstekt	grillert/grilstehkt
marinated	marinert	mahrināy^rt
poached	pochert/kokt	pooshāy^rt/kookt
simmered	lettkokt	lehtkookt
smoked	røkt	rurkt
steamed	dampet/dampkokt	dahmpert/dahmpkookt

fiskeboller / fiskepudding
(fiskerbollerr / fiskerpewding)

fish balls / fish pudding; served poached and laid in a béchamel or shrimp sauce, or fried, with boiled potatoes and vegetables

fritert flyndrefilet
(fritāy'rt flewndrerfillāy)

(deep) fried fillets of flounder; usually served with boiled potatoes or chips (French fries), a cucumber or mixed salad and a herb-flavoured mayonnaise sauce

gravet laks / gravlaks
(graavert lahkss / graavlahkss)

salt-and-sugar-cured salmon flavoured with dill; often served with sliced potatoes in a white sauce

kokt torsk
(kookt toshk)

poached cod; normally served with cod liver, boiled potatoes, lemon and melted butter

kokt / dampet ørret
(kookt / dahmpert urrert)

poached trout; usually served with boiled potatoes, hollandaise sauce or thick sour cream and cucumber salad

lutefisk
(lēwterfisk)

stockfish soaked in lye; simmered and served with boiled potatoes, peas, mustard, pepper and melted butter or dripping or alternatively a béchamel sauce (a traditional Christmas dish)

seibiff med løk
(sæibif meh[d] lūrk)

fried fillets of coalfish (pollack) with onions, served with boiled potatoes and vegetables or salad

spekesild
(spāykersil)

salted herring; served with boiled potatoes, onion rings, pickled beetroot, butter and often cabbage or mashed swedes (rutabaga)

Meat *Kjøtt*

What kind of meat is this?	**Hva slags kjøtt er dette?**	vaa shlahkss khurt ær dehter
beef	**oksekjøtt**	ookserkhurt
lamb	**lammekjøtt**	lahmerkhurt
mutton	**fårekjøtt**	fawrerkhurt
pork	**svinekjøtt**	sveenerkhurt
veal	**kalvekjøtt**	kahlverkhurt
I'd like some ...	**Jeg vil gjerne ha ...**	yæi vil yæ'ner haa
biff	bif	beef steak
frikadeller	frikahdehlerr	meat balls
fårestek	fawrerstāyk	roast leg of mutton or lamb

kalvebrissel	kahlverbrisserl	sweetbread
kalverlever	kahlverlehverr	calf's liver
kalvemedaljonger	kahlvermehdahlyongerr	small round fillets of veal
kalvenyrestek	kahlvernewrerstayk	roast loin of veal
karbonade(kake)	kahrboonaader(kaaker)	hamburger
kjøttboller	khurtbollerr	meat balls
kjøttkaker	khurtkaakerr	small hamburgers
kjøttpudding	khurtpewding	meat loaf
-knoke	-knooker	... bone
-kotelett	-kotterleht	... chop
lammebog	lahmerboog	shoulder of lamb
lammebryst	lahmerbrewst	brisket of lamb
lammelår	lahmerlawr	leg of lamb
lammesadel	lahmersaaderl	saddle of lamb
lammestek	lahmerstayk	roast lamb
-lever	-lehverr	... liver
lungemos	loongermoos	minced pork lungs and onions
medisterkaker	mehdisterrkaakerr	small pork-and-veal hamburgers
medisterpølse	mehdisterrpurlser	pork-and-veal sausage
mørbradstek	murrbraadstayk	roast sirloin
-nyrer	-newrerr	... kidneys
oksebryst	ookserbrewst	brisket of beef
oksefilet	ookserfillay	fillet of beef
oksekam	ookserkahm	loin
okserulader	ookserrewlaaderr	braised beef rolls
oksestek	ookserstayk	roast beef
pølse	purlser	sausage
-ragu	-rahgew	... ragout
roastbiff	rostbif	roast beef
skinke	shingker	ham
kokt	kookt	boiled
røkt	rurkt	smoked
spekeskinke	spaykershingker	smoked, cured ham
-stek	-stayk	roast ...
svinefilet	sveenerfillay	fillet of pork
svinekam	sveenerkahm	loin of pork
svineribbe	sveenerribber	sparerib
svinestek	sveenerstayk	roast pork
svor	svoor	crackling
sylte	sewlter	brawn (headcheese)
tartarbiff	tahˊtaarbif	steak tartare
T-benstek	tay-baynstayk	T-bone steak
-tunge	-toonger	... tongue
wienerschnitzel	veenershnitserl	breaded veal escalope

boiled	kokt	kookt
braised	braisert	brahss$\overline{ay}^r$t
breaded	griljert/panert	grily$\overline{ay}^r$t/pahn$\overline{ay}^r$t
fried	stekt	stehkt
grilled (broiled)	grillet/grillstekt	grillert/grilstehkt
roast	ovnsstekt	ovnsstehkt
sautéed	sautert/brunet	sot$\overline{ay}^r$t/br$\overline{ew}$nert
smoked	røkt	rurkt
stuffed	fylt	fewlt
whole roasted	helstekt	h$\overline{ay}$lstehkt
underdone (rare)	råstekt	rawstehkt
medium	medium stekt	m$\overline{ay}$diewm stehkt
well-done	godt stekt	got stehkt

benløse fugler
(b$\overline{ay}$nlu$\overline{r}$sser f$\overline{ew}$lerr)

fried rolled slices of veal or beef stuffed with forcemeat, served with gravy, potatoes and vegetables or salad

biff med løk
(bif meh[d] l$\overline{u}$rk)

thick beef steak topped with fried onion, usually served with chips (French fries) and salad

fårikål
(fawrikawl)

mutton or lamb in cabbage stew, cooked in a big pot and served with boiled potatoes (a national dish)

kjøttkaker med løk
(khurtkaakerr meh[d] l$\overline{u}$rk)

small hamburgers with fried onions, boiled potatoes and vegetables

lapskaus
(lahpskouss)

a tasty stew that comes either "brown" (*brun* or *bifflapskaus*), with diced fried beef, potatoes and onions, or "white" (*lys* or *saltkjøttlapskaus*), with diced, salted boiled meat (usually pork), potatoes and different root vegetables; traditionally eaten with *flatbrød*

pinnekjøtt
(pinnerkhurt)

salted and dried ribs of mutton steamed on twigs; usually served with boiled potatoes and mashed swedes (rutabaga) or as a *koldtbord* dish (a Christmas speciality)

stekt ribbe/juleribbe
(stehkt ribber/
y$\overline{ew}$lerribber)

roast spareribs; usually served with sweet-and-sour cabbage stew and boiled potatoes or as a *koldtbord* dish (a Christmas speciality)

Game and poultry *Vilt og fugl*

Game is normally served with a rich and heavy cream sauce, boiled potatoes, vegetables and cranberries.

I'd like some game.	**Jeg vil gjerne ha en viltrett.**	yæi vil yǣ^rner haa ehn viltreht
What poultry dishes do you serve?	**Hva slags fugleretter har dere?**	vah shlahkss fēwlerrehterr haar dayrer
and	ahn	duck
bekkasin	berkahseen	snipe
broiler	broylerr	chicken
dyrestek	dēwrerstāyk	roast venison
elg	ehlg	elk
elgbiff	ehlgbif	elk steak
elgfilet	ehlgfillāy	fillet of elk
elgstek	ehlgstāyk	roast elk
fasan	fahssaan	pheasant
gås	gawss	goose
hane	haaner	cock
hare	haarer	hare
harestek	haarerstāyk	roast hare
hjort	yo^rt	deer
hjortesadel	yo^rtersaaderl	saddle of deer
høne	hūrner	hen
jerpe	yærper	hazelhen
kalkun	kahlkēwn	turkey
kanin	kahneen	rabbit
kylling	khewling	chicken
orre/orrfugl	orrer/orfewl	black grouse
rapphøne	rahphūrner	partridge
reinsdyr/rensdyr	ræinsdēwr/rāynsdēwr	reindeer
reinsdyrmedal- jonger	ræinsdēwrmehdahl- yongerr	small, round fillets of reindeer
reinsdyrstek	ræinsdēwshtāyk	roast reindeer
rugde	rewgder	woodcock
rype	rēwper	ptarmigan
rådyr	rawdēwr	venison
rådyrsadel	rawdēwshaaderl	saddle of venison
rådyrstek	rawdēwshtāyk	roast venison
tiur	teeēwr	woodgrouse (caper- caillie)
vaktel	vahkterl	quail
villand	vilahn	wild duck
årfugl	awrfēwl	black grouse

Vegetables   *Grønnsaker*

Could I have some vegetables?	**Kan jeg få litt grønnsaker?**	kahn yæi faw lit grurnsaakerr
agurk	ahgewrk	cucumber
artisjokker	ah**r**tishokkerr	artichokes
asparges	ahspahrggers	asparagus
aubergine	obæsheen	aubergine (eggplant)
blomkål	blomkawl	cauliflower
brekkbønner	bre**h**kburnerr	French (cut green) beans
bønner	burnerr	beans
erter	æ**r**terr	peas
gresskar	gre**h**skaar	marrow
grønnkål	grurnkawl	curly kale
gulrøtter	gewlrurterr	carrots
hodesalat	hōōdersahlaat	lettuce
kantareller	kahntahre**h**lerr	chanterelle mushrooms
kål	kawl	cabbage
kålrabi/kålrot	kawlraabi/kawlrōōt	swede (rutabaga)
løk	lūrk	onions
linser	linserr	lentils
mais	maayss	sweet corn (corn)
maiskolbe	**maay**skolber	corn on the cob
nepe	nā̄yper	turnips
paprika	paaprikkah	sweet pepper
purre	pewrer	leeks
reddiker	re**h**dikkerr	radishes
rosenkål	rōōssernkawl	Brussels sprouts
rødbeter	rū̄behterr	beetroot
rødkål	rū̄rkawl	red cabbage
salat	sah**l**aat	salad
selleri	sehlerree	celery
sjampinjonger	shahmpin**y**ongerr	button mushrooms
sopp	sop	mushrooms
sylteagurk	se**w**lterahgewrk	pickled gherkin
tomater	too**maa**terr	tomatoes
spinat	spinnaat	spinach

baked	**bakte**	bahkter
boiled	**kokte**	kookter
au gratin	**gratinerte**	grahtinā̄y**r**ter
in a sauce	**stuede**	stā̄werder
stuffed	**fylte**	fewlter

Potatoes, rice and pasta *Poteter, ris og pasta*

bakt potet	bahkt pootāyt	baked potato
komper	koomperr	potato dumplings
kokte poteter	kookter pootāyterr	boiled potatoes
kumler	koomlerr	potato dumplings
nudler	newdlerr	noodles
nypoteter	nēwpootāyterr	new potatoes
pommes frites	pom frit	chips (French fries)
potet	pootāyt	potato
potetgull	pootāytgewl	potato crisps (chips)
potetkroketter	pootāytkrookehterr	potato croquettes
potetmos/-puré/ -stappe	pootāytmōōss/-pewrāy/ -stahper	mashed potatoes
potetsalat	pootāytsahlaat	potato salad
raspeball	rahsperbahl	potato dumplings
ris	reess	rice
stekte poteter	stehkter pootāyterr	sautéed potatoes
stuede poteter	stēwerder pootāyterr	potatoes in a white sauce
sildeball (sillerbahl)		potato dumplings with a filling of minced salted herring, onion, bacon and flour; served with melted butter and pickled beetroot

Sauces *Sauser*

ansjossmør	ahngshōōssmurr	butter with chopped marinated sprats
brun saus	brūrn souss	gravy
dillsaus	dilsouss	sweet-and-sour béchamel sauce with dill
fløtesaus	flūrtersouss	cream sauce
hvitløksmør	veetlūrksmurr	garlic butter
hvit saus	veet souss	béchamel sauce
kryddersmør	krewderrsmurr	herb butter
løksaus	lūrksouss	onion sauce
majones	mahyoonāyss	mayonnaise
pepperrotsaus	pehperrōōtsouss	horseradish sauce
persillesmør	pæshillersmurr	parsley butter
rekesaus	rāykersouss	prawn (shrimp) sauce
rømme	rurmer	thick sour cream
smeltet smør	smehltert smurr	melted butter
viltsaus	viltsouss	rich cream sauce served with game

Some of the herbs, *urter*, and spices, *krydder*, you may come across:

dill	dil	dill
eine(r)bær	æiner(r)bǣr	juniper berries
gressløk	grehslūrk	chives
hvitløk	veetlūrk	garlic
ingefær	ingerfǣr	ginger
kanel	kahnāyl	cinnamon
kapers	kaapersh	capers .
karri	kahri	curry seasoning
karve	kahrver	caraway seeds
nellik	nehlik	clove
persille	pæshiller	parsley
pepper	pehperr	pepper
salvie	sahlvee	sage
salt	sahlt	salt
timian	teemeeahn	thyme

Cheese   *Ost*

Cheese is mostly eaten on *smørbrød*. Some cheeses are home-grown versions of well-known continental cheeses, while others are indigenous Norwegian.

gammelost (gahmerloost)	"old-fashioned" pungent "cheese" made with skimmed milk
Jarlsbergost (yaaˈlsbærgoost)	mild, slightly sweet, semi-hard; a taste that falls between Gouda and Emmental
normannaost (noormahnahoost)	blue-veined cow's milk cheese; sharp taste
ridderost (ridderroost)	semi-hard with nutty flavour; eaten young or mature

The square brown (goat's) cheeses found on Norwegian breakfast and lunch tables come in different varieties:

ekte geitost (ehkter yæitoost)	"real" goat's cheese, the most pungent, is made from the whey of goat's milk
Gudbrandsdalsost (gewdbrahnsdaalsoost)	milder, consists of goat's and cow's milk
fløtemysost (flūrtermēwssoost)	mild and sweet, made from the whey of cow's milk with cream added

Fruit *Frukt*

Do you have (fresh) fruit?	**Har dere (frisk) frukt?**	haar dāÿrer (frisk) frewkt
I'd like a fruit salad.	**Jeg vil gjerne ha en fruktsalat.**	yæi vil yǣᵣner haa ehn frøwktsahlaat
ananas	ahnahnahss	pineapple
appelsin	ahperl**seen**	orange
aprikos	ahprik**kooss**	apricot
banan	bah**naan**	banana
bjørnebær	byūrᵣnerbær	blackberries
blåbær	blawbær	bilberries (blueberries)
bringebær	bringerbær	raspberries
dadler	dahdlerr	dates
druer	drēwerr	grapes
blå	blaw	black
grønne	grurner	white
eple	ehpler	apple
fersken	fæshkern	peach
fikener	feekernerr	figs
grapefrukt	grāÿpfrewkt	grapefruit
hasselnøtter	hahsserlnurterr	hazelnuts
jordbær	yoorbær	strawberries
kastanjer	kahstahnyerr	chestnuts
kirsebær	khisherbær	cherries
kokosnøtt	kookoosnurt	coconut
korinter	koorinterr	currants
mandler	mahndlerr	almonds
markjordbær	mahrkyoorbær	wild strawberries
melon	mehlōōn	melon
moreller	moorehlerr	morello cherries
multer	mewlterr	arctic cloudberries
nøtter	nurterr	nuts
plommer	ploommerr	plums
pære	pǣrer	pear
rabarbra	rahbahrbrah	rhubarb
rips	ripss	redcurrants
rognebær	rongnerbær	rowanberries
rosiner	roosseenerr	raisins
sitron	sitrōōn	lemon
solbær	sōōlbær	blackcurrants
stikkelsbær	stikkerlsbær	gooseberries
svisker	sviskerr	prunes
tyttebær	tewterbær	cranberries
valnøtter	vaalnurterr	walnuts
vannmelon	vahnmehlōōn	watermelon

Dessert *Dessert*

I'd like a dessert, please.	**Jeg vil gjerne ha en dessert.**	yæi vil yǣᴿner haa ehn dehssǣr
Something light, please.	**Noe lett, takk.**	nōōer leht tahk
With / Without ...	**Med / Uten ...**	meh(d) / ēwtern
cream	**fløte**	flūrter
whipped cream	**krem**	krāym
jam	**syltetøy**	sewltertoy
(varm) eplekake med krem	(vahrm) **e**hplerkaaker meh(d) krāym	(hot) apple pie with whipped cream
frityrstekt camembert med solbær- syltetøy	fritēwshtehkt kahmang-bǣr meh(d) sōōlbǣr-sewltertoy	deep-fried camembert with blackcurrant jam
fruktkompott	**frewkt**koompot	stewed fruit
is(krem)	eess(krāym)	ice cream
jordbær-	yoorbǣr-	strawberry
sjokolade-	shookoolaader-	chocolate
vanilje-	vahnilyer-	vanilla
karamellpudding	kahrah**mehl**pewding	creme caramel
mandelkake	**mahn**derlkaaker	almond cake
multer med krem	**mewl**terr meh(d) krāym	arctic cloudberries with whipped cream
pannekaker	**pahn**erkaakerr	pancakes
riskrem	rees**krāym**	creamed rice with red berry sauce
rødgrøt	rūrgrūrt	fruit pudding with cream
sjokoladepudding	shookoolaader**pew**ding	chocolate mousse
sorbett	sor**beht**	sorbet (sherbet)
sufflé	sew**flāy**	soufflé
terte	**tæ**ᴿter	fruit cake
vafler med syltetøy	**vahf**lerr meh(d) **sewl**tertoy	waffles with jam
Hoffdessert (hofdehssǣr)		layers of meringue and whipped cream, topped with chocolate sauce and toasted almonds
pære Belle Helene (pǣrer behl hehlāyn)		poached pears with vanilla ice cream and chocolate
tilslørte bondepiker (tilshlūrᴿter boonnerpeekerr)		layers of stewed apples, biscuit (cookie) crumbs, sugar and whipped cream

Drinks   *Drikkevarer*

Alcohol* is expensive because of high taxes. Elegant restaurants are licensed to serve spirits (liquor), but only after 3 p.m., and never on Sundays. Beer and wine are served in a larger number of restaurants — but by no means all of them — even on Sundays, after 12 noon.

Beer   *Øl*

Norwegian beer meets international standards. *Pils* (pilss) is the generic term for lager, *bayerøl* (**bah**yerrurl) is medium-strong and dark, *bokkøl* (**book**url) is strong and dark, and *exportøl* (ehks**po**^rturl) is strong and light-coloured. If you're driving, stick to low-alcohol beer (*lettøl*—**leht**url or *lagerøl*—**laa**gerrurl) or the nonalcoholic *Zero* (**say**roo). *Vørterøl* (**vur**^r-terrurl) is a nonalcoholic dark and rather sweet "beer".

I'd like a beer, please.	Jeg vil gjerne ha en øl.	yæi vil yæ^rner haa ehn url
Do you have ...?	Har dere ...?	haar da͞yrer
bottled beer	flaskeøl	flahskerurl
draught (tap) beer	fatøl	faaturl
foreign beer	utenlandsk øl	e͞wternlahnsk url
light/dark beer	lyst/mørkt øl	le͞wst/murrkt url
A bottle of ...	En flaske ...	ehn flahsker
A glass of ...	Et glass ...	eht glahss
Half a litre of lager, please.	En halv pils, takk.	ehn hahl pilss tahk

Aquavit   *Akevitt*

This traditional Norwegian drink is served ice-cold in tiny glasses and goes well with herring hors d'œuvres, *spekemat* and rich food. *Akevitt* (ahker**vit**), which is usually served with a beer chaser, contains about 40% pure alcohol. It is distilled from potatoes or grain, flavoured with aromatic seeds (mostly

---

* If you want to buy wine or spirits, a branch of *Vinmonopolet* (**veen**moonoopo͞oler), the State Wine Monopoly, is the place to go to.

caraway) and spices and matured in oak casks. *Linjeakevitt*
(**lin**yerahkervit—"line" aquavit) is aquavit which has crossed
the equator circle stored in the holds of a Norwegian ship;
the rolling motion of the ship is said to produce a unique
taste.

Wine   *Vin*

Wine is imported from many countries. You'll find excellent
Bordeaux and Burgundy vintages in better hotels and restaurants, together with less expensive wines which can be
ordered by the carafe or the glass.

Do you have a wine list?	**Har dere et vinkart?**	haar **dāy**rer eht **veen**kah**ʳ**t
May I have the wine list, please?	**Kan jeg få se vinkartet?**	kahn yæi faw sāy **veen**kah**ʳ**ter
Do you have any open wines?	**Har dere åpne viner?**	haar **dāy**rer **awp**ner **vee**nerr
I'd like to try a glass of ...	**Jeg vil gjerne prøve et glass ...**	yæi vil y**ǣ**ʳner pr**ur**ver eht glahss
Can you recommend a good white wine?	**Kan du anbefale en god hvitvin?**	kahn dew **ahn**berfaaler ehn gōō(d) **veet**veen
I'd like a ... of red wine.	**Jeg vil gjerne ha ... rødvin.**	yæi vil y**ǣ**ʳner haa ... **rur**veen
bottle	**en flaske**	ehn **flahs**ker
carafe	**en karaffel**	ehn kah**rah**ferl
glass	**et glass**	eht glahss
half bottle	**en halv flaske**	ehn hahl **flahs**ker
A bottle of champagne, please.	**En flaske champagne, takk.**	ehn **flahs**ker shahm**pah**nyer tahk
Please bring me another ...	**Kan jeg få en ... til?**	kahn yæi faw ehn ... til
Where does this wine come from?	**Hvor kommer denne vinen fra?**	voor **kom**merr **deh**ner **vee**nern fraa
It's excellent.	**Den er meget god.**	dehn ær **māy**gert gōō(d)
Do you have any nonalcoholic wines?	**Har dere alkoholfrie viner?**	haar **dāy**rer ahlkooh**ōōl**freeyer **vee**nerr

red	rødvin	rūrveen
white	hvitvin	veetveen
rosé	rosévin	roossāyveen
dry	tørr	turr
full-bodied	fyldig	fewldi
sparkling	musserende	mewssāyrehner
very dry	meget tørr	māygert turr
sweet	søt	sūrt
chilled	avkjølt	aavkhurlt
at room temperature	værelses-temperert	vāērerlsers-tehmperrāy'rt

Other alcoholic drinks *Andre alkoholholdige drikker*

You can get almost all the drinks you're used to at home. The customary international names are used, and the drinks are mixed the same way.

I'd like a/an ..., please.	**Jeg vil gjerne ha ...**	yæi vil yāē'rner haa
aperitif	en aperitiff	ehn ahperritif
brandy	brandy	"brandy"
cognac	et glass konjakk	eht glahss konyahk
gin and tonic	en gin tonic	ehn "gin tonic"
liqueur	et glass likør	eht glahss likūrr
port	et glass portvin	eht glahss poo'tveen
rum	rom	room
sherry	et glass sherry	eht glahss shæri
vermouth	et glass vermut	eht glahss værmewt
vodka	vodka	vodkah
whisky	whisky	viski
neat (straight)	bar	baar
on the rocks	med is	meh(d) eess
with water	med vann	meh(d) vahn
with soda water	med soda	me(h)d sōodah

SKÅL!
(skawl)
CHEERS!

Nonalcoholic drinks *Alkoholfrie drikker*

Of course, you don't have to order wine or spirits. If you prefer, ask for a soft drink.

I don't drink alcohol.	**Jeg drikker ikke alkohol.**	yæi **drikkerr ikker** ahlkoo**hōōl**
A bottle of mineral (spring) water, please.	**En flaske naturlig mineralvann, takk.**	ehn **flah**sker nah**tēw**ʳli minerraalvahn tahk
fizzy (sparkling)	**med kullsyre**	meh(d) **kewl**sēwrer
still (natural)	**uten kullsyre**	**ēw**tern **kewl**sēwrer
I'd like a/an ...	**Jeg vil gjerne ha ...**	yæi vil **yǣ**ʳner haa
apple juice	**eplesaft**	**ehp**lersahft
grapefruit juice	**grapefruktjuice**	**grāy**pfrewktyēwss
iced tea	**iste**	**ees**tāy
lemonade	**sitronbrus**	sit**rōōn**brēwss
(glass of) milk	**(et glass) melk**	(eht glahss) mehlk
low-fat milk	**lettmelk**	**leht**mehlk
milkshake	**en milkshake**	ehn "milkshake"
orange juice	**appelsinjuice**	ahperl**seen**yēwss
pineapple juice	**ananasjuice**	ah**nah**nahsyēwss
soft drink	**leskedrikk**	**lehs**kerdrik

Hot drinks *Varme drikker*

The best place to go for your afternoon tea or coffee is a *konditori*, teashop (coffee shop). Pay for your cake or pastry at the counter and then take it through to the seating area. In more elegant or old-fashioned cafés you'll be served at the table.

I'd like a/an ...	**Jeg vil gjerne ha ...**	yæi vil **yǣ**ʳner haa
(hot) chocolate	**(varm) sjokolade**	(vahrm) shookoo**laa**der
coffee	**kaffe**	**kah**fer
a pot of	**en kanne**	ehn **kah**ner
decaffeinated	**koffeinfri**	koffer**een**free
espresso	**en espresso**	ehn ehs**preh**ssoo
with cream	**med fløte**	meh(d) **flūr**ter
tea	**te**	tāy
a cup of	**en kopp**	ehn kop
with lemon	**med sitron**	meh(d) sit**rōōn**
with milk	**med melk**	meh(d) mehlk

Complaints *Klager*

There's a ... missing.	**Det mangler ...**	deh mahnglerr
plate	**en tallerken**	ehn tahlærkern
glass	**et glass**	eht glahss
I don't have a ...	**Jeg har ikke noen ...**	yæi haar ikker nōōern
knife	**kniv**	kneev
fork	**gaffel**	gahferl
spoon	**skje**	shāy
That's not what I ordered.	**Dette er ikke det jeg bestilte.**	dehter ær ikker deh yæi berstilter
I asked for ...	**Jeg ba om ...**	yæi baa om
There must be a mistake.	**Det må være en misforståelse.**	deh maw værer ehn misfoshtawerlser
May I change this?	**Kan jeg få byttet dette?**	kahn yæi faw bewtert dehter
I asked for a small portion (for the child).	**Jeg ba om en liten porsjon (til barnet).**	yæi baa om ehn leetern pooshōōn (til baarner)
The meat is ...	**Kjøttet er ...**	khurter ær
overdone	**for mye stekt**	for mēwer stehkt
underdone	**for lite stekt**	for leeter stehkt
too rare	**for blodig**	for blōōdi
too tough	**for seigt**	for sæit
This is too ...	**Dette er for ...**	dehter ær for
bitter	**beskt**	behskt
salty	**salt**	sahlt
sweet	**søtt**	surt
This doesn't taste right.	**Dette smaker ikke godt.**	dehter smaakerr ikker got
The food is cold.	**Maten er kald.**	maatern ær kahl
This isn't fresh.	**Dette er ikke ferskt.**	dehter ær ikker fæshkt
What's taking so long?	**Hvorfor tar det så lang tid?**	voorfor taar deh saw lahng teed
Have you forgotten our drinks?	**Har du glemt drinkene våre?**	haar du glehmt dringkerner vawrer
The wine doesn't taste right.	**Vinen smaker ikke godt.**	veenern smaakerr ikker got

| This isn't clean. | **Dette er ikke rent.** | dehter ær ikker rāynt |
| I'd like to speak to the head waiter/ manager. | **Kan jeg få snakke med hovmesteren/ bestyreren?** | kahn yæi faw snahker meh(d) hawvmehsterrern/ berstēwrerren |

The bill (check) *Regningen*

The service charge is automatically included in restaurant bills. You can add a little extra if you are satisfied with the meal and the service.

The bill, please.	**Regningen, takk.**	rǣiningern tahk
I'd like to pay.	**Jeg vil gjerne betale.**	yæi vil yǣˉner bertaaler
We'd like to pay separately.	**Vi vil gjerne betale hver for oss.**	vee vil yǣˉner bertaaler vǣr for oss
I think there's a mistake in this bill.	**Jeg tror det er en feil på regningen.**	yæi trōor deh ær ehn fæil paw rǣiningern
What's this amount for?	**Hva står dette beløpet for?**	vah stawr dehter berlūrper for
Is everything included?	**Er alt inkludert?**	ær ahlt inklewdāyˉt
Do you accept traveller's cheques/ Eurocheques?	**Tar dere reisesjekker/ eurosjekker?**	taar dāyrer rǣissershehkerr/ yēwrooshehkerr
Can I pay with this credit card?	**Kan jeg betale med dette kreditt-kortet?**	kahn yæi bertaaler meh(d) dehter krehdit-koˉter
This is for you.	**Vær så god.**	vǣr saw gōo(d)
Keep the change.	**Behold veksle-pengene.**	berhol vehkshler-pehngerner
That was a delicious meal.	**Det var et utsøkt måltid.**	deh vaar eht ēwtsurkt mawlteed
We enjoyed it, thank you.	**Det var meget godt.**	deh vaar māygert got

SERVICE INKLUDERT
SERVICE INCLUDED

TIPPING, see inside back cover

Snacks *Småretter*

For a quick snack, go to a *gatekjøkken*, "street kitchen", where you can get everything from a hot dog to chicken and spring rolls, ice cream and soft drinks. At cafés and cafeterias, you can have pastries, open sandwiches and maybe a salad.

I'll have one of those.	**Jeg vil gjerne ha en av dem.**	yæi vil y**ǣ**ʳner haa ehn ahv dehm
Can I have two of these, please?	**Kan jeg få to av disse?**	kahn yæi faw t**oo** ahv disser
to the right/left above/below	**til høyre/venstre ovenfor/nedenfor**	til h**oy**rer/**vehn**strer **aw**vernfor/n**ay**dernfor
It's to take away.	**Jeg tar det med meg.**	yæi taar deh meh(d) mæi
I'll eat it here.	**Jeg spiser det her.**	yæi **spee**sserr deh h**ǣ**r
A frankfurter with ..., please.	**En pølse med ...**	ehn **pu**rlser meh(d)
mashed potatoes	**potetstappe**	poot**ay**tstahper
a potato pancake	**lompe**	**loom**per
I'd like a/an/ some ...	**Jeg vil gjerne ha ...**	yæi vil y**ǣ**ʳner haa
fried sausage	**en grillpølse**	ehn **gril**purlser
in a roll	**med brød**	meh(d) br**ur**
with chips (fries)	**med pommes frites**	meh(d) pom frit
with onion	**med løk**	meh(d) l**ur**k
ice cream	**en is(krem)**	ehn **ees**(kr**ay**m)
(slice of) pizza	**en (skive) pizza**	ehn (**shee**ver) pitsah
soft ice cream	**en softis**	ehn **soft**eess
with nuts	**med nøtter**	meh(d) **nu**rterr
with chocolate	**med sjokolade**	meh(d) shookool**aa**der
spring (egg) roll	**vårrull**	**vawr**rewl
water ice	**en fruktis**	ehn fr**ew**kteess
Can I have an open sandwich with eggs and marinated sprats?	**Kan jeg få et smør-brød med egg og ansjos?**	kahn yæi faw eht **smurr**-br**ur** meh(d) ehg o(g) ahng**shoo**s
cheese	**ost**	oost
cod roe	**torskerogn**	**tosh**kerrongn
fish pudding	**fiskepudding**	**fisk**erpewding
ham	**kokt skinke**	kookt **shing**ker
liver paté	**leverpostei**	**lehv**errpoost**æ**i

Pastries and cakes *Bakverk og kaker*

I'd like a piece of ...	**Jeg vil gjerne ha et stykke ...**	yæi vil yǣ^rner haa eht stewker
gâteau (layer cake)	**bløtkake**	blū̄rtkaaker
with marzipan	**med marsipan**	meh(d) mahshippaan
I'd like a/an/ some ...	**Jeg vil gjerne ha ...**	yæi vil yǣ^rner haa
apple pie	**en eplekake**	ehn ehplerkaaker
biscuits (cookies)	**noen småkaker**	nōōern smawkaakerr
bun	**en bolle**	ehn boller
with raisins	**med rosiner**	meh(d) roosseenerr
chocolate cake	**en sjokoladekake**	ehn shookoolaaderkaaker
coconut macaroons	**noen kokos- makroner**	nōōern kookooss- mahkrōōnerr
cream horn	**et fløtehorn**	eht flūrterhōō^rn
custard slice (napo- leon)	**en napoleonskake**	ehn nahpōōlehonskaaker
Danish pastry	**et wienerbrød**	eht veenerrbrū̄r
doughnut	**en smultring**	ehn smewltring
fruit tart	**en fruktterte**	ehn frewkttæ^rter
meringues	**noen marengs**	nōōern mahrehngss
shortbread	**en sandkake**	ehn sahnkaaker
sponge cake	**et sukkerbrød**	eht sookkerrbrū̄r
Swiss roll	**en rullekake**	ehn rewlerkaaker
with vanilla butter	**med vaniljefyll**	meh(d) vahnilyerfewl
with jam	**med syltetøy**	meh(d) sewltertoy
with chocolate cream	**med sjokoladefyll**	meh(d) shookoolaader- fewl

fastelavnsbolle
(**fahsterlaavns-
boller**)

lenten bun; bun cut in half, filled with whipped cream and topped with icing (confectioners') sugar

julekake
(**yēw̄lerkaaker**)

rich fruit cake (a Christmas speciality)

kransekake
(**krahnserkaaker**)

cone-shaped pile of almond-macaroon rings decorated with icing (frosting), marzipan flowers, etc.

kringle
(**kringler**)

twisted sweet yeast-bread ring

krumkake
(**kroomkaaker**)

wafer cone filled with whipped cream and jam or berries

vaniljebolle
(**vahnilyerboller**)

bun filled with vanilla custard and topped with icing sugar

Picnic *Picnic*

Here's a basic list of food and drink that might come in useful when shopping for a picnic.

I'd like a/an/ some ...	**Jeg vil gjerne ha ...**	yæi vil yǣ'ner haa
apples	**epler**	ehpler
bananas	**bananer**	bahnaanerr
beer	**øl**	url
bread	**brød**	brūr
rye	**rug**	rēwg
white	**loff**	loof
butter	**smør**	smurr
cake	**en kake**	ehn **kaa**ker
cheese	**ost**	oost
cheese spread	**smøreost**	smūrreroost
chips (Am.)	**potetgull**	pootāytgewl
chocolate bar	**en sjokoladeplate**	ehn shookoolaaderplaater
coffee	**kaffe**	kahfer
instant coffee	**pulverkaffe**	pewlverrkahfer
cold cuts	**kjøttpålegg**	khurtpawlehg
crackers	**salte kjeks**	sahlter khehkss
crisps	**potetgull**	pootāytgewl
eggs	**egg**	ehg
grapes	**druer**	drēwerr
ham	**skinke**	shingker
lemon	**en sitron**	ehn sitrōōn
liver paté	**leverpostei**	lehverrpoostæi
liver sausage	**leverpølse**	lehverrpurlser
milk	**melk**	mehlk
mustard *	**sennep**	sehnerp
oranges	**appelsiner**	ahperlseenerr
pastries	**kaker**	kaakerr
pepper	**pepper**	pehperr
pickled gherkins	**sylteagurker**	sewlterahgewrkerr
rolls	**rundstykker**	rewnstewkerr
salt	**salt**	sahlt
sausage	**pølse**	purlser
soft drink	**leskedrikk**	lehskerdrik
sugar	**sukker**	sookkerr
tea	**te**	tāy
wine	**vin**	veen

---

* Norwegian mustard is sweet; if you want a sharp one, ask for French mustard (*fransk sennep* – frahnsk **seh**nerp).

Travelling around

Plane *Fly*

Is there a flight to Tromsø?	Går det et fly til Tromsø?	gawr deh eht flew til troomsur
Is it a direct flight?	Er det et direkte fly?	ær deh eht deerehkter flew
When's the next flight to Alta?	Når går neste fly til Alta?	nor gawr nehster flew til ahltah
Is there a connection to Kirkenes?	Fins det en forbindelse til Kirkenes?	finss deh ehn forbinerlser til khirkernayss
I'd like to make a reservation for Stavanger.	Jeg vil gjerne reservere en plass til Stavanger.	yæi vil yæ'ner rehssærvayrer ehn plahss til stahvahngerr
I'd like a ticket to Bergen.	Jeg vil gjerne ha en billett til Bergen.	yæi vil yæ'ner haa ehn billeht til bærgern
single (one-way)	enkeltbillett	ehngkerltbilleht
return (round-trip)	tur-returbillett	tewr-rehtewrbilleht
aisle seat	plass ved midtgangen	plahss veh(d) mitgahngern
window seat	vindusplass	vindewsplahss
What time ...?	Når ...?	nor
do we take off	går flyet	gawr flewer
should I check in	må jeg sjekke inn	maw yæi shehker in
do we arrive	er vi fremme	ær vee frehmer
This is cabin luggage.	Dette er håndbagasje.	dehter ær honbahgaasher
Is there a bus to/from the airport?	Går det buss til/fra flyplassen?	gawr deh bewss til/fraa flewplahssern
I'd like to ... my reservation.	Jeg vil gjerne ... reservasjonen.	yæi vil yæ'ner ... rehssærvahshoonern
cancel/change confirm	annullere/endre bekrefte	ahnewlayrer/ehndrer berkrehfter
How long is the ticket valid?	Hvor lenge er billetten gyldig?	voor lehnger ær billehtern yewldi

ANKOMST	**AVGANG**
ARRIVAL	DEPARTURE

Train   *Tog*

Trains in Norway are operated by Norwegian State Railways—Norges Statsbaner (NSB). From Oslo central station (*Oslo Sentralstasjon*) there are connections to Sweden and the Continent via Copenhagen. The main inland destinations are Stavanger, Bergen and Trondheim, with connections to Bodø, Norway's northernmost station (apart from Narvik, which has connections to Sweden only).

Children under four years old travel free. Travellers under 16 pay half price.

Except on local trains, food is available either from a snack trolley (cart; *serveringsvogn*), a kiosk (*togkiosk*), a buffet car (*kafeteriavogn*) or a dining car (*restaurantvogn*). In sleeping cars, men and women can be accommodated separately; there are also family compartments. Most long-distance trains have carriages specially equipped for parents with babies and for disabled people. It's worth reserving a seat, particularly on long-distance trains.

EuroCity-tog (EC) (yēwroosítti-tawg)	International express train with first and second class
Inter-City-tog (''intercity''-tawg)	Day train connecting major towns in southern Norway with Oslo
Ekspresstog (ehksprehstawg)	Long-distance express train stopping at few stations
Hurtigtog (hew^rtitawg)	Long-distance express train stopping at more stations than the *ekspresstog*
Lokaltog (lookaaltawg)	Local train stopping at all stations

Coach (Long-distance bus)   *Rutebil/Ekspressbuss*

Areas not served by NSB are covered by regional and local bus companies. Tourist information offices and travel agencies have timetables and other details.

Note: Most of the phrases on the following pages can be used for both train and coach travel.

To the railway station *Til jernbanestasjonen*

Where's the railway station?	**Hvor er jernbanestasjonen?**	voor ær yǣ^rnbaaner-stahshōonern
Where's the coach station?	**Hvor er buss-stasjonen?**	voor ær bews-stahshōonern
Taxi!	**Drosje!**	drosher
Take me to the ..., please.	**Kjør meg til ...**	khūrr mæi til

INNGANG	ENTRANCE
UTGANG	EXIT
TIL TOGENE	TO THE TRAINS
INFORMASJON	INFORMATION

Where's the ...? *Hvor er ...?*

Where is/are (the) ...?	**Hvor er ...?**	voor ær
booking office	**billettkontoret**	billehtkoontōorer
cafeteria	**kafeteriaen**	kahfertāyreeahern
currency exchange office	**vekslingskontoret**	vehkshlingskoontōorer
left-luggage office (checkroom)	**bagasje-oppbevaringen**	bahgaasher-opbervaaringern
lost property (lost and found) office	**hittegodskontoret**	hittergoodskoontōorer
luggage (baggage) lockers	**oppbevarings-boksene**	opbervaarings-bokserner
newsstand	**aviskiosken**	ahveeskhyoskern
platform 2	**perrong 2**	pehrong 2
reservations office	**billettkontoret**	billehtkoontōorer
restaurant	**restauranten**	rehstewrahngern
snack bar	**snackbaren**	snækbaarern
ticket office	**billettluken**	billehtlēwkern
track 5	**spor 5**	spōor 5
waiting room	**ventesalen**	vehntersaalern
Where are the toilets?	**Hvor er toalettet?**	voor ær tooahlehter

TAXI, see page 21

Inquiries *Forespørsler*

In Norway the sign [i] means information office.

When is the ....train to Halden?	**Når går ... tog til Halden?**	nor gawr ... tawg til hahldern
first/last	**første/siste**	furshter/sister
When is the next train to Hamar?	**Når går neste tog til Hamar?**	nor gawr nehster tawg til haamahr
What time does the train to Oslo leave?	**Når går toget til Oslo?**	nor gawr tawger til ooshloo
What's the fare to Trondheim?	**Hvor mye koster det it Trondheim?**	voor mewer kosterr deh til tronhæim
Is it a through train?	**Er det et gjennom-gående tog?**	ær deh eht yehnom-gawehner tawg
Is there a connection to Elverum?	**..... en forbin-delse til Elverum?**	finss deh ehn forbin-erlser til ehlverrewm
Do I have to change trains?	**Må jeg bytte tog?**	maw yæi bewter tawg
Is there enough time to change?	**Rekker jeg å bytte tog?**	rehkerr yæi aw bewter tawg
Is the train running on time?	**Er toget i rute?**	ær tawger ee rewter
What time does the train arrive in Åndalsnes?	**Når er toget fremme i Åndalsnes?**	nor ær tawger frehmer ee ondahlsnayss
Is there a dining car/sleeping car on the train?	**Er det en spise-vogn/sovevogn i toget?**	ær deh ehn speesser-vongn/sawvervongn ee ....er
Does the train stop in Asker?	**Stanser toget i Asker?**	stahnserr tawger ee ahskerr
Which platform does the train to Skien leave from?	**Fra hvilken perrong går toget til Skien?**	fraa vilkern pehrong gawr tawger til shayern
Which track does the train from Gjøvik arrive at?	**På hvilket spor kommer toget fra Gjøvik inn?**	paw vilkert spoor kommerr tawger fraa yurveek in
I'd like a time-table, please.	**Jeg vil gjerne ha en rutetabell.**	yæi vil yæᶠner haa ehn rewtertahbehl

Det er et gjennomgående tog.	It's a through train.
Du må bytte i ...	You have to change at ...
Bytt i ... og ta lokaltoget.	Change at ... and get a local train.
Perrong 2 er ...	Platform 2 is ...
der borte/opp trappen til høyre/til venstre	over there/upstairs on the right/on the left
Det går et tog til Tønsberg kl. 16.00.	There's a train to Tønsberg at 16.00 (4 p.m.).
Toget går fra spor 8.	Your train will leave from track 8.
Det er ... minutter forsinket.	It's running ... minutes late.
Første klasse er foran/i midten/bakerst.	First class at the front/in the middle/at the rear.

Tickets—Reservation *Billetter – Bestilling*

I'd like a ticket to ...	Jeg vil gjerne ha en billett til ...	yæi vil yāē'rner haa ehn billeht til
single (one-way)	enkeltbillett	ehngkerltbilleht
return (round-trip)	tur-returbillett	tewr-rehtēwrbilleht
first class	første klasse	furshter klahsser
second class	andre/annen klasse	ahndrer/aaern klahsser
half price	halv pris	hahl preess
Must the child pay full fare?	Må barnet betale full takst?	maw baa'rner bertaaler fewl tahkst
I'd like a window seat.	Jeg vil gjerne ha vindusplass.	yæi vil yāē'rner hah vindewsplahss
I'd like to reserve a ...	Jeg vil gjerne reservere en ...	yæi vil yāē'rner rehssærvāȳrer ehn
couchette	køye i liggevognen	koyer ee liggervongnern
berth in the sleeping car	køye i sovevognen	koyer ee sawvervongnern
upper berth	overkøye	awverrkoyer
middle berth	midtkøye	mitkoyer
lower berth	underkøye	ewnerrkoyer

TIME, see page 153

On the platform *På perrongen*

Is this the platform for the train to Kongsberg?	**Er dette perrongen for toget til Kongsberg?**	ær **deh**ter peh**rong**ern for **taw**ger til **kongs**bærg
Is this the train to Geilo?	**Er dette toget til Geilo?**	ær **deh**ter **taw**ger til **yæi**loo
Is the train from Levanger late?	**Er toget fra Levanger forsinket?**	ær **taw**ger fraa **ler**vahngerr fo**shing**kert
What track does the train to Gol arrive on?	**På hvilket spor kommer toget til Gol inn?**	paw **vil**kert spōor **kom**merr **taw**ger til gōol in

All aboard *Ta plass*

Excuse me. Could I get by?	**Unnskyld. Kan jeg få komme forbi?**	**ewn**shewl. kahn yæi faw **kom**mer for**bee**
Is this seat taken?	**Er denne plassen opptatt?**	ær **deh**ner **plahss**ern op**taht**

RØYKING TILLATT	RØYKING FORBUDT/ RØYKING IKKE TILLATT
SMOKER	NONSMOKER

I think that's my seat.	**Jeg tror at det er min plass.**	yæi trōor aht deh ær meen plahss
Would you let me know before we get to Røros?	**Kan du si fra før vi kommer til Røros?**	kahn dew see fraa fūrr vee **kom**merr til **rūr**rawss
What station is this?	**Hvilken stasjon er dette?**	**vil**kern stah**shōon** ær **deh**ter
How long does the train stop here?	**Hvor lenge står toget her?**	voor **leh**nger stawr **taw**ger hǣr
When do we get to Voss?	**Når kommer vi til Voss?**	nor **kom**merr vee til voss
Where are we now?	**Hvor er vi nå?**	voor ær vee naw
Where's the ...?	**Hvor er ...**	voor ær
dining car	**spisevognen**	**spee**sservongnern
buffet car	**kafeteriavognen**	kahfer**tay**reeahvongnern
kiosk	**togkiosken**	**tawg**khyoskern

Sleeping   *I sovevognen*

Are there any free compartments in the sleeping car?	**Fins det noen ledige kupéer i sove-vognen?**	finss deh nōōern lāy-deeyer kewpāyerr ee **saw**vervongnern
Where's the sleeping car?	**Hvor er sovevognen?**	voor ær **saw**vervongnern
Where's my berth?	**Hvor er min køye?**	voor ær meen **koy**er
I'd like a lower berth.	**Jeg vil gjerne ha en underkøye.**	yæi vil yǣ^rner haa ehn ewnerrkoyer
Would you make up our berths?	**Kan du gjøre i stand køyene våre?**	kahn dew yūrrer ee stahn koyerner vawrer
Would you wake me at 7 o'clock?	**Kan du vekke meg kl. 7?**	kahn dew vehker mæi klokkern 7

Baggage and porters   *Bagasje og bærere*

Can you help me with my luggage?	**Kan du hjelpe meg med bagasjen?**	kahn dew yehlper mæi meh(d) bahgaashern
Are there any ...?	**Fins det ... her?**	finss deh ... hǣr
luggage trolleys (carts)	**bagasjetraller**	bahgaashertrahlerr
luggage (baggage) lockers	**oppbevarings-bokser**	opbervaaringsbokserr
Where are they?	**Hvor er de?**	voor ær dee
Where's the left-luggage office (checkroom)?	**Hvor er bagasje-oppbevaringen?**	voor ær bahgaasher-opbervaaringern
I'd like to leave my luggage, please.	**Jeg vil gjerne levere inn bagasjen til oppbevaring.**	yæi vil yǣ^rner lehvāyrer in bahgaashern til opbervaaring
I'd like to register (check) my luggage.	**Jeg vil gjerne ekspe-dere bagasjen.**	yæi vil yǣ^rner ehksper-dāyrer bahgaashern
I'd like to take out luggage insurance.	**Jeg vil gjerne tegne en reisegods-forsikring.**	yæi vil yǣ^rner tæiner ehn ræissergoods-foshikring

---

REISEGODSEKSPEDISJON
REGISTERING LUGGAGE (BAGGAGE CHECKING)

PORTERS, see also page 18

Bus—Tram (Streetcar)   *Buss – Trikk*

Single tickets are available from the driver. In Oslo, it's worth buying a booklet of tickets (valid for transfers within one hour) if you plan to travel around.

I'd like a booklet of tickets.	**Jeg vil gjerne ha et billetthefte.**	yæi vil yǣ^{r}ner haa eht billehthehfter
Which tram (streetcar) goes to the town centre?	**Hvilken trikk går til sentrum?**	vilkern trik gawr til sehntrewm
Does this bus stop at ...?	**Stanser denne bussen ved ...?**	stahnserr dehner bewssern veh(d)
Where can I get a bus to the Folk Museum?	**Hvorfra går bussen til Folkemuseet?**	voorfra gawr bewssern til folkermewssǟyer
Which tram do I take to Vigeland Park?	**Hvilken trikk går til Vigelandsparken?**	vilkern trik gawr til veegerlahnspahrkern
Where's the ...?	**Hvor er ...?**	voor ær
bus stop	**bussholdeplassen**	bewshollerplahssern
tram stop	**trikkeholdeplassen**	trikkerhollerplahssern
When is the ... bus to the town centre?	**Når går ... buss til sentrum?**	nor gawr ... bewss til sehntrewm
first/next/last	**første/neste/siste**	furshter/nehster/sister
How much is the fare to ...?	**Hvor mye koster det til ...?**	voor mēwer kosterr deh til
Do I have to change buses?	**Må jeg bytte buss?**	maw yæi bewter bewss
How many stops are there to ...?	**Hvor mange holdeplasser er det til ...?**	voor mahnger hollerplahsserr ær deh til
Will you tell me when to get off?	**Kan du si fra når jeg skal gå av?**	kahn dew see fraa nor yæi skahl gaw ahv
I want to get off at ...	**Jeg skal av ved ...**	yæi skahl ahv veh(d)

> **BUSSHOLDEPLASS**
> BUS STOP

Underground (Subway)   *T-bane*

Oslo's underground railway extends from the centre of the city to the suburbs. Maps of the system are displayed at stations and aboard trains. You can transfer from bus or tram to underground (subway) on the same ticket.

Where's the nearest underground station?	**Hvor er nærmeste T-banestasjon?**	voor ær nærmehster tāy-baanerstahshōōn
Does this train go to Holmenkollen?	**Går denne banen til Holmenkollen?**	gawr dehner baanern til holmernkollern
Where do I change for ...?	**Hvor må jeg bytte for å komme til ...?**	voor maw yæi bewter for aw kommer til
Is the next station ...?	**Er neste stasjon ...?**	ær nehster stahshōōn
Which line should I take to ...?	**Hvilken linje skal jeg ta til ...?**	vilkern linyer skahl yæi taa til

Boat—Ship   *Båt – Skip*

Travelling by car in western Norway involves numerous fjord crossings by ferry. The frequency of services depends on the season. In rural areas, local hotels will always be able to tell you exact ferry times. At the height of the summer tourist season, try to reserve a place for your car or you may find yourself spending hours in queues. Fares vary according to size and weight of vehicle.

In Oslo, there are guided cruises of the harbour and around the islands, as well as regular boat services to the museums on the Bygdøy peninsula.

When does the boat/ferry for ... leave?	**Når går båten/ fergen til ...?**	nor gawr bawtern/ færggern til
Where's the embarkation point?	**Ved hvilken kai legger båten til?**	veh(d) vilkern kahy lehgerr bawtern til
How long does the crossing take?	**Hvor lang tid tar overfarten?**	voor lahng teed taar awverrfah'tern

When do we call at Molde?	Når legger vi til i Molde?	nor lehgerr vee til ee molder
I'd like to take a boat trip/harbour tour.	Jeg vil gjerne ta en båttur/havne-rundtur.	yæi vil yǣᵣner taa ehn bawttēwr/hahvner-rewntēwr
boat	en båt	ehn bawt
cabin	en lugar	ehn lewgaar
single/double	enkel/dobbel	ehngkerl/dobberl
canoe	en kano	ehn kaanoo
cruise	et cruise	eht "cruise"
deck	et dekk	eht dehk
ferry	en ferge/ferje	ehn færgger/færyer
car ferry	bilferge	beelfærgger
gangway	en landgang	ehn lahngahng
hydrofoil	en hydrofoil	ehn hewdroofoil
jetty	en brygge	ehn brewger
kayak	en kajakk	ehn kahyahk
life belt	et livbelte	eht leevbehlter
life boat	en livbåt	ehn leevbawt
life jacket	en flytevest	ehn flēwtervehst
motorboat	en motorbåt	ehn mōōtoorbawt
pier	en pir	ehn peer
port	en havn	ehn hahvn
rowing boat	en robåt	ehn roobawt
sailing boat	en seilbåt	ehn sæilbawt
ship	et skip	eht sheep
steamer	en dampbåt	ehn dahmpbawt

Other means of transport *Andre transportmidler*

bicycle	en sykkel	ehn sewkerl
cable car	en taubane	ehn toubaaner
helicopter	et helikopter	eht hehlikopterr
moped	en moped	ehn moopāyd
motorbike	en motorsykkel	ehn mōōtooshewkerl
scooter	en scooter	ehn skēwterr
I'd like to hire (rent) a bicycle.	Jeg vil gjerne leie en sykkel.	yæi vil yǣᵣner læier ehn sewkerl

Or perhaps you prefer:

to hike	å vandre	aw vahndrer
to hitchhike	å haike	aw hahyker
to walk	å spasere	aw spahssāyrer

Car *Bil*

All the basic rules for right-hand traffic apply. The use of seat belts (*bilbelte*) is obligatory, and that includes back-seat passengers if the car is so equipped. A red reflector warning triangle must be carried. Crash helmets are compulsory for both drivers and passengers on motorcycles and scooters. Fines for drinking and driving are prohibitive and may involve loss of licence and imprisonment.

Where's the nearest filling station?	**Hvor er nærmeste bensinstasjon?**	voor ær nærmehster behnseenstahshōōn
Fill it up, please.	**Full tank, takk.**	fewl tahngk tahk
Give me ... litres of petrol (gasoline).	**... liter bensin, takk.**	... leeterr behnseen tahk
super (premium)	**super**	sēwperr
regular	**normal**	noormaal
unleaded	**blyfri**	blēwfree
diesel	**diesel**	deesserl
Please check the ...	**Vær snill å kontrollere ...**	vær snil aw koontroolāyrer
battery	**batteriet**	bahterreeyer
brake fluid	**bremsevæsken**	brehmservehskern
oil/water	**oljen/vannet**	olyern/vahner
Would you check the tyre pressure?	**Kan du kontrollere trykket i dekkene?**	kahn dew koontroolāyrer trewker ee dehkerner
1.6 front, 1.8 rear.	**1,6 foran, 1,8 bak.**	1 kommah 6 forahn 1 kommah 8 baak
Could you check the spare tyre, too?	**Kan du kontrollere reservedekket også?**	kahn dew koontroolāyrer rehsærverdehker osso
Can you mend this puncture (fix this flat)?	**Kan du reparere denne punkte-ringen?**	kahn dew rehpahrāyrer dehner poongtāy-ringern
Would you change the ..., please?	**Kan du skifte ...**	kahn dew shifter
bulb	**pæren**	pæærern
fan belt	**vifteremmen**	vifterrehmern
spark(ing) plugs	**tennstiftene**	tehnstifterner
tyre	**dekket**	dehker
wipers	**vindusviskerne**	vindewsviskæ{r}ner

Would you clean the windscreen (windshield)?	**Kan du vaske frontruten?**	kahn dew **vah**sker front<u>rew</u>tern
Where can I get my car cleaned?	**Hvor kan jeg få vasket bilen?**	voor kahn yæi faw **vah**skert **bee**lern
Is there a car wash here/nearby?	**Er det en bilvask her/i nærheten?**	ær deh ehn **beel**vahsk h<u>ær</u>/ee **nær**hehtern

Asking the way   *Spørre om veien*

In which direction is ...?	**I hvilken retning ligger ...?**	ee **vil**kern **reht**ning **ligg**err
Can you tell me the way to ...?	**Kan du vise meg veien til ...?**	kahn dew **vee**sser mæi **væi**ern til
Can you tell me where ... is?	**Kan du si meg hvor ... ligger?**	kahn dew see mæi voor ... **ligg**err
How do I get to ...?	**Hvordan kommer jeg til ...?**	voo**r**dahn **komm**err yæi til
this place	**dette stedet**	**deh**ter **stay**der
this address	**denne adressen**	**deh**ner ah**dreh**ssern
Am I on the right road for ...?	**Er dette veien til ...?**	ær **deh**ter **væi**ern til
How far is the next village?	**Hvor langt er det til neste tettsted?**	voor lahngt ær deh til **neh**ster **teht**st<u>ay</u>(d)
How far is it to ... from here?	**Hvor langt er det til ... herfra?**	voor lahngt ær deh til ... **hær**frah
Is there a motorway (expressway) to ...?	**Fins det en motorvei til ...?**	finss deh ehn <u>moo</u>toorvæi til
Is there a road with little traffic?	**Fins det en vei med lite trafikk?**	finss deh ehn væi meh(d) **lee**ter trah**fik**
Can I drive to the centre of town?	**Kan jeg kjøre inn i sentrum?**	kahn yæi **khür**rer in ee **sehn**trewm
How long does it take by car/on foot?	**Hvor lang tid tar det med bil/til fots?**	voor lahng teed taar deh meh(d) beel/til **foot**ss
Where does this road lead to?	**Hvor fører denne veien?**	voor **für**rerr **deh**ner **væi**ern
Can you show me on the map where I am?	**Kan du vise meg på kartet hvor jeg er?**	kahn dew **vee**sser mæi paw **kah**r**ter** voor yæi ær

Du har kjørt feil.	You're on the wrong road.
Kjør rett frem.	Go straight ahead.
Det er der borte til høyre/venstre.	It's down there on the right/left.
midt imot/bak ...	opposite/behind ...
ved siden av/etter ...	next to/after ...
nord/sør/øst/vest	north/south/east/west
Kjør til første/annet kryss.	Go to the first/second crossroads (intersection).
Sving til venstre ved trafikklyset.	Turn left at the traffic lights.
Ta til høyre ved neste kryss.	Turn right at the next corner.
Ta E 6.	Take the E 6.
Det er en enveisgate.	It's a one-way street.
Du må kjøre tilbake til ...	You have to go back to ...
Følg skiltene til Moss.	Follow signs for Moss.

Parking *Parkering*

Where can I park?	**Hvor kan jeg parkere?**	voor kahn yæi pahrkāyrer
Is there a ... nearby?	**Fins det en ... i nærheten?**	finns deh ehn ... ee nǣrhehtern
car park (parking lot)	**parkeringsplass**	pahrkāyringsplahss
multistorey car park (parking garage)	**parkeringshus**	pahrkāyringshēwss
May I park here?	**Kan jeg parkere her?**	kahn yæi pahrkāyrer hær
How long can I park here?	**Hvor lenge kan jeg stå her?**	voor lehnger kahn yæi staw hær
What's the charge per hour?	**Hvor mye koster det pr. time?**	voor mēwer kosterr deh pær teemer
Do you have some change for the parking meter?	**Har du vekslepenger til parkometeret?**	haar dew vehkshlerpehn- gerr til pahrkoomāyterrer

Breakdown—Road assistance   *Motorstopp – Hjelp på veien*

Where's the nearest garage (auto repair shop)?	**Hvor er nærmeste bilverksted?**	voor ær **nær**mehster **beel**værksteh(d)
My car has broken down.	**Jeg har fått motorstopp.**	yæi haar fot **moo**tooshtop
I've had a breakdown at ...	**Jeg har fått motorstopp ved ...**	yæi haar fot **moo**tooshtop veh(d)
Can you send a mechanic?	**Kan du sende en mekaniker?**	kahn dew **seh**ner ehn meh**kaa**nikkerr
My car won't start.	**Bilen starter ikke.**	**bee**lern staa^rterr **ik**ker
The battery is dead.	**Batteriet er flatt.**	bahter**ree**eyer ær flaht
I've run out of petrol (gas).	**Jeg har kjørt tom.**	yæi haar khû^rt tom
I have a flat tyre.	**Jeg har punktert.**	yæi haar poong**tay**^rt
The engine is overheating.	**Motoren har gått varm.**	**moo**toorern haar got vahrm
There is something wrong with the ...	**Det er noe i veien med ...**	deh ær **noo**er ee **væ**iern meh(d)
brakes	**bremsene**	**brehm**serner
carburettor	**forgasseren**	for**gahs**serrern
exhaust (tail) pipe	**eksosrøret**	ehk**soos**rûrrer
ignition	**tenningen**	**teh**ningern
indicator	**blinklyset**	**bling**klêwsser
radiator	**kjøleren**	**khû**lerrern
steering	**styringen**	**stêw**ringern
wheel	**hjulet**	**yû**ler
Can you send a breakdown van (tow truck)?	**Kan du sende en kranbil?**	kahn dew **seh**ner ehn **kraan**beel
How long will you be?	**Når kommer du?**	nor **kom**merr dew
Can you lend me a/some ...?	**Kan du låne meg ...?**	kahn dew **law**ner mæi
jack	**en jekk**	ehn yehk
jerry can	**en bensinkanne**	ehn behn**seen**kahner
pliers	**en tang**	ehn tahng
spanner	**en skrunøkkel**	ehn skrêw**nur**kerl
tools	**noe verktøy**	**noo**er værktoy
towrope	**et slepetau**	eht **shlay**pertou

Accident—Police *Ulykke – Politi*

Please call the police.	**Vær så snill å ringe politiet.**	vær saw snil aw **ringer** polit**teey**er
There's been an accident.	**Det har skjedd en ulykke.**	deh haar shehd ehn $\overline{ew}$**lew**ker
It's about 2 km. from ...	**Det er ca. 2 km. fra ...**	deh ær **sirr**kah 2 khilloom$\overline{ay}$terr fraa
Where's there a telephone?	**Hvor fins det en telefon?**	voor finss deh ehn tehler**foon**
Call a doctor/an ambulance quickly.	**Ring etter lege/ sykebil!**	ring **eh**terr l$\overline{ay}$ger/ s$\overline{ew}$**ker**beel
There are people injured.	**Det er noen som er skadet.**	deh ær **noo**ern som ær **skaa**dert
Here's my driving licence.	**Her er førerkortet mitt.**	hær ær f**ur**rerrko'ter mit
What's your name and address?	**Kan jeg få navn og adresse?**	kahn yæi faw nahvn o(g) ah**drehss**er
What's your insurance company?	**Hvilket forsikrings- selskap har du?**	**vil**kert fo**shik**rings- **sehl**skaap haar dew

Road signs *Trafikkskilt*

ALL STANS FORBUDT	No stopping
DATOPARKERING	Parking according to date *
FERIST	Cattle grid
GRUSVEI	Gravelled road
INNKJØRSEL FORBUDT	No entry
KJØR SAKTE	Drive slowly
LØS GRUS	Gravelled road
MØTEPLASS	Road passing place
FORBIKJØRING FORBUDT	No overtaking (passing)
OMKJØRING	Diversion (Detour)
PARKERING (FORBUDT)	(No) Parking
RASFARE	Falling rocks
SVAKE KANTER	Soft shoulders
TELELØSNING/TELELØYSE	Potholes due to frost
TOLL	Customs
UTKJØRSEL	Exit
VEIARBEID/VEGARBEID	Roadworks (Men working)

* Night parking on one side of the street only (even numbers on even days, odd numbers on odd days).

Sightseeing

Where's the tourist office?	**Hvor er turist-kontoret?**	voor ær tewrist-koontōōrer
What are the main points of interest?	**Hva er hoved-severdihetene?**	vah ær hōōverd-sehværdihehterner
We're here for ...	**Vi skal være her ...**	vee skahl værer hær
a few hours a day/a week	**et par timer en dag/en uke**	eht pahr teemerr ehn daag/ehn ēwker
Can you recommend a/an ...?	**Kan du anbefale en ...?**	kan dew ahnberfaaler ehn
sightseeing tour excursion	**sightseeingtur utflukt**	"sightseeing"tēwr ēwtflewkt
Where do we leave from?	**Hvor starter vi fra?**	voor staarterr vee fraa
Will the bus pick us up at the hotel?	**Kommer bussen og henter oss ved hotellet?**	kommerr bewssern o(g) hehnterr oss veh(d) hootehler
How much does the tour cost?	**Hvor mye koster turen?**	voor mēwer kosterr tēwrern
What time does the tour start?	**Når starter turen?**	nor staarterr tēwrern
Is lunch included?	**Er lunsj inkludert?**	ær lurnsh inklewdayrt
What time do we get back?	**Når er vi tilbake?**	nor ær vee tilbaaker
Do we have free time in ...?	**Har vi fri tid til disposisjon i ...?**	haar vee free teed til dispoosishōōn ee
Is there an English-speaking guide?	**Fins det en engelsk-talende guide der?**	finss deh ehn ehngerlsk-taalerner "guide" dær
I'd like to hire a private guide for ...	**Jeg vil gjerne ha en privat guide for ...**	yæi vil yærner haa ehn preevaat "guide" for
half a day a day	**en halv dag en dag**	ehn hahl daag ehn daag
I'd like to see the ...	**Jeg vil gjerne se ...**	yæi vil yærner sāy
Are there any special events going on?	**Foregår det noen spesielle begiven-heter her for tiden?**	fawrergawr deh nōōern spehsseeyehler beryee-vernhehterr hær for teedern

Where is/are the ...?	Hvor er ...?	voor ær
amusement park	fornøyelsesparken	fo'noyerlserspahrkern
aquarium	akvariet	ahkvaareeyer
art gallery	kunstgalleriet	kewnstgahlerreeyer
botanical gardens	den botaniske hagen	dehn bootaanisker haagern
bridge	broen	brōōern
building	bygningen	bewgningern
business district	forretningskvarteret	forrehtningskvah'tayrer
castle	slottet	shlotter
cathedral	domkirken	domkhirkern
cave	hulen	hēwlern
cemetery	gravlunden	graavlewnern
chapel	kapellet	kahpehler
church	kirken	khirkern
citadel	festningen	fehstningern
city centre	sentrum	sehntrewm
concert hall	konserthuset	koonsæ'thewsser
conference centre/ congress hall	kongresshallen	konggrehshahlern
court house	tinghuset	tinghēwsser
downtown area	sentrum	sehntrewm
exhibition	utstillingen	ēwtstillingern
factory	fabrikken	fahbrikkern
fair	messen	mehssern
flea market	loppemarkedet	loppermahrkerder
fortress	borgen	borggern
fountain	fontenen	fontaynern
gardens	hagene	haagerner
grotto	grotten	grottern
harbour	havnen	hahvnern
lake	(inn)sjøen	(in)shūrern
library	biblioteket	biblyootayker
market	torghandelen	torghahnderlern
memorial	minnesmerket	minnersmærker
monastery	klostret	klostrer
monument	monumentet	moonewmehnter
museum	museet	mewssayer
observatory	observatoriet	obsærvahtōōryer
old town	gamlebyen	gahmlerbēwern
opera house	operahuset	ooperrahhēwsser
palace	slottet	shlotter
park	parken	pahrkern
parliament building	Stortinget	stōō'tinger
planetarium	planetariet	plahnertaaryer
royal palace	det kongelige slott	deh kongerleeyer shlot

ruins	**ruinene**	reweenerner
shopping area	**handlestrøket**	hahndlerstrürker
square	**plassen/torget**	plahssern/torgger
stadium	**stadion**	staadyoon
statue	**statuen**	staatewern
stave church	**stavkirken**	staavkhirkern
stock exchange	**børsen**	bürshern
theatre	**teatret**	tāyaatrer
tomb	**graven**	graavern
tower	**tårnet**	taw^rner
town (city) hall	**rådhuset**	rawdhew̄sser
university	**universitetet**	ewnivæshitāyter
zoo	**dyrehagen**	dēw̄rerhaagern

Admission *Adgang*

Is ... open on Sundays?	**Er ... åpent på søndager?**	ær ... awpernt paw surndaagerr
When is it open?	**Når er det åpent?**	nor ær deh awpernt
When does it open/close?	**Når åpner/stenger det?**	nor awpnerr/stehngerr deh
What's the entrance fee?	**Hva koster inngangs-billetten?**	vah kosterr ingahngs-billehtern
2 adults and 1 child	**2 voksne og 1 barn**	2 voksner o(g) 1 baa^rn
Is there any reduction for (the) ...?	**Er det noen rabatt for ...?**	ær deh nōōern rahbaht for
children	**barn**	baa^rn
disabled	**bevegelseshemmede**	bervāygerlsershehmerder
groups	**grupper**	grewperr
pensioners (senior citizens)	**pensjonister**	pahngshoonisterr
students	**studenter**	stewdehnterr
Do you have a guidebook (in English)?	**Har du en guidebok (på engelsk)?**	haar dew ehn "guide"-bōōk (paw ehngerlsk)
Can I buy a catalogue?	**Kan jeg få kjøpt en katalog?**	kahn yæi faw khurpt ehn kahtahlawg
Is it all right to take pictures?	**Er det tillatt å fotografere?**	ær deh tillaht aw footoograhfāyrer

---

GRATIS ADGANG ADMISSION FREE
FOTOGRAFERING FORBUDT NO CAMERAS ALLOWED

Who—What—When? *Hvem – Hva – Når?*

What's that building?	**Hvilken bygning er det?**	vilkern bewgning ær dāy
Who was the ...?	**Hvem var ...?**	vehm vaar
architect	**arkitekten**	ahrkitehktern
artist	**kunstneren**	kewnstnerrern
painter	**maleren**	maalerrern
sculptor	**billedhuggeren**	billerdhewgerrern
Who built it?	**Hvem har bygd den?**	vehm haar bewgd dehn
Who painted that picture?	**Hvem har malt det bildet?**	vehm haar maalt dāy bilder
When did he live?	**Når levde han?**	nor lehvder hahn
When was it built?	**Når ble det bygd?**	nor bleh deh bewgd
Where's the house where ... lived?	**Hvor er huset hvor ... bodde?**	vohr ær hēwsser voor ... boodder
We're interested in ...	**Vi interesserer oss for ...**	vee interrehssāyrerr oss for
antiques	**antikviteter**	ahntikvittāyterr
archaeology	**arkeologi**	ahrkehoolooggee
art	**kunst**	kewnst
botany	**botanikk**	bootahnik
ceramics	**keramikk**	khærahmik
coins	**mynter**	mewnterr
folk art	**folkekunst**	folkerkewnst
furniture	**møbler**	murblerr
geology	**geologi**	gāyoolooggee
handicrafts	**kunsthåndverk**	kewnsthonværk
history	**historie**	histōōryer
maritime history	**sjøfartshistorie**	shūrfah'tshistōōryer
medicine	**medisin**	mehdisseen
modern art	**moderne kunst**	moodǣ'ner kewnst
music	**musikk**	mewssik
natural history	**naturhistorie**	nahtēwrhistōōryer
ornithology	**ornitologi**	oornitoolooggee
painting	**maleri**	mahlerree
pottery	**pottemakerkunst**	pottermaakerrkewnst
religion	**religion**	rehliggeeōōn
sculpture	**skulptur**	skewlptēwr
zoology	**zoologi**	soolooggee
Where's the ... department?	**Hvor er avdelingen for ...?**	voor ær ahvdāylingern for

It's ...	Det er ...	deh ær
amazing	**praktfullt**	**prahktfewlt**
awful	**forferdelig**	forfærderli
beautiful	**vakkert**	**vahker**^rt
fantastic	**fantastisk**	fahntahstisk
gloomy	**dystert**	**dewster**^rt
impressive	**imponerende**	impoonayrerner
interesting	**interessant**	interehssahngt
magnificent	**storslagent**	stooshlaagernt
pretty	**søtt**	surt
romantic	**romantisk**	roomahntisk
strange	**underlig**	ewnderli
superb	**ypperlig**	ewperli
terrible	**forferdelig**	forfærderli
tremendous	**forskrekkelig**	foshkrehkerli
ugly	**stygt**	stewkt

Churches—Religious services *Kirker – Gudstjenester*

Norway has a Lutheran state church, but freedom of religion is assured, and other denominations have their own places of worship.

Most churches are open to visitors except, of course, when a service is being conducted.

Is there a ...	Fins det en ...	finss deh ehn ...
nearby?	**i nærheten?**	ee nærhehtern
Catholic church	**katolsk kirke**	kahtoolsk khirker
Protestant church	**protestantisk kirke**	prooterstahntisk khirker
mosque	**moské**	mooskay
synagogue	**synagoge**	sewnahgoogger
At what time is ...?	**Når begynner ...?**	nor beryewnerr
mass	**messen**	mehssern
the service	**gudstjenesten**	gewdstyehnerstern
Where can I find a ... who speaks English?	**Hvor kan jeg få tak i en ... som snakker engelsk?**	voor kahn yæi faw taak ee ehn ... som snahkerr ehngerlsk
priest	**katolsk prest**	kahtoolsk prehst
minister	**protestantisk prest**	prooterstahntisk prehst
rabbi	**rabbiner**	rahbeenerr
I'd like to visit the church.	**Jeg vil gjerne se kirken.**	yæi vil yæ^rner say khirkern

In the countryside *På landet*

Is there a scenic route to ...?	**Fins det en natur- skjønn vei til ...?**	finss deh ehn nahtewr- shurn væi til
How far is it to ...?	**Hvor langt er det til ...?**	voor lahngt ær deh til
Can we walk there?	**Kan man spasere dit?**	kahn mahn spahssayrer deet
How high is that mountain?	**Hvor høyt er det fjellet?**	voor hoyt ær day fyehler
What kind of ... is that?	**Hva slags ... er det?**	vaa shlahkss ... ær day
animal/bird	**dyr/fugl**	dewr/fewl
flower/tree	**blomst/tre**	blomst/tray

Landmarks *Landemerker*

cliff	**en klippe**	ehn klipper
coast	**en kyst**	ehn khewst
farm	**en bondegård**	ehn boonergawr
field	**et jorde**	eht yoorer
fjord	**en fjord**	ehn fyoor
footpath	**en sti**	ehn stee
forest	**en skog**	ehn skoog
garden	**en hage**	ehn haager
hill	**en høyde**	ehn hoyder
house	**et hus**	eht hewss
inlet	**en vik**	ehn veek
island	**en øy**	ehn oy
meadow	**en eng**	ehn ehng
mountain	**et fjell**	eht fyehl
ocean	**et hav**	eht haav
path	**en sti**	ehn stee
peak	**en topp**	ehn top
pond	**en dam**	ehn dahm
ridge	**en ås**	ehn awss
river	**en elv**	ehn ehlv
sea	**en sjø**	ehn shur
spring	**en kilde**	ehn khilder
stream	**en bekk**	ehn behk
valley	**en dal**	ehn daal
wall	**en mur**	ehn mewr
waterfall	**en foss**	ehn foss
well	**en brønn**	ehn brurn

ASKING THE WAY, see page 76

Relaxing

Cinema (Movies)—Theatre   *Kino – Teater*

To find out what's on, check the newspapers and advertizing posters, or the weekly/monthly tourist publication in Oslo and other towns.

All films are shown in the original language with Norwegian subtitles. Advance booking is essential for theatres and the opera.

I'd like to ... tonight.	**Jeg har lyst til å ... i kveld.**	yæi haar lewst til aw ... ee kvehl
go to the cinema	**gå på kino**	gaw paw **khee**noo
go to the teatre	**gå i teatret**	gaw ee tā̄yaatrer
What's on at the cinema tonight?	**Hvilke filmer vises på kino i kveld?**	vilker filmerr **vee**ssers paw **khee**noo ee kvehl
What's playing at the National Theatre?	**Hva spilles på Nationaltheatret?**	vah **spill**erss paw nahshoo**naal**tā̄yaatrer
What sort of play is it?	**Hva slags stykke er det?**	vah shlahkss **stew**ker ær deh
Who's it by?	**Hvem har skrevet det?**	vehm haar **skrā̄y**vert deh
Can you recommend a ...?	**Kan du anbefale en ...?**	kahn dew **ahn**berfaaler ehn
good film	**god film**	goo(d) film
comedy	**komedie**	koo**mā̄y**dyer
musical	**musikal**	mewssi**kaal**
revue	**revy**	reh**vew**
Where's that new film directed by ... being shown?	**Hvor går den nye filmen av ...?**	voor gawr dehn **new**er filmern ahv
Who's in it?	**Hvem spiller i den?**	vehm **spill**err ee dehn
Who's playing the lead?	**Hvem spiller hoved-rollen?**	vehm **spill**err **hōō**verd-rollern
Who's the director?	**Hvem har regissert den?**	vehm haar rehshiss**ā̄y**ᵗt dehn

At which theatre is that new play by ... being performed?	På hvilket teater går det nye stykket av ...?	paw vilkert tāyaaterr gawr deh nēwer stewker ahv
What time does it begin/finish?	Når begynner/ slutter det?	nor beryewnerr/ shlewterr deh
How long does it last?	Hvor lenge varer det?	voor lehnger vaarerr deh
Are there any tickets for tonight?	Fins det fremdeles billetter til i kveld?	finss deh frehmdāylerss billehterr til ee kvehl
How much are the tickets?	Hvor mye koster billettene?	voor mēwer kosterr billehterner
I'd like to reserve 2 tickets for the show on Friday evening.	Jeg vil gjerne be- stille 2 billetter til forestillingen på fredag kveld.	yæi vil yǣ'ner ber- stiller 2 billehterr til fawrerstillingern paw frāydah(g) kvehl
Can I have a ticket for the matinée on Tuesday?	Kan jeg få en billett til matinéen på tirsdag?	kahn yæi faw ehn billeht til mahtināyern paw teeshdah(g)
I'd like a seat in the stalls (orchestra).	Jeg vil gjerne ha en plass i parkett.	yæi vil yǣ'ner haa ehn plahss ee pahrkeht
Not too far back.	Ikke for langt bak.	ikker for lahngt baak
Somewhere in the middle.	Et sted i midten.	eht stāy(d) ee mittern
How much are the tickets for the circle (mezzanine)?	Hvor mye koster billettene på bal- kongen?	voor mēwer kosterr billehterner paw bahl- kongern
May I have a pro- gramme, please?	Kan jeg få et program?	kahn yæi faw eht proograhm
Where's the cloakroom?	Hvor er garderoben?	voor ær gahrderrōōbern

---

Dessverre, det er utsolgt.	I'm sorry, we're sold out.
Det er bare noen få plasser igjen på balkongen.	There are only a few seats left in the circle (mezzanine).
Kan jeg få se billetten?	May I see your ticket?
Dette er din plass.	This is your seat.

DAYS OF THE WEEK, see page 150

Opera—Ballet—Concert   *Opera – Ballett – Konsert*

Can you recommend a/an ...?	**Kan du anbefale en ...?**	kahn dew **ahn**berfaaler ehn
ballet/concert opera/operetta	**ballett/konsert opera/operette**	bah**leht**/koon**sær**t **oo**perrah/**oo**perr**eh**ter
Where's the opera house/the concert hall?	**Hvor er operahuset/ konserthuset?**	voor ær **oo**perrah**hew**sser/ koon**sær**t**hew**sser
What's on at the opera tonight?	**Hva spilles på operaen i kveld?**	vah **spil**lerss paw **oo**perrahern ee kvehl
Who's singing/ dancing?	**Hvem synger/ danser?**	vehm **sew**ngerr/ **dahn**serr
Which orchestra is playing?	**Hvilket orkester spiller?**	**vil**kert or**keh**sterr **spil**lerr
What are they playing?	**Hva spilles?**	vah **spil**lerss
Who's the conduc-tor/soloist?	**Hvem er dirigent/ solist?**	vehm ær dirri**ggeh**nt/ soo**list**

Nightclubs   *Nattklubber*

Can you recommend a good nightclub?	**Kan du anbefale en bra nattklubb?**	kahn dew **ahn**berfaaler ehn braa **naht**klewb
Is there a floor show?	**Vises det noe show?**	**vee**sserss deh **noo**er ''show''
What time does the show start?	**Når begynner showet?**	nor ber**yew**nerr ''schow''er
Do I have to wear a tie?	**Er det slipstvang?**	ær deh **shlips**tvahng

Discos   *Diskoteker*

Where can we go dancing?	**Hvor kan man gå og danse?**	voor kahn mahn gaw o(g) **dahn**ser
Is there a disco-theque in town/ nearby?	**Fins det et diskotek i byen/i nærheten?**	finss deh eht disko**otayk** ee **bew**ern/ee **nær**rheh-tern
Would you like to dance?	**Skal vi danse?**	skahl vee **dahn**ser

Sports *Sport*

Are there any sporting events going on?	**Holdes det noe sportsstevne her for tiden?**	hollerss deh nooer spo^rtsstehvner hær for teedern

athletics (track-and-field) meeting	**friidrettsstevne**	freeeedrehtsstehvner
bicycle racing	**sykkelløp**	sewkerllūrp
car racing	**billøp**	beellūrp
football (soccer) match	**fotballkamp**	footbahlkahmp
horse racing	**hesteveddeløp**	hehstervehderlūrp
ice hockey match	**ishockeykamp**	eeshokkikahmp
regatta	**regatta**	rehgahtah
speed skating	**skøyteløp**	shoyterlūrp
ski race	**skirenn**	sheerehn
ski jumping	**skihopping**	sheehopping
tennis match	**tenniskamp**	tehniskahmp

Is there a football (soccer) match anywhere this Saturday?	**Er det en fotballkamp noe sted på lørdag?**	ær deh ehn footbahlkahmp nooer stāy(d) paw lūr^rdah(g)
Which teams are playing?	**Hvilke lag spiller?**	vilker laag spillerr
Can you get me a ticket?	**Kan du skaffe meg en billett?**	kahn dew skahfer mæi ehn billeht
I'd like to see an ice-hockey match.	**Jeg vil gjerne se en ishockeykamp**	yæi vil yæ^rner sāy ehn eeshokkikahmp
What's the admission charge?	**Hva koster inngangsbilletten?**	vah kosterr ingahngsbillehtern
Where's the race course (track)?	**Hvor er hesteveddeløpsbanen?**	voor ær hehstervehderlūrpsbaanern

And if you want to take a more active part:

Is there a golf course/tennis court nearby?	**Fins det en golfbane/tennisbane i nærheten?**	finss deh ehn golfbaaner/tehnisbaaner ee nærhehtern
I'd like to play golf/tennis.	**Jeg vil gjerne spille golf/tennis.**	yæi vil yæ^rner spiller golf/tehniss

What's the charge per ...?	**Hva koster det pr. ....?**	vah **kosterr** deh pær
day/round/hour	**dag/runde/time**	daag/**rewnder**/teemer
Can I hire (rent) rackets?	**Kan man leie racketer?**	kahn mahn **læier rehkeh**'terr
Is there any good fishing around here?	**Fins det en bra fiske-plass i nærheten?**	finss deh ehn braa **fisker-**plahss ee **nǣrhehtern**
Do I need a permit?	**Må man ha fiske-kort?**	maw mahn haa **fiskerko**'t
Can one swim in the lake/river?	**Kan man bade i (inn)sjøen/elven?**	kahn mahn **baader** ee (in)**shūrern**/**ehlvern**
Is there a swimming pool here?	**Er det et svømme-basseng her?**	ær deh eht **svurmer-**bahssehng hǣr
Is it an open-air or indoor pool?	**Er det utendørs eller innendørs?**	ær deh **ēwterndūrsh ehlerr** innerndūrsh
Is it heated?	**Er det oppvarmet?**	ær deh **opvahrmert**
Is there a sandy beach?	**Fins det en sand-strand her?**	finss deh ehn **sahn-**strahn hǣr

bicycling	**sykling**	**sewk**ling
(horse-back) riding	**ridning**	**reed**ning
fishing	**fiske**	**fisker**
mountain climbing	**fjellklatring**	**fyehlk**lahtring
rowing	**roing**	**rōō**ing
sailing	**seiling**	**sæi**ling
swimming	**svømming**	**svur**ming

On the beach *På stranden*

Is it safe to swim/dive here?	**Er det trygt å bade/dykke her?**	ær deh trewkt aw **baader**/**dew**ker hǣr
Is there a lifeguard?	**Fins det badevakt?**	finss deh **baader**vahkt
Is it safe for children?	**Er det trygt for barn?**	ær deh trewkt for baa'n
Could I have swimming lessons?	**Kan man ta svømme-timer?**	kahn mahn taa **svurmer-**teemerr
Are there any dangerous currents?	**Fins det noen farlige strømmer?**	finss deh **nōō**ern faa'-leeyer **strurmerr**
How deep is it?	**Hvor dypt er det?**	voor dewpt ær deh

Is it shallow?	**Er det langgrunt?**	ær deh **lahng**grewnt
What's the temperature of the water?	**Hvor mange grader er det i vannet?**	voor **mahng**er **graad**err ær deh ee **vah**ner
I want to hire (rent) a/some ...	**Jeg vil gjerne leie ...**	yæi vil yæͬner **læi**er
bathing hut (cabana)	**et badehus**	eht **baad**erhewss
skin-diving equipment	**et dykkerutstyr**	eht **dew**kerrewtstewr
sunshade	**en parasoll**	ehn pahrah**sol**
water-skis	**vannski**	**vahn**shee
windsurfer	**et seilbrett**	eht **sæil**breht

| **BADING FORBUDT** | NO SWIMMING |
| **FISKING FORBUDT** | NO FISHING |

Winter sports *Vintersport*

Is there a skating rink near here?	**Fins det en skøyte-bane i nærheten?**	finss deh ehn **shoyter**baaner ee **nær**hehtern
I'd like to ski.	**Jeg vil gjerne gå på ski.**	yæi vil yæͬner gaw paw shee
downhill	**utforkjøring**	**ewt**forkhūrring
cross-country skiing	**langrenn**	**lahng**rehn
Are there any ski runs for ...?	**Fins det noen skibakker for ...?**	finss deh **nōō**ern **shee**bahkerr for
beginners	**begynnere**	ber**yew**nerrer
average skiers	**middelsgode skiløpere**	**midderls**gōō(d)er **shee**lūrperrer
good skiers	**gode skiløpere**	**gōō**(d)er **shee**lūrperrer
Which way are the ski lifts?	**I hvilken retning ligger skiheisene?**	ee **vil**kern **reht**ning **ligg**err **shee**hæisserner
Are there any good ski tracks (trails) nearby?	**Fins det noen gode skiløyper i nær-heten?**	finss deh **nōō**ern **gōō**(d)er **shee**loyperr ee **nær**hehtern
Are there floodlit ski tracks?	**Fins det lysløyper?**	finss deh **lews**loyperr
I'd like to hire ...	**Jeg vil gjerne leie ...**	yæi vil yæͬner **læi**er
skates/skis	**skøyter/ski**	**shoy**terr/shee
ski boots/poles	**skistøvler/staver**	**shee**sturvlerr/**staa**verr

Making friends

Introduction   *Presentasjon*

May I introduce ...?	**Får jeg presentere ...?**	fawr yæi prehssern-tayrer
John, this is ...	**John, dette er ...** *	John dehter ær
My name is ...	**Mitt navn er ...**	mit nahvn ær
Pleased to meet you!	**Hyggelig å treffes!**	hewgerli aw trehferss
What's your name?	**Hva heter du?**	vah hayterr dew
How are you?	**Hvordan står det til?**	voordahn stawr deh til
Fine, thanks. And you?	**Bare bra, takk. Og med deg?**	baarer braa tahk. o(g) meh(d) dæi

Follow up   *Nærmere bekjentskap*

How long have you been here?	**Hvor lenge har du vært her?**	voor lehnger haar dew vært hær
I've been here a week.	**Jeg har vært her en uke.**	yæi haar vært hær ehn ewker
We're on a 3-day visit.	**Vi er her på et 3-dagers besøk.**	vee ær hær paw eht 3-daagersh bersurk
Is this your first visit to Oslo?	**Er det første gang du er i Oslo?**	ær deh furshter gahng dew ær ee ooshloo
How do you like Norway?	**Hva synes du om Norge?**	vah sewnerss dew om norgger
We like it here.	**Vi liker oss her.**	vee leekerr oss hær
What do you think of the country/the people?	**Hva synes du om landet/folket?**	vah sewnerss dew om lahner/folker
The scenery is beautiful.	**Naturen er vakker.**	nahtewrrern ær vahkerr
Where do you come from?	**Hvor kommer du fra?**	voor kommer dew fraa
I'm from ...	**Jeg er fra ...**	yæi ær fraa

* The terms Mr., Mrs. and Miss (*herr* – hærr, *fru* – frew, *frøken* – frürkern) are very rarely used. People are introduced by their full name.

COUNTRIES, see page 146

What nationality are you?	**Hvilken nasjonalitet har du?**	vilkern nahshoonahlitäyt haar dew
I'm ...	**Jeg er ...**	yæi ær
American	**amerikaner**	ahm(er)rikaanerr
British	**brite**	breeter
Canadian	**kanadier**	kahnaadyer
English	**englender**	ehnglehnder
Irish	**irlender**	eerlehnderr
Where are you staying?	**Hvor bor du her?**	voor bōōr dew hær
Are you on your own?	**Er du her alene?**	ær dew hær ahlāyner
I'm with my ...	**Jeg er her med ...**	yæi ær hær meh(d)
wife/husband	**min kone/min mann**	meen kōōner/meen mahn
family	**min familie**	meen fahmeelyer
children	**mine barn**	meener baaʳn
parents	**mine foreldre**	meener forehldrer
boyfriend/girlfriend	**min venn/venninne**	meen vehn/vehninner

father/mother	**far/mor**	faar/mōōr
son/daughter	**sønn/datter**	surn/dahterr
brother/sister	**bror/søster**	brōōr/sursterr
uncle/aunt	**onkel/tante**	oongkerl/tahnter
nephew/niece	**nevø/niese**	nehvūr/neeäysser
cousin	**fetter*/kusine****	fehterr/kewsseener

* masc., ** fem.

Are you married/single?	**Er du gift/ugift?**	ær dew yift/ēwyift
Do you have children?	**Har du barn?**	haar dew baaʳn
What do you do?	**Hvilket yrke har du?**	vilkert ewrker haar dew
I'm a student.	**Jeg er student.**	yæi ær stewdehnt
What are you studying?	**Hva studerer du?**	vah stewdāyrerr dew
I'm here on a business trip.	**Jeg er her på forretningsreise.**	yæi ær hær paw forrehtningsræisser
Do you travel a lot?	**Reiser du mye?**	ræisserr dew mēwer
Do you play cards/chess?	**Spiller du kort/sjakk?**	spillerr dew koʳt/shahk

The weather   *Været*

What a lovely day!	**Hvilken herlig dag!**	vilkern hæ^rli daag
What awful weather!	**For et forferdelig vær!**	for eht forfærderli vær
Isn't it cold/hot today?	**Er det ikke kaldt/ varmt i dag?**	ær deh ikker kahlt/ vahrmt ee daag
Is it usually as rainy/warm as this?	**Pleier det å være så regnfullt/varmt?**	plæierr deh aw værer saw ræinfewlt/vahrmt
Do you think it's going to ... tomorrow?	**Tror du det kommer til å ... i morgen?**	trōōr dew deh kommerr til aw ... ee mawer^rn
be a nice day	**bli pent vær**	blee pāynt vær
rain	**regne**	ræiner
snow	**snø**	snūr
What's the weather forecast?	**Hva er vær- utsiktene?**	vah ær værewtsikterner

cloud	**sky**	shēw
fog	**tåke**	tawker
frost	**frost**	frost
hail	**hagl**	hahgl
ice	**is**	eess
lightning	**lyn**	lēwn
midnight sun	**midnattssol**	midnahtssōōl
moon	**måne**	mawner
rain	**regn**	ræin
sky	**himmel**	himmerl
snow	**snø**	snūr
star	**stjerne**	styæ^rner
sun	**sol**	sōōl
thunder	**torden**	toordern
thunderstorm	**tordenvær**	toordernvær
wind	**vind**	vin

Invitations   *Innbydelser*

Would you like to have dinner with us on ...?	**Vil du spise middag med oss på ...?**	vil dew speesser mid- dah(g) meh(d) oss paw
May I invite you to lunch?	**Får jeg by på lunsj?**	fawr yæi bēw paw lurnsh

DAYS OF THE WEEK, see page 150

Can you come round for a drink this evening?	**Kan du komme til en drink i kveld?**	kahn dew **kom**mer til ehn dringk ee kvehl
We're having a party. Can you come?	**Vi skal ha fest. Kan du komme?**	vee skahl haa fehst. kahn dew **kom**mer
Great. I'd love to come.	**Mange takk. Jeg kommer gjerne.**	**mahng**er tahk. yæi **kom**merr yǣ**r**ner
What time shall I come?	**Når skal jeg komme?**	nor skahl yæi **kom**mer
May I bring a friend?	**Kan jeg ta med en venn?**	kahn yæi taa meh(d) ehn vehn
I'm afraid we've got to leave now.	**Vi må dessverre gå nå.**	vee maw **dehs**værer gaw naw
Next time you (pl.) must come to visit us.	**Neste gang må dere besøke oss.**	**neh**ster gahng maw **dāy**rer ber**sū**rker oss
Thanks for the evening.	**Takk for i kveld.**	tahk for ee kvehl
It was great.	**Det var veldig hyggelig.**	det vaar **veh**ldi **hew**gerli

Dating *Stevnemøte*

Do you mind if I smoke?	**Har du noe imot at jeg røyker?**	haar dew **nōō**er eem**ōō**t aht yæi **roy**kerr
Would you like a cigarette?	**Vil du ha en sigarett?**	vil dew haa ehn sigga**reht**
Do you have a light, please?	**Har du fyr?**	haar dew fēwr
Why are you laughing?	**Hvorfor ler du?**	**voor**for lāyr dew
Is my Norwegian that bad?	**Snakker jeg så dårlig norsk?**	**snah**kerr yæi saw **daw**rli noshk
Do you mind if I sit down here?	**Har du noe imot at jeg setter meg her?**	haar dew **nōō**er eem**ōō**t aht yæi **seh**terr mæi hāēr
Would you like a drink?	**Har du lyst på en drink?**	haar dew lewst paw ehn dringk
Are you waiting for someone?	**Venter du på noen?**	**vehn**terr dew paw **nōō**ern

Are you free this evening?	**Er du ledig i kveld?**	ær dew lāydi ee kvehl
Would you like to go out with me tonight?	**Skal vi gå ut i kveld?**	skahl vee gaw ēwt ee kvehl
Would you like to go dancing?	**Har du lyst til å gå ut og danse?**	haar dew lewst til aw gaw ēwt o(g) dahnser
I know a good discotheque.	**Jeg vet om et bra diskotek.**	yæi vāyt om eht braa diskootāyk
Shall we go to the cinema (movies)?	**Skal vi gå på kino?**	skahl vee gaw paw **kee**noo
Would you like to go for a drive?	**Har du lyst til å kjøre en tur?**	haar dew lewst til aw **khū**rrer ehn tēwr
Where shall we meet?	**Hvor skal vi møtes?**	voor skahl vee **mū**rterss
I'll pick you up at your hotel.	**Jeg henter deg på hotellet.**	yæi **hehn**terr dæi paw hoo**teh**ler
I'll call for you at 8.	**Jeg henter deg kl. 8.**	yæi **hehn**terr dæi **klok**kern 8
May I take you home?	**Kan jeg få følge deg hjem?**	kahn yæi faw **fur**ler dæi yehm
Can I see you again tomorrow?	**Skal vi ses igjen i morgen?**	skahl vee **sāy**ss ee**yehn** ee **maw**er^{r}n
I hope we'll meet again.	**Jeg håper vi ses igjen.**	yæi **haw**perr vee **sāy**ss ee**yehn**

... and you might answer:

I'd love to, thank you.	**Takk, det vil jeg gjerne.**	tahk deh vil yæi **yā̈r**ner
That's very kind of you.	**Det er veldig snilt av deg.**	deh ær **veh**ldi snilt ahv dæi
Thank you, but I'm busy.	**Takk, men jeg er dessverre opptatt.**	tahk mehn yæi ær dehs**vær**er **op**taht
Leave me alone, please.	**Vær så snill å la meg være i fred.**	vær saw snill aw laa mæi **vā̈r**er ee frā̈y(d)
Thank you, it's been a wonderful evening.	**Takk, det har vært en veldig hyggelig kveld.**	tahk deh haar vær^{r}t ehn **veh**ldi **hew**gerli kvehl

Shopping guide

This shopping guide is designed to help you find what you want with ease, accuracy and speed. It features:

1. A list of all major shops, stores and services (p. 98).
2. Some general expressions required when shopping to allow you to be specific and selective (p. 100).
3. Full details of the shops and services most likely to concern you. Here you'll find advice, alphabetical lists of items and conversion charts listed under the headings below.

		page
Bookshop/ Stationer's	books, magazines, newspapers, stationery	104
Camping equipment	all items required for camping	106
Chemist's (Drugstore)	medicine, first-aid, cosmetics, toilet articles	108
Clothes	clothes and accessories, shoes	112
Electrical appliances	hi-fi equipment, household appliances	119
Grocer's/ Supermarket	some general expressions, weights, measures and packaging	120
Jeweller's Watchmaker's	jewellery, watches, watch repairs	121
Optician	glasses, lenses, binoculars	123
Photography	cameras, films, developing, accessories	124
Tobacconist's	smoker's supplies	126
Miscellaneous	souvenirs, records, cassettes, toys	127

LAUNDRY, see page 29/HAIRDRESSER, see page 30

Shops, stores and services *Butikker og servicenæringer*

Hours vary, but most shops are open from 9 a.m. to 5 p.m., Monday to Friday, and from 9 a.m. to 2 p.m. on Saturdays. Centrally located kiosks selling newspapers, tobacco and sweets may stay open till 11 p.m. Fruit, vegetable and flower markets normally open from 7 or 8 a.m. to 2 or 3 p.m., Monday to Saturday.

Where can I find a/an ...?	Hvor er det ...?	voor ær deh
antique shop	en antikvitets-forretning	ehn ahntikvittayts-forrehtning
art gallery	et kunstgalleri	eht kewnstgahlerree
baker's	et bakeri	eht baakerree
bank	en bank	ehn bahngk
barber's	en herrefrisør	ehn hærerfrissurr
beauty salon	en skjønnhetssalong	ehn shurnhehtssahlong
bookshop	en bokhandel	ehn bookhahnderl
butcher's	en slakter	ehn shlahkterr
cake shop	et konditori	eht koondittooree
camera shop	en fotoforretning	ehn footooforrehtning
candy store	en godtebutikk	ehn goterbewtik
cheese shop	en osteforretning	ehn oosterforrehtning
chemist's	et apotek	eht ahpootayk
china shop	et glassmagasin	eht glahsmahgahsseen
dairy	en melkebutikk	ehn mehlkerbewtik
delicatessen	en delikatesse-forretning	ehn dehlikkatehsser-forrehtning
dentist	en tannlege	ehn tahnlayger
department store	et stormagasin	eht stoormahgahsseen
doctor	en lege	ehn layger
drugstore	et apotek	eht ahpootayk
dry cleaner's	et renseri	eht rehnserree
electrical goods shop	en elektrisitets-forretning	ehn ehlehktrissitayts-forrehtning
fishmonger's	en fiskebutikk	ehn fiskerbewtik
flea market	et loppemarked	eht loppermahrkerd
florist's	en blomsterbutikk	ehn blomsterrbewtik
furrier's	en pelsforetning	ehn pehlsforrehtning
greengrocer's	en grønnsakhandel	ehn grurnsaakhahnderl
grocer's	en matvarehandel	ehn maatvaarerhahnderl
hairdresser (ladies/men)	en frisør (dame-/herre-)	ehn frissurr (daamer-/hærer-)
hardware store	en jernvarehandel	ehn yærnvaarerhahnderl

health food shop	**en helsekost-forretning**	ehn **hehl**serkost-forrehtning
hospital	**et sykehus**	eht **sew**kerhewss
ironmonger's	**en jernvarehandel**	ehn yǣ**r**nvaarerhahnderl
jeweller's	**en gullsmed**	ehn **gewl**smāy(d)
launderette	**et selvbetjenings-vaskeri**	eht **sehl**bertyāynings-vahskerree
laundry	**et vaskeri**	eht vahsker**ree**
library	**et bibliotek**	eht biblyootāyk
liquor store	**et vinmonopol**	eht **veen**moonoopōōl
market	**en torghandel**	ehn **torg**hahnderl
newsstand	**en aviskiosk**	ehn ahveeskhyosk
optician	**en optiker**	ehn **op**tikkerr
pastry shop	**et konditori**	eht koondittoo**ree**
perfumery	**et parfymeri**	eht pahrfewmer**ree**
pharmacy	**et apotek**	eht ahpootāyk
photographer	**en fotograf**	ehn footoo**graaf**
police station	**en politistasjon**	ehn poolit**tee**stahshōōn
post office	**et postkontor**	eht **post**koontōōr
second-hand shop	**en marsjandise-forretning**	ehn mahshahnd**eess**er-forrehtning
shoemaker's (repairs)	**en skomaker**	ehn skōōmaakerr
shoe shop	**en skoforretning**	ehn skōōforrehtning
shopping centre	**et butikksenter**	eht bewtiksehnterr
souvenir shop	**en suvenirbutikk**	ehn sewverneerbewtik
sporting goods shop	**en sportsforretning**	ehn spo**r**tsforrehtning
stationer's	**en papirhandel**	ehn pah**peer**hahnderl
supermarket	**et supermarked**	eht **sew**perrmahrkerd
sweet shop	**en godtebutikk**	ehn goterbewtik
tailor's	**en skredder**	ehn **skreh**derr
telegraph office	**et telesenter**	eht **tāy**lerssehnterr
tobacconist's	**en tobakkshandel**	ehn too**bahks**hahnderl
toy shop	**en leketøysbutikk**	ehn lāykertoysbewtik
travel agency	**et reisebyrå**	eht rǣisserbewraw
vegetable store	**en grønnsakhandel**	ehn grurnsaakhahnderl
veterinarian	**en dyrlege**	ehn **dewr**lāyger
watchmaker's	**en urmaker**	ehn **ēwr**maakerr
wine merchant	**et vinmonopol**	eht **veen**moonoopōōl

INNGANG	ENTRANCE
UTGANG	EXIT
NØDUTGANG	EMERGENCY EXIT

General expressions *Vanlige uttrykk*

Where? *Hvor?*

Where's there a good ...?	**Hvor fins det en god ...?**	voor finss deh ehn goo(d)
Where can I find a ...?	**Hvor finner jeg en ...?**	voor finnerr yæi ehn
Where's the (main) shopping area?	**Hvor er (det største) handlestrøket?**	voor ær (deh sturshter) hahndlerstrurker
Is it far from here?	**Er det langt herfra?**	ær deh lahngt hærfrah
How do I get there?	**Hvordan kommer jeg dit?**	voordahn kommerr yæi deet

(UT)SALG	SALE
TILBUDSVARE	BARGAIN

Service *Betjening*

Can you help me?	**Kan du hjelpe meg?**	kahn dew yehlper mæi
I'm just looking.	**Jeg bare ser meg omkring.**	yæi baarer sāyr mæi omkring
Do you sell ...?	**Selger dere ...?**	sehlerr dāyrer
I'd like to buy ...	**Jeg vil gjerne kjøpe ...**	yæi vil yǣrner khurper
Can you show me ...?	**Kan du vise meg ...?**	kahn dew veesser mæi
this/that	**dette/det**	dehter/deh
the one in the window	**den i vinduet**	dehn ee vindewer
the one in the display case	**den i monteren**	dehn ee monterrern
Do you have any ...?	**Har du noen ...?**	har dew nōōern
Where's the ...?	**Hvor er ...?**	voor ær
... department	**-avdelingen**	-ahvdāylingern
lift (elevator)	**heisen**	hæissern
escalator	**rulletrappen**	rewlertrahpern
Where do I pay?	**Hvor betaler man?**	voor bertaalerr mahn

Defining the article   *Varebeskrivelse*

I'd like a ... one.	**Jeg vil gjerne ha en ...**	yæi vil yǣ͞rner haa ehn
big	**stor**	sto͞or
cheap	**rimelig**	reemerli
dark	**mørk**	murrk
good	**god**	goo(d)
heavy	**tung**	toong
large	**stor**	sto͞or
light (weight)	**lett**	leht
light (colour)	**lys**	le͞wss
oval	**oval**	oovaal
rectangular	**rektangulær**	rehktahngewlǣr
round	**rund**	rewn
small	**liten**	leetern
square	**firkantet**	firkahntert
sturdy	**robust/solid**	roobewst/sooleed

I don't want any-thing too expensive.	**Jeg vil ikke ha noe for dyrt.**	yæi vil ikker haa no͞oer for dew͞ʳt

Preference   *Jeg foretrekker ...*

Can you show me some others?	**Kan du vise meg noen andre?**	kahn dew veesser mæi no͞oern ahndrer
Don't you have anything ...?	**Har du ikke noe ...?**	haar dew ikker no͞oer
cheaper/better	**rimeligere/bedre**	reemerleeyerrer/bay͞drer
larger/smaller	**større/mindre**	sturrer/mindrer
It's too ...	**Den er for ...**	den ær for
big/small	**stor/liten**	sto͞or/leetern
dark/light	**mørk/lys**	murrk/le͞wss

How much?   *Hvor mye?*

How much is this?	**Hvor mye koster dette?**	voor me͞wer kosterr dehter
How much are they?	**Hvor mye koster de?**	voor me͞wer kosterr dee
I don't understand.	**Jeg forstår ikke.**	yæi foshtawr ikker
Please write it down.	**Kan du skrive det?**	kahn dew skreever deh
I don't want to spend more than... kroner.	**Jeg vil ikke gi mer enn ... kroner.**	yæi vil ikker yee may͞r ehn ... kro͞onerr

COLOURS, see page 113

Decision   *Avgjørelse*

I'll take it.	**Jeg tar det.**	yæi taar deh
No, I don't like it.	**Nei, jeg liker det ikke.**	næi yæi **lee**kerr deh **ik**ker
It's not quite what I want.	**Det er ikke akkurat det jeg hadde tenkt meg.**	deh ær **ik**ker ahkew**raat** deh yæi **hah**der **tehngkt** mæi

Ordering—Delivery   *Bestilling – Levering*

Can you order it for me?	**Kan du bestille det til meg?**	kahn dew ber**stil**ler deh til mæi
How long will it take?	**Hvor lang tid tar det?**	voor lahng teed taar deh
I'll take it with me.	**Jeg tar det med meg.**	yæi taar deh meh(d) mæi
Deliver it to the ... Hotel.	**Kan du levere det til ... hotell?**	kahn dew leh**vay**rer deh til ... hoo**tehl**
Please send it to this address.	**Kan du sende det til denne adressen?**	kahn dew **seh**ner deh til **deh**ner ah**dreh**ssern
Will I have any difficulties with the customs?	**Kan jeg få problemer i tollen?**	kahn yæi faw proo**blay**merr ee **tol**lern

Paying   *Betaling*

How much is it?	**Hvor mye blir det?**	voor **mew**er bleer deh
Can I pay by traveller's cheque?	**Kan jeg betale med reisesjekk?**	kahn yæi ber**taa**ler meh(d) **ræis**sershehk
Do you accept dollars/pounds?	**Tar dere dollar/pund?**	taar **day**rer **dol**lahr/pewn
Do you accept credit cards?	**Tar dere kreditt-kort?**	taar **day**rer kreh**dit**ko^rt
Can I get the VAT (sales tax) back?	**Får jeg tilbakebetalt momsen?**	fawr yæi til**baa**kerber**taalt** **moom**sern
Could I have a receipt?	**Kan jeg få kvittering?**	kahn yæi faw kvit**tay**ring
I think there's a mistake in the bill.	**Jeg tror det er en feil på regningen.**	yæi **troor** deh ær ehn fæil paw **ræi**ningern

Anything else? *Noe annet?*

No, thanks, that's all.	**Nei takk. Det var alt.**	næi tahk. deh vaar ahlt
Yes, I'd like ...	**Ja, jeg vil gjerne ha ...**	yaa yæi vil yǣ^rner haa
May I have a bag, please?	**Kan jeg få en bærepose?**	kahn yæi faw ehn bǣrerpōōsser
Could you wrap it up for me, please?	**Kan du pakke det inn for meg?**	kahn dew pahker deh in for mæi

Dissatisfied? *Misfornøyd?*

Can you exchange this, please?	**Kan jeg få byttet dette?**	kahn yæi faw bewtert dehter
I want to return this.	**Jeg vil gjerne levere tilbake dette.**	yæi vil yǣ^rner lehvāyrer tilbaaker dehter
Could I have a refund?	**Kan jeg få pengene tilbake?**	kahn yæi faw pehngerner tilbaaker.
Here's the receipt.	**Her er kvitteringen.**	hǣr ær kvittāyringern

---

Kan jeg hjelpe deg?	Can I help you?
Hva skal det være?	What would you like?
Hvilken ... vil du ha?	What ... would you like?
farge/form	colour/shape
Jeg beklager. Det har vi ikke.	I'm sorry, we don't have any.
Det er vi utsolgt for.	We're out of stock.
Skal vi bestille det?	Shall we order it for you?
Tar du det med eller skal vi sende det?	Will you take it with you or shall we send it?
Skal det være noe annet?	Anything else?
Det blir ... kroner, takk.	That comes to ... kroner.
Kassen er der borte.	The cash desk is over there.

Bookshop—Stationer's *Bokhandel – Papirhandel*

In Norway, books and stationery are usually sold in the same shop. You'll find newspapers, magazines and paperbacks at newsstands and tobacconists.

Where's the nearest ...?	**Hvor er nær-meste ...?**	voor ær nær-mehster
bookshop	**bokhandel**	bookhahnderl
stationer's	**papirhandel**	pahpeerhahnderl
newsstand	**aviskiosk**	ahveeskhyosk
Where can I buy an English-language newspaper?	**Hvor kan jeg få kjøpt en engelsk-språklig avis?**	voor kahn yæi faw khurpt ehn ehngerlsk-sprawkli ahveess
Where's the guide-book section?	**Hvor står reise-håndbøkene?**	voor stawr ræisser-honbūrkerner
Where are the English books?	**Hvor står de engelske bøkene?**	voor stawr dee ehngerlsker būrkerner
Do you have any of ...'s books in English?	**Har dere noen av ...s bøker på engelsk?**	haar dāyrer nōoern ahv ...s būrkerr paw ehngerlsk
I'd like a/an/some ...	**Jeg vil gjerne ha ...**	yæi vil yǣ'rner haa
address book	**en adressebok**	ehn ahdrehsserbook
adhesive tape	**limbånd**	leembon
ball-point pen	**en kulepenn**	ehn kēwlerpehn
blotting paper	**trekkpapir**	trehkpahpeer
book	**en bok**	ehn book
calendar	**en kalender**	ehn kahlehnderr
carbon paper	**blåpapir**	blawpahpeer
chalk	**kritt**	krit
crayons	**fargeblyanter**	fahrggerblēwahnterr
dictionary	**en ordbok**	ehn ōorbook
pocket Norwegian-English	**lomme-norsk-engelsk**	loommer-noshk-ehngerlsk
drawing pad	**en tegneblokk**	ehn tæinerblok
drawing pins	**tegnestifter**	tæinerstifterr
envelopes	**noen konvolutter**	nōoern koonvoolewterr
eraser	**et viskelær**	eht viskerlǣr
exercise book	**en skrivebok**	ehn skreeverbook
felt-tip pen	**en tusjpenn**	ehn tewshpehn
fountain pen	**en fyllepenn**	ehn fewlerpehn
gift wrapping paper	**gavepapir**	gaaverpahpeer

glue	lim	leem
grammar book	en grammatikk	ehn grahmahtik
guidebook	en reisehåndbok	ehn ræisserhonbook
ink	blekk	blehk
(self-adhesive) labels	noen (selvklebende) etiketter	nooern (sehlklayberner) ehtikehterr
magazine	et ukeblad	eht ewkerblaa(d)
map	et kart	eht kahrt
street map of ...	et kart over ...	eht kahrt aw_verr
road map of ...	et veikart over ...	eht væikahrt aw_verr
mechanical pencil	en skrublyant	ehn skrewblewahnt
newspaper	en avis	ehn ahveess
American	amerikansk	ahm(eh)rikaansk
English	engelsk	ehngerlsk
notebook	en notiskbok	ehn nooteessbook
note paper	brevpapir	brayvpahpeer
phrase book	en parlør	ehn pahrlurr
paintbox	et malerskrin	eht maalerrskreen
paper	papir	pahpeer
paperback	en pocketbok	ehn pokkertbook
paperclips	binders	bindersh
paper napkins	papirservietter	pahpeersærvyehterr
pen	penn	pehn
pencil	en blyant	ehn blewahnt
pencil sharpener	en blyantspisser	ehn blewahntspisserr
picturebook	en billedbok	ehn billerdbook
playing cards	spillkort	spilkort
pocket calculator	en lommekalkulator	ehn lommerkahlkewlaatoor
postcard	et postkort	eht postkort
propelling pencil	en skrublyant	ehn skrewblewahnt
refill (for a pen)	en refill	ehn "refill"
rubber	et viskelær	eht viskerlær
rubber bands	gummistrikker	gewmistrikkerr
ruler	en linjal	ehn linyaal
stapler	en heftemaskin	ehn hehftermahsheen
staples	heftestifter	hehfterstifterr
string	hyssing	hewssing
thumbtacks	tegnestifter	tæinerstifterr
tissue paper	silkepapir	silkerpahpeer
travel guide	en reisehåndbok	ehn ræisserhonbook
typewriter ribbon	et fargebånd (til skrivemaskin)	eht fahrggerbon (til skreevermahsheen)
typing paper	skrivemaskinpapir	skreevermahsheenpahpeer
(box of) watercolors	et malerskrin	eht maalerrskreen
wrapping paper	innpakningspapir	inpahkningspahpeer
writing pad	en skriveblokk	ehn skreeverblok
writing paper	skrivepapir	skreeverpahpeer

Camping equipment   *Campingutstyr*

I'd like a/an/ some ... | **Jeg vil gjerne ha ...** | yæi vil yæ^rner haa

I'd like a/an/ some ...	**Jeg vil gjerne ha ...**	yæi vil yæ^rner haa
air bed (mattress)	en luftmadrass	ehn lewftmahdrahss
aluminum foil (Am.)	aluminiumsfolie	ahlewmeenyewmsfoolyer
backpack	en ryggsekk	ehn rewgsehk
bottle-opener	en flaskeåpner	ehn flahskerawpnerr
bucket	en bøtte	eht burter
butane gas	butangass	bewtaangahss
camp bed	en campingseng	ehn kæmpingsehng
candles	stearinlys	stehahreenlewss
can opener	en boksåpner	ehn boksawpnerr
charcoal briquets	trekullbriketter	trāykewlbrikkehterr
clothes pegs (pins)	klesklyper	klāysklewperr
compass	et kompass	eht koompahss
cool bag	en kjøleboks	ehn khūrlerbokss
corkscrew	en korketrekker	ehn korkertrehkerr
crockery	et servise	eht særveesser
deck chair	en fluktstol	ehn flewktstōōl
dish detergent	et oppvaskmiddel	eht opvahskmidderl
fire lighter	tennvæske	tehnvehsker
fishing tackle	fiskeutstyr	fiskerewtstewr
flashlight	en lommelykt	ehn loommerlewkt
folding chair	en klappstol	ehn klahpstōōl
folding table	et klappbord	eht klahpbōōr
food box	en matboks	ehn maatbokss
frying pan	en stekepanne	ehn stāykerpahner
groundsheet	et teltunderlag	eht tehltewnerrlaag
hammer	en hammer	ehn hahmerr
hammock	en hengekøye	ehn hehngerkoyer
ice chest	en kjøleboks	ehn khūrlerbokss
(cooler) ice packs	kjøleelementer	khurlerehlermehnterr
insect spray (killer)	en insektgift	ehn insehktyift
kerosene	parafin	pahrahfeen
(oil) lamp	en (olje)lampe	ehn (olyer)lahmper
lantern	en lykt	ehn lewkt
matches	fyrstikker	fewshtikkerr
(foam rubber) mattress	en (skumgummi-) madrass	ehn (skoomgewmi-) mahdrahss
mosquito net	et myggnett	eht mewgneht
paper napkins	papirservietter	pahpeersærvyehterr
paper towel	husholdningspapir	hewsholningspahpeer
paraffin	parafin	pahrahfeen
penknife	en lommekniv	ehn lommerkneev
picnic basket	en picnickurv	ehn piknikkewrv

CAMPING, see page 32

plastic bags	plastposer	plahstpōosserr
pliers	en tang	ehn tahng
pocketknife	en lommekniv	ehn lommerkneev
pot holders	grytekluter	grēwterklēwterr
primus stove	en primus	ehn preemewss
pump	en pumpe	ehn poomper
rope	et tau	eht tou
rucksack	en ryggsekk	ehn rewgsehk
saucepan	en kasserolle	ehn kahsserroller
scissors	en saks	ehn sahkss
screwdriver	en skrutrekker	ehn skrēwtrehkerr
sleeping bag	en sovepose	ehn sawverpōosser
stew pot	en gryte	ehn grēwter
tent	et telt	eht tehlt
tent pegs	teltplugger	tehltplewgerr
tent pole	en teltstang	ehn tehltstahng
tinfoil	aluminiumsfolie	ahlewmeenyewmsfōolyer
tin opener	en boksåpner	ehn boksawpnerr
torch	en lommelykt	ehn loommerlewkt
vacuum flask	en termosflaske	ehn tærmoosflahsker
washing powder	vaskepulver	vahskerpewlverr
water flask	en feltflaske	ehn fehltflahsker

Crockery   Servise

cups	kopper	kopperr
mugs	krus	krēwss
dishes	fat	faat
bowls	skåler	skawlerr
plates	tallerkener	tahlærkernerr
saucers	skåler (til kopper)	skawlerr (til kopperr)
tumblers	drikkeglass	drikkerglahss
(made of) cardboard	(av) papp	(ahv) pahp

Cutlery (Flatware)   Bestikk

forks	gafler	gahflerr
knives	kniver	kneeverr
spoons	skjeer	shāyerr
teaspoons	teskjeer	tāyshāyerr
(made of) plastic	(av) plast	(ahv) plahst
(made of) stainless steel	(av) rustfritt stål	(ahv) rewstfrit stawl

Chemist's (Drugstore) *Apotek*

Norwegian pharmacies don't stock the wide range of goods that you'll find in Britain or the U.S. For example, they don't sell photographic equipment or toys. And for perfume, cosmetics, etc., you have to go to a *parfymeri* (pahrfewmer**ree**). You need a prescription for most medicine.

In the window you'll see a notice telling you where the nearest all-night pharmacy is.

This section is divided into two parts:

1. Pharmaceutical—medicine, first-aid, etc.
2. Toiletry—toilet articles, cosmetics

General *Allment*

Where's the nearest (all-night) chemist's?	**Hvor er nærmeste (vakthavende) apotek?**	voor ær nærmehster (**vahk**thaaverner) ahpoo**tayk**
What time does the chemist's open/ close?	**Når åpner/stenger apoteket?**	nor **awp**nerr/**stehng**err ahpoo**tay**ker

1. Pharmaceutical *Medisiner*

I'd like something for ...	**Jeg vil gjerne ha noe mot ...**	yæi vil y**æ**ᵣner haa n**oo**er m**oo**t
a cold	**forkjølelse**	forkh**ur**lerlser
a cough	**hoste**	**hoo**ster
a headache	**hodepine**	h**oo**derpeener
hay fever	**høysnue**	**hoy**sn**ew**er
insect bites	**insektstikk**	in**sehk**tstik
sunburn	**solforbrenning**	**sool**forbrehning
travel sickness	**reisesyke**	**ræi**ssers**ew**ker
an upset stomach	**urolig mage**	ew**roo**li **maa**ger
Can you make up this prescription for me?	**Kan du gjøre i stand denne resepten for meg?**	kahn dew y**ur**rer ee stahn **dehn**er reh**sseh**ptern for mæi
Can I get it without a prescription?	**Kan jeg få det uten resept?**	kahn yæi faw deh **ew**tern reh**sseh**pt
Shall I wait?	**Skal jeg vente?**	skahl yæi **vehn**ter

DOCTOR, see page 137

Can I have a/an/some ...?	**Kan jeg få ...?**	kahn yæi faw
absorbent cotton	**bomull**	boomewl
analgesic	**et analgetikum**	eht ahnahlgāytikewm
antiseptic cream	**en antiseptisk salve**	ehn ahntissehptisk sahlver
aspirin	**aspirin**	ahspirreen
bandage	**en bandasje**	ehn bahndaasher
elastic bandage	**et elastisk bind**	eht ehlahstisk bin
Band-Aids	**plaster**	plahsterr
... capsules	**-kapsler**	-kahpshlerr
charcoal tablets	**kulltabletter**	kewltahblehterr
condoms	**kondomer**	koondoomerr
contraceptives	**et preventivmiddel**	eht prāyvahngteevmidderl
corn plasters	**liktornplaster**	leektoo'nplahsterr
cotton wool	**bomull**	boomewl
cough drops	**halspastiller**	hahlspahstillerr
cough syrup	**hostesaft**	hoostersahft
disinfectant	**et desinfeksjons-middel**	eht dehssinfehkshoons-midderl
ear drops	**øredråper**	ūrrerdrawperr
Elastoplast	**plaster**	plahsterr
eye drops	**øyendråper**	oyerndrawperr
first-aid kit	**et førstehjelpsskrin**	eht furshteryehlpsskreen
(roll of) gauze	**(en rull) gasbind**	(ehn rewl) gahsbin
insect repellent	**et insektmiddel**	eht insehktmidderl
iodine	**jod**	yod
laxative	**et laksermiddel**	eht lahksāyrmidderl
mouthwash	**et munnvann**	eht mewnvahn
nose drops	**nesedråper**	nāysserdrawperr
... ointment	**-salve**	-sahlver
painkiller	**et smertestillende middel**	eht smæ'terstillerner midderl
sanitary towels (napkins)	**sanitetsbind**	sahnitāytsbin
suppositories	**stikkpiller**	stikpillerr
... tablets	**-tabletter**	-tahblehterr
tampons	**tamponger**	tahmpongerr
thermometer	**termometer**	tærmoomāyterr
throat lozenges	**halstabletter**	hahlstahblehterr
vitamin pills	**vitaminpiller**	vittahmeenpillerr

GIFT	POISON
KUN TIL UTVENDIG BRUK	FOR EXTERNAL USE ONLY

2. Toiletry *Toalettartikler*

I'd like a/an/some ...	Jeg vil gjerne ha ...	yæi vil yǣ'ner haa
after-shave lotion	et etterbarberings-vann	eht ehterrbahrbāyrings-vahn
bath salts	et badesalt	eht baadersahlt
blusher	en rouge	ehn rōōsh
bubble bath	et skumbad	eht skoombaad
cosmetics	noe kosmetikk	nōōer koosmertik
cream	en krem	ehn krāym
cleansing cream	en rensekrem	ehn rehnserkrāym
foot cream	en fotkrem	ehn fōōtkrāym
foundation cream	en underlagskrem	ehn ewnerrlaagskrāym
hand cream	en håndkrem	ehn honkrāym
moisturizing cream	en fuktighetskrem	ehn fooktihehtskrāym
night cream	en nattkrem	ehn nahtkrāym
sun-tan cream	en solkrem	ehn sōōlkrāym
cuticle remover	en neglebåndsfjerner	ehn nǣilerbonsfyǣ'nerr
deodorant	en deodorant	ehn dehoodoorahnt
emery boards	sandpapirfiler	sahnpahpeerfeelerr
eyebrow pencil	en øyenbrynsstift	ehn oyernbrēwnsstift
eye liner	en eyeliner	ehn "eyeliner"
eye shadow	en øyenskygge	ehn oyernshewger
face flannel	en ansiktsklut	ehn ahnsiktsklēwt
face powder	pudder	pewderr
lipbrush	en leppestiftpensel	ehn lehperstiftpehnserl
lipsalve (balm)	en leppepomade	ehn lehperpoomaader
lipstick	en leppestift	ehn lehperstift
make-up bag	en sminkepung	ehn smingkerpoong
make-up remover pads	bomullspads	boomewls"pads"
mascara	en øyensverte	ehn oyernsvær'ter
nail brush	en neglebørste	ehn nǣilerburshter
nail clippers	en negleklipper	ehn nǣilerklipperr
nail file	en neglefil	ehn nǣilerfeel
nail polish	en neglelakk	ehn nǣilerlahk
nail polish remover	en neglelakkfjerner	ehn nǣilerlahkfyǣ'nerr
nail scissors	en neglesaks	ehn nǣilersahkss
perfume	en parfyme	ehn pahrfēwmer
powder	pudder	pewderr
powder puff	en pudderkvast	ehn pewderrkvahst
razor	en barberhøvel	ehn bahrbāyrhurverl
razor blades	barberblader	bahrbāyrblaaderr
safety pins	sikkerhetsnåler	sikkerrhehtsnawlerr
shaving brush	en barberkost	ehn bahrbāyrkoost

shaving cream	**en barberkrem**	ehn bahr**bāy**rkraym
soap	**en såpe**	ehn **saw**per
sponge	**en svamp**	ehn svahmp
sponge bag	**en toalettmappe**	ehn tooah**leht**mahper
sun-tan oil	**en sololje**	ehn **sōōl**olyer
talcum powder	**en talkum**	ehn **tahl**kewm
(facial) tissues	**papirlommetørklær**	pah**peer**loommerturrklǣr
toilet paper	**toalettpapir**	tooah**leht**pahpeer
toiletries bag	**en toalettmappe**	ehn tooah**leht**mahper
toilet water	**en eau de toilette**	en aw deh tooah**leht**
toothbrush	**en tannbørste**	ehn **tahn**burshter
toothpaste	**en tannpasta**	ehn **tahn**pahstah
towel	**et håndkle**	eht **hong**kleh
tweezers	**en pinsett**	ehn **pin**seht
washcloth	**en ansiktsklut**	ehn **ahn**siktsklewt

For your hair   *For håret*

barrette	**en hårspenne**	ehn **haws**hpehner
bobby pins	**hårklemmer**	**hawr**klehmerr
colour shampoo	**en fargesjampo**	ehn **fahr**ggershahmpoo
comb	**en kam**	ehn kahm
curlers (rollers)	**hårruller**	**hawr**rewlerr
dry shampoo	**tørrsjampo**	**turr**shahmpoo
hairbrush	**en hårbørste**	ehn **hawr**burshter
hair dye	**et hårfargingsmiddel**	eht **hawr**fahrgingsmidderl
hair (styling) gel	**en hårgelé**	ehn **hawr**shehlāy
hairgrips	**hårklemmer**	**hawr**klehmerr
hair lotion	**hårvann**	**hawr**vahn
hair mousse	**et hårskum**	eht **haws**hkoom
hairpins	**hårnåler**	**haw**ʳnawlerr
hair slide	**en hårspenne**	ehn **haws**hpehner
hair spray	**hårlakk**	**haw**ʳlahk
setting lotion	**et leggevann**	eht **leh**gervahn
shampoo	**en sjampo**	ehn **shahm**poo
for dry/greasy (oily) hair	**for tørt/fett hår**	for turʳt/feht hawr
tint	**et hårtoningsmiddel**	eht **haw**ʳtōōningsmidderl
wig	**en parykk**	ehn pah**rewk**

For the baby   *For babyen*

baby food	**barnemat**	**baa**ʳnermaat
dummy (pacifier)	**en narresmokk**	ehn **nah**rersmook
feeding bottle	**en tåteflaske**	ehn **taw**terflahsker
nappies (diapers)	**bleier**	**blæi**err

Clothing   *Klær*

If you want to buy something specific, prepare yourself in advance. Look at the list of clothing on page 116. Get some idea of the colour, material and size you want. They're all listed on the next few pages.

General   *Allment*

I'd like ...	**Jeg vil gjerne ha ...**	yæi vil yǣ^rner haa
I'm just looking.	**Jeg bare ser meg omkring.**	yæi baarer sāȳr mæi omkring
I'd like ... for a 10-year-old boy/girl.	**Jeg vil gjerne ha ... til en gutt/pike på 10 år.**	yæi vil yǣ^rner haa ... til ehn gewt/peeker paw 10 awr
I'd like something like this.	**Jeg vil gjerne ha noe i denne stilen.**	yæi vil yǣ^rner haa nōōer ee dehner steelern
I like the one in the window.	**Jeg liker den i vinduet.**	yæi leeker dehn ee vindewer
How much is that per metre?	**Hvor mye koster det pr. meter?**	voor mēw̄er kosterr deh pær māȳterr

1 centimetre (cm.) = 0.39 in.	1 inch = 2.54 cm.
1 metre (m.) = 39.37 in.	1 foot = 30.5 cm.
10 metres = 32.81 ft.	1 yard = 0.91 m.

Colour   *Farge*

I'd like something in ...	**Jeg vil gjerne ha noe i ...**	yæi vil yǣ^rner haa nōōer ee
I'd like a darker/lighter shade.	**Jeg vil gjerne ha en mørkere/lysere nyanse.**	yæi vil yǣ^rner haa en murrkerrer/lēw̄sserrer newahngser
I'd like something to match this.	**Jeg vil gjerne ha noe som står til dette.**	yæi vil yǣ^rner haa nōōer som stawr til dehter
I don't like the colour/pattern.	**Jeg liker ikke fargen/mønstret.**	yæi leekerr ikker fahrggern/murnstrer

beige	**beige**	bāysh
black	**svart**	svah{r}t
blue	**blå**	blaw
brown	**brun**	brēwn
golden	**gullfarget**	gewlfahrggert
green	**grønn**	grurn
grey	**grå**	graw
mauve	**lilla**	lillah
orange	**oransje**	oorahngsh
pink	**rosa**	rōossah
purple	**fiolett**	feeooleht
red	**rød**	rūr
scarlet	**skarlagenrød**	skah{r}laagernrūr
silver	**sølvfarget**	surlfahrggert
turquoise	**turkis**	tewrkeess
white	**hvit**	veet
yellow	**gul**	gēwl
light ...	**lyse-**	lēwsser-
dark ...	**mørke-**	murrker-

ensfarget	**stripet**	**prikket**	**rutet**	**mønstret**
(āynsfahrggert)	(streepert)	(prikkert)	(rēwtert)	(murnstrert)

Fabric   *Tøystoff*

Do you have anything in ...?	**Har du noe i ...?**	haar dew nōōer ee
Is that ...?	**Er det ...?**	ær deh
handmade	**håndlaget**	honlaagert
imported	**importert**	impo{r}tāy{r}t
made in Norway	**laget i Norge**	laagert ee norgger
What fabric/material is it?	**Hva slags stoff/ materiale er det?**	vah shlahkss stof/ maht(er)reeaaler ær deh
I'd like something thinner.	**Jeg vil gjerne ha noe tynnere.**	yæi vil yǣ{r}ner haa nōōer tewnnerer
Do you have anything of better quality?	**Har du en bedre kvalitet?**	haar dew ehn bāydrer kvahlitāyt

What's it made of? **Hva er det laget av?** vaa ær deh **laa**gert ahv

cambric	**batist**	bahtist
camelhair	**kamelhår**	kahm$\overline{ay}$lhawr
chiffon	**chiffon**	shiffong
corduroy	**kordfløyel**	kaw^{r}dfloyerl
cotton	**bomull**	boomewl
crepe	**krepp**	krehp
denim	**denim**	dehneem
felt	**filt**	filt
flannel	**flanell**	flåhnehl
gabardine	**gabardin**	gahbah^{r}deen
lace	**knipling**	knipling
leather	**lær**	l$\overline{æ}$r
linen	**lin**	leen
poplin	**poplin**	poplin
satin	**sateng**	sahtehng
silk	**silke**	silker
suede	**semsket skinn**	sehmskert shin
towelling	**frotté**	froot$\overline{ay}$
velvet	**fløyel**	floyerl
velveteen	**bomullsfløyel**	boomewlsfloyerl
wool	**ull**	ewl
worsted	**kamgarn**	kahmgaa^{r}n

Is it ...?	**Er det ...?**	ær deh
pure cotton/wool	**ren bomull/ull**	r$\overline{ay}$n boomewl/ewl
synthetic	**syntetisk**	sewnt$\overline{ay}$tisk
colourfast	**fargeekte**	fahrggerehkter
crease resistant (wrinkle-free)	**krøllfritt**	krurlfrit

Is it hand washable/ machine washable?	**Skal det vaskes for hånd/i maskin?**	skahl deh **vahs**kerss for hon/ee mah**sheen**
Will it shrink?	**Krymper det?**	krewmperr deh

Size *Størrelse*

I take size 38.	**Jeg bruker størrelse 38.**	yæi br$\overline{ew}$kerr sturrerlser 38
Could you measure me?	**Kan du ta mål av meg?**	kahn dew taa mawl ahv mæi
I don't know the Norwegian sizes.	**Jeg kjenner ikke de norske størrelsene.**	yæi khehnerr ikker dee noshker sturrerlserner

Sizes vary from country to country and from one manufacturer to another, so be sure to try on the clothes before you buy.

Women *Kvinner*

Dresses/Suits					
American	8	10	12	14	16	18
British	10	12	14	16	18	20
Continental	36	38	40	42	44	46

Stockings							Shoes			
American } British	8	$8\frac{1}{2}$	9	$9\frac{1}{2}$	10	$10\frac{1}{2}$	$5\frac{1}{2}$	$6\frac{1}{2}$	$7\frac{1}{2}$	$8\frac{1}{2}$
							4	5	6	7
Continental		1		2		3	37	38	39	40

Men *Menn*

Suits/Overcoats							Shirts			
American } British	36	38	40	42	44	46	15	16	17	18
Continental	46	48	50	52	54	56	38	40	42	44

Shoes							
American	$6\frac{1}{2}$	7	$7\frac{1}{2}$	8	$8\frac{1}{2}$	9	10	11
British	5	6	7	8	9	10	11	12
Continental	38	39	40	41	42	43	44	45

A good fit? *Passer det?*

Can I try it on?	**Kan jeg få prøve den?**	kahn yæi faw prūrver dehn
Where's the changing room?	**Hvor er prøverommet?**	voor ær prūrver-roommer
Is there a mirror?	**Fins det et speil her?**	finss deh eht spæil hǣr
It fits very well.	**Den passer meget bra.**	dehn pahsserr māygert braa
It doesn't fit.	**Den passer ikke.**	dehn pahsser ikker

NUMBERS, see page 147

It's too ...	Den er for ...	dehn ær for
short/long	kort/lang	ko^{r}t/lahng
tight/loose	trang/vid	trahng/vee(d)
How long will it take to alter it?	Hvor lang tid tar det å endre den?	voor lahng teed taar deh aw ehndrer dehn

Clothes and accessories *Klær og tilbehør*

I would like a/an/ some ...	Jeg vil gjerne ha ...	yæi vil yǣ^{r}ner haa
anorak	en anorakk	ehn ahnoorahk
bathing cap	en badehette	ehn baaderhehter
bathrobe	en badekåpe	ehn baaderkawper
blouse	en bluse	ehn blewsser
bow tie	en flue	ehn flewer
bra	en behå	ehn bayhaw
braces	et par seler	eht pahr saylerr
cap	en lue	ehn lewer
cardigan	en golfjakke	ehn golfyahker
children's ...	barne-	baa^{r}ner-
coat (man's)	en frakk	ehn frahk
coat (woman's)	en kåpe	ehn kawper
dress	en kjole	ehn khooler
with long sleeves	med lange ermer	meh(d) laanger ærmerr
with short sleeves	med korte ermer	meh(d) ko^{r}ter ærmerr
sleeveless	uten ermer	ewtern ærmerr
dressing gown	en morgenkåpe	ehn mawer^{r}nkawper
evening dress (woman's)	en aftenkjole	ehn ahfternkhooler
fur coat	en pels	ehn pehlss
girdle	en hofteholder	ehn hofterhollerr
gloves	et par hansker	eht pahr hahnskerr
handbag	en håndveske	ehn honvehsker
handkerchief	et lommetørkle	eht loommerturrkler
hat	en hatt	ehn haht
jacket	en jakke	ehn yahker
jeans	et par jeans	eht pahr ''jeans''
kneesocks	et par knestrømper	eht pahr knaystrurmperr
man's ...	herre-	hærer-
nightdress (night-gown)	en nattkjole	ehn nahtkhooler
overalls	en overall	ehn awverrol
pair of ...	et par ...	eht pahr
panties	et par truser	eht pahr trewsserr

pants (Am.)	et par langbukser	eht pahr **lahng**bookserr
panty hose	en strømpebukse	ehn **strurmper**bookser
parka	en anorakk	ehn ahn**oor**ahk
pullover	en genser	ehn **gehn**serr
crew-neck	med rund hals	meh(d) rewn hahlss
polo (turtle)-neck	høyhalset	**hoy**hahlset
V-neck	V-genser	vāy-**gehn**serr
pyjamas	en pyjamas	ehn pew**shaa**mahss
raincoat	en regnfrakk	ehn **ræin**frahk
scarf	et skjerf	eht shærf
shirt	en skjorte	ehn **shoo**ʳter
shorts	et par shorts	eht pahr "shorts"
skirt	et skjørt	eht shurʳt
slip	en underkjole	ehn **ewner**khōoler
socks	et par sokker	eht pahr **sokk**err
sportswear	sportsklær	spoʳts**klær**
stockings	et par strømper	eht pahr **strurm**perr
suit (man's)	en dress	ehn drehss
suit (woman's)	en drakt	ehn drahkt
suspenders (Am.)	et par seler	eht pahr **sāy**lerr
sweater	en genser	ehn **gehn**serr
sweat suit	en treningsdrakt	ehn **trāy**ningsdrahkt
swimming trunks	en badebukse	ehn **baader**bookser
swimsuit	en badedrakt	ehn **baader**drahkt
tie	et slips	eht shlipss
tights	en strømpebukse	ehn **strurm**perbookser
tracksuit	en treningsdrakt	ehn **trāy**ningsdrahkt
trousers	et par langbukser	eht pahr **lahng**bookserr
T-shirt	en T-skjorte	ehn tāy-**shoo**ʳter
umbrella	en paraply	ehn pahrahp**lēw**
underpants	en underbukse	ehn **ewner**rbookser
undershirt	en trøye	ehn **troy**er
vest (Am.)	en vest	ehn vehst
vest (Br.)	en trøye	ehn **troy**er
waistcoat	en vest	ehn vehst
woman's ...	dame-	**daa**mer-

belt	et belte	eht **behl**ter
buckle	en spenne	ehn **spehn**er
button	en knapp	ehn knahp
collar	en krage	ehn **kraag**er
pocket	en lomme	ehn **loom**mer
press stud (snap fastener)	en trykknapp	ehn **trewk**knahp
zip (zipper)	en glidelås	ehn **gleeder**lawss

Shoes *Sko*

I'd like a pair of ...	**Jeg vil gjerne ha et par ...**	yæi vil yǣ^rner haa eht pahr
athletic shoes	**turnsko**	tēw^rnskoo
boots	**støvler**	sturvler
lined/unlined	**forede/uforede**	foorerder/ēwfoorerder
moccasins	**mokkasiner**	mookahsseenerr
plimsolls	**turnsko**	tēw^rnskoo
sandals	**sandaler**	sahndaalerr
shoes	**sko**	skoo
flat	**lavhælte**	laavhāylter
with a heel	**mod hæl**	meh(d) hayl
with leather soles	**med lærsåler**	meh(d) lǣ^rsawlerr
with rubber soles	**med gummisåler**	meh(d) gewmissawlerr
slippers	**tøfler**	turflerr
These are too ...	**Disse er for ...**	disser ær for
narrow/wide	**smale/vide**	smaaler/vee(d)er
big/small	**store/små**	stoorer/smaw
Do you have a smaller/larger size?	**Har du et nummer mindre/større?**	haar dew eht noommerr mindrer/sturrer
Do you have the same in black?	**Har du de samme i svart?**	haar dew dee sahmer ee svah^rt
cloth/leather/rubber/ suede	**tøy/lær/gummi/ semsket skinn**	toy/lǣr/gewmi/ sehmskert shin
Is it real leather?	**Er det ekte lær?**	ær deh ehkter lǣr
I need some ...	**Jeg trenger ...**	yæi trehngerr
insoles	**innleggssåler**	inlehgssawlerr
shoe polish	**skokrem**	skookrāym
shoelaces	**skolisser**	skoolisserr

Shoe repairs *Skoreparasjon*

Can you repair these shoes?	**Kan du reparere disse skoene?**	kahn dew rehpahrāyrer disser skooerner
Can you stitch this?	**Kan du sy sammen dette?**	kahn dew sēw sahmern dehter
I want new soles and heels.	**Jeg vil ha nye såler og hæler.**	yæi vil haa nēwer sawler o(g) hāylerr
When will they be ready?	**Når blir de ferdig?**	nor bleer dee fǣ^rdi

COLOURS, see page 113

Electrical appliances   *Elektrisk utstyr*

Standard voltage (*strømstyrke*) is 220 volts, 50 cycles A.C.

Do you have a battery for this?	**Har du et batteri til denne?**	haar dew eht bahterree til dehner
This is broken. Can you repair it?	**Denne er gått i stykker. Kan du reparere den?**	dehner ær got ee stewkerr. kahn dew rehpahrāyrer dehn
Can you show me how it works?	**Kan du vise meg hvordan den fungerer?**	kahn dew veesser mæi vooͬdahn dehn fewngāyrerr
How do I switch it on?	**Hvordan setter man den i gang?**	vooͬdahn sehterr mahn dehn ee gahng
I'd like to hire (rent) a video cassette.	**Jeg vil gjerne leie en videokassett.**	yæi vil yǣͬner læier ehn veedyookahsseht
I'd like a/an/ some ...	**Jeg vil gjerne ha ...**	yæi vil yǣͬner haa
adaptor	**en adapter**	ehn ahdahpterr
amplifier	**en forsterker**	ehn foshtærkerr
bulb	**en lyspære**	ehn lēwspærer
cassette player	**en kassettspiller**	ehn kahssehtspillerr
(radio) cassette recorder	**en (radio)kassett-opptaker**	ehn (raadyoo)kahsseht-optaakerr
clock-radio	**en klokkeradio**	ehn klokkerraadyoo
electric toothbrush	**en elektrisk tannbørste**	ehn ehlehktrisk tahnburshter
extension lead (cord)	**en skjøteledning**	ehn shūrterlāydning
hair dryer	**en hårføner**	ehn hawrfūrnerr
headphones	**et par høre-telefoner**	eht pahr hūrrer-tehlerfōōnerr
(travelling) iron	**et (reise)strykejern**	eht (ræisser)strēwkeryǣͬn
lamp	**en lampe**	ehn lahmper
personal stereo (pocket radio)	**en lommeradio**	ehn loommerraadyoo
portable ...	**bærbar ...**	bǣrbaar
radio	**en radio**	ehn raadyoo
record player	**en platespiller**	ehn plaaterspillerr
shaver	**en barbermaskin**	ehn bahrbāyrmahsheen
speakers	**høyttalere**	hoyttaalerrer
(colour) television	**en (farge)TV**	ehn (fahrgger)tāyveh
transformer	**en transformator**	ehn trahnsformaatoor
video recorder	**en videokassett-opptaker**	ehn veedyookahsseht-optaakerr

Grocer's   *Matvarehandel*

I'd like some bread, please.	**Jeg vil gjerne ha litt brød.**	yæi vil yǣᵣner haa lit brūr
crispbread	**knekkebrød**	knehkerbrūr
sliced bread	**oppskåret brød**	opskawrert brūr
white bread	**loff**	loof
What sort of cheese do you have?	**Hva slags ostesorter har du?**	vaa shlakss oostersoᵣterr haar dew
A piece of that one, please.	**Et stykke av den, takk.**	eht stewker ahv dehn tahk
I'll have one of those, please.	**Kan jeg få en av dem?**	kahn yæi faw ehn ahv dehm
May I help myself?	**Kan jeg ta selv?**	kahn yæi taa sehl
I'd like ...	**Jeg vil gjerne ha ...**	yæi vil yǣᵣner haa ...
a kilo of apples	**1 kg epler**	ehn kheeloo ehplerr
half a kilo of tomatoes	**½ kg tomater**	ehn hahl kheeloo toomaaterr
250 grams of coffee	**¼ kg kaffe**	ehn kvahᵣt kheeloo kahfer
3 hg. (300 g.) of salami	**3 h salami**	trāy hehktoo sahlaami
a litre of milk	**1 l melk**	ehn leeterr mehlk
4 slices of ham	**4 skiver skinke**	feerer sheeverr shingker
a packet of tea	**en pakke te**	ehn pahker tāy
a jar of jam	**et glass syltetøy**	eht glahss sewltertoy
a tin (can) of peaches	**en boks fersken**	ehn bokss fæshkern
a tube of mustard	**en tube sennep**	ehn tēwber sehnerp,
a box of chocolates	**en eske sjokolade**	ehn ehsker shookoolaader

Weights and measures		
1 kilogram or kilo (kg.) = 1,000 grams (g.)		
100 g. = 3.5 oz.	½ kg. = 1.1 lb.	
200 g. = 7.0 oz.	1 kg. = 2.2 lb.	
1 oz. = 28.35 g.		
1 lb. = 453.60 g.		
1 litre (l.) = 0.88 imp. qt. or 1.6 U.S. qt.		
1 imp. qt. = 1.14 l.	1 U.S. qt. = 0.95 l.	
1 imp. gal. = 4.55 l.	1 U.S. gal. = 3.80 l.	

FOOD, see also page 64

Jeweller's—Watchmaker's   *Gullsmed – Urmaker*

Can you show me some jewellery, please?	**Kan jeg få se på noen smykker?**	kahn yæi faw sāy paw nōōern smewkerr
I want a present for ...	**Jeg vil gjerne ha en presang til ...**	yæi vil yǣᵉrner haa ehn prehssahng til
Could I see that, please?	**Kan jeg få se på det?**	kahn yæi faw sāy paw dāy
Do you have anything in gold?	**Har du noe i gull?**	haar dew nōōer ee gewl
How many carats is this?	**Hvor mange karat har dette?**	voor mahnger kahraat haar dehter
Is this real silver?	**Er dette ekte sølv?**	ær dehter ehkter surl
Can you engrave these initials on it?	**Kan du gravere disse initialene?**	kahn dew grahvāyrer disser ini(t)seeaalerner
Can you repair this watch?	**Kan du reparere denne klokken?**	kahn dew rehpahrāyrer dehner klokkern
I'd like a/an/some ...	**Jeg vil gjerne ha ...**	yæi vil yǣᵉrner haa
alarm clock	**en vekkeklokke**	ehn vehkerklokker
bangle	**en armring**	ehn ahrmring
battery	**et batteri**	eht bahterree
bracelet	**et armbånd**	eht ahrmbon
chain bracelet	**en armlenke**	ehn ahrmlehngker
charm bracelet	**et berlokkarmbånd**	eht bærlokahrmbon
brooch	**en brosje**	ehn brōōsher
chain	**et kjede**	eht khāyder
charm	**en berlokk**	ehn bærlok
clock	**en klokke**	ehn klokker
cross	**et kors**	eht kosh
cuff links	**et par mansjett-knapper**	eht pahr mahnsheht-knahperr
earrings	**et par øreringer**	eht pahr ūrrerringerr
gem	**en edelsten**	ehn āyderlstāyn
jewel box	**et smykkeskrin**	eht smewkerskreen
mechanical pencil	**en skrublyant**	ehn skrewblewahnt
music box	**en spilledåse**	ehn spillerdawsser
necklace	**et halskjede**	eht hahlskhāyder
pendant	**et hengesmykke**	eht hehngersmewker
pocket watch	**et lommeur**	eht loommerēwr
powder compact	**en pudderdåse**	ehn pewderrdawsser
propelling pencil	**en skrublyant**	ehn skrewblewahnt

ring	en ring	ehn ring
engagement ring	en forlovelsesring	ehn forlawverlsersring
signet ring	en signetring	ehn singnaytring
wedding ring	en giftering	ehn yifterring
silverware	noe sølvtøy	nooer surltoy
string (strand)	et perlekjede	eht pærlerkhayder
of pearls		
tie clip	en slipsklype	ehn shlipsklewper
tie pin	en slipsnål	ehn shlipsnawl
watch	en klokke	ehn klokker
automatic	automatisk	outoomaatisk
digital/analogue	digital/analog	diggitaal/ahnahlawg
quartz	kvarts	kvahʳtss
with a second	med sekundviser	meh(d) sehkewn-
hand		veesserr
waterproof	vanntett	vahnteht
watchstrap	en klokkerem	ehn klokkerrehm
wristwatch	et armbåndsur	eht ahrmbonsewr

amber	rav	raav
amethyst	ametyst	ahmertewst
brass	messing	mehssing
bronze	bronse	brongser
chromium	krom	kroom
copper	kopper	kopperr
coral	korall	koorahl
crystal	krystall	krewstahl
cut glass	slepet glass	shlaypert glahss
diamond	diamant	deeahmahnt
emerald	smaragd	smahrahgd
enamel	emalje	ehmahlyer
gold	gull	gewl
gold plate	gullbelagt	gewlberlahkt
jade	jade	yaader
mother-of-pearl	perlemor	pæʳlermoor
onyx	onyks	oonewkss
pearl	perle	pæʳler
pewter	tinn	tin
platinum	platina	plaateenah
ruby	rubin	rewbeen
sapphire	safir	sahfeer
silver	sølv	surl
silver plate	sølvplett	surlpleht
topaz	topas	toopaass
turquoise	turkis	tewrkeess

Optician   *Optiker*

I've broken my glasses.	**Brillene mine er gått i stykker.**	brillerner meener ær got ee stawkerr
Can you repair them for me?	**Kan du reparere dem for meg?**	kahn dew rehpahrāyrer dehm for mæi
When will they be ready?	**Når blir de ferdig?**	nor bleer dee fæᵣdi
Can you change the lenses?	**Kan du skifte ut glassene?**	kahn dew shifter ēwt glahsserner
I'd like tinted lenses.	**Jeg vil gjerne ha fargede glass.**	yæi vil yæᵣner haa fahrggerder glahss
The frame is broken.	**Innfatningen er brukket.**	infahtningern ær brookkert
I'd like a glasses case.	**Jeg vil gjerne ha et brillefutteral.**	yæi vil yæᵣner haa eht brillerfewterraal
I'd like to have my eyesight checked.	**Jeg vil gjerne få kontrollert synet.**	yæi vil yæᵣner faw koontroolāyᵣt sēwner
I'm ...	**Jeg er ...**	yæi ær
short-sighted long-sighted	**nærsynt langsynt**	næᵣsēwnt lahngsēwnt
I'd like some contact lenses.	**Jeg vil gjerne ha kontaktlinser.**	yæi vil yæᵣner haa koontahktlinserr
I've lost one of my contact lenses.	**Jeg har mistet en kontaktlinse.**	yæi haar mistert ehn koontahktlinser
Could you give me another one?	**Kan jeg få en ny?**	kahn yæi faw ehn nēw
I have hard/soft lenses.	**Jeg har harde/ myke linser.**	yæi haar haarer/ mēwker linserr
Do you have any contact-lens fluid?	**Har du en kontakt- linsevæske?**	haar dew ehn koontahkt- linservehsker
I'd like to buy a pair of sunglasses.	**Jeg vil gjerne kjøpe et par solbriller.**	yæi vil yæᵣner khūᵣper eht pahr sōolbrillerr
May I look in the mirror?	**Kan jeg få se meg i speilet?**	kahn yæi faw sāy mæi ee spæiler
I'd like to buy a pair of binoculars.	**Jeg vil gjerne kjøpe en kikkert.**	yæi vil yæᵣner khūᵣper ehn khikkeᵣt

Photography   *Fotografering*

I'd like a(n) ... camera.	**Jeg vil gjerne ha et ... fotoapparat.**	yæi vil yǣ^rner haa eht ... fōōtooahpahraat
automatic	**helautomatisk**	hāyloutoomaatisk
compact	**kompakt**	koompahkt
simple	**enkelt**	ehngkehrlt
Can you show me some video cameras, please?	**Kan jeg få se på noen video-kameraer?**	kahn yæi faw sāy paw nōōern veedyoo-kaamerraherr
I'd like to have some passport photos.	**Jeg vil gjerne få tatt noen passfoto.**	yæi vil yǣ^rner faw taht nōōern pahsfōōtoo

Film   *Film*

I'd like a film (for this camera).	**Jeg vil gjerne ha en film (til dette apparatet).**	yæi vil yǣ^rner haa ehn film (til dehter ahpahraater)
black and white	**svart-hvitt**	svah^rt-vit
colour	**farge**	fahrgger
colour negative	**fargenegativ**	fahrggernāygahteev
cartridge	**en kassett**	ehn kahsseht
disc film	**en disc**	ehn disk
roll film	**en rullefilm**	ehn rewlerfilm
slide film	**film for lysbilder**	film for lēwsbilderr
video cassette	**en videokassett**	ehn veedyookahsseht
24/36 exposures	**24/36 bilder**	khēwerfeerer/trehtisehkss bilderr
this size	**dette formatet**	dehter formaater
this ASA/DIN number	**dette ASA-/DIN-nummeret**	dehter aassah-/din-noommerrer
artificial light type	**for kunstig belysning**	for kewnsti berlēwsning
daylight type	**for dagslys**	for dahkslēwss
fast (high-speed)	**hurtig**	hew^rti
fine grain	**finkornet**	feenkōō^rnert

Processing   *Fremkalling*

Does the price include processing?	**Er fremkalling inkludert i prisen?**	ær frehmkahling inklewdāy^rt ee preessern
How much do you charge for processing?	**Hvor mye koster fremkallingen?**	voor mēwer kosterr frehmkahlingern

I'd like ... prints of each negative.	Jeg vil gjerne ha ... kopier av hvert negativ.	yæi vil yæ^rner haa ... koopeeyerr ahv væ^rt nāygahteev
with a mat finish	med matt overflate	meh(d) maht awverflaater
with a glossy finish	med blank overflate	meh(d) blahngk awverflaater
Will you enlarge this, please?	Kan du forstørre dette?	kahn dew foshturrer dehter
When will the photos be ready?	Når blir bildene ferdig?	nor bleer bilderner fæ^rdi

Accessories and repairs   *Tilbehør og reparasjon*

I'd like a/an/ some ...	Jeg vil gjerne ha ...	yæi vil yæ^rner haa
battery	et batteri	eht bahterree
cable release	en snorutløser	ehn snōōrewtlürsserr
camera case	en kameraveske	ehn kaamerrahvehsker
(electronic) flash	en (elektronisk) blitz	ehn (ehlehktrōōnisk) blitss
filter	et filter	eht filterr
for black and white	for svart-hvitt	for svah^rt-vit
for colour	for farge	for fahrgger
lens	et objektiv	eht obyehkteev
telephoto lens	et teleobjektiv	eht tāylerobyehkteev
wide-angle lens	et vidvinkel-objektiv	eht vee(d)vinkerl-obyehkteev
lens cap	en linsebeskytter	ehn linserbershewterr
slide projector	et lysbildeapparat	eht lēwsbilderahpahraat
Can you repair this camera?	Kan du reparere dette apparatet?	kahn dew rehpahrāyrer dehter ahpahraater
The film is jammed.	Filmen sitter fast.	filmern sitter fahst
There's something wrong with the ...	Det er noe i veien med ...	deh ær nōōer ee væiern meh(d)
exposure counter	telleverket	tehlervær̄ker
film winder	fremtrekkeren	frehmtrehkerrern
flash attachment	blitzaggregatet	blitsahgrergaater
lens	objektivet	obyehkteever
light meter	lysmåleren	lēwsmawlerrern
rangefinder	avstandsmåleren	aavstahnsmawlerrern
self-timing release	selvutløseren	sehlewtlürsserrern
shutter	lukkeren	lookkerrern

NUMBERS, see page 147

Tobacconist's *Tobakkshandel*

Virtually all international brands of cigarettes, cigars and tobacco are available at tobacconists, in kiosks and supermarkets. Local cigarettes are quite good, and Norwegian pipe tobacco is noted for its quality.

A packet of cigarettes, please.	En pakke sigaretter, takk.	ehn **pahker** siggah-**rehterr** tahk
How much are they per ...?	Hvor mye koster de pr. ...?	voor **mēwer kosterr** dee pær
packet/carton	pakke/kartong	**pahker**/kah**'tong**
Could I have a carton, please?	Kan jeg få en kartong?	kahn yæi faw ehn kah**'tong**
I'd like a/some ...	Jeg vil gjerne ha ...	yæi vil yǣ**'ner** haa
candy	noen godter	**nōōern goterr**
chewing gum	en pakke tyggegummi	ehn **pahker tewger-gewmi**
chewing tobacco	litt skråtobakk	lit **skrawtoobahk**
chocolate bar	en sjokoladeplate	ehn **shookoolaaderplaater**
cigarette case	et sigarettetui	eht **siggahrehtehtewee**
cigarette holder	et sigarett-munnstykke	eht **siggahreht-mewnstewker**
cigarettes	sigaretter	**siggahrehter**
filter-tipped	med filter	meh(d) **filterr**
without filter	uten filter	**ēwtern filterr**
light/dark tobacco	lys/mørk tobakk	**lēwss**/murrk **toobahk**
mild/strong	milde/sterke	**miller/stærker**
menthol	mentol-	**mehntōōl-**
king-size	king-size	"king-size"
cigars	noen sigarer	**nōōern siggaarerr**
lighter	en lighter	ehn "lighter"
lighter fluid	lighterbensin	"lighter"**behnseen**
lighter gas	lightergass	"lighter"**gahss**
matches	fyrstikker	**fewshtikkerr**
pipe	en pipe	ehn **peeper**
pipe cleaners	piperensere	**peeperrehnserrer**
pipe tobacco	pipetobakk	**peepertoobahk**
postcards	noen postkort	**nōōern postko'rt**
snuff	en eske snus	ehn **ehskoor snēwss**
stamps	noen frimerker	**nōōern freemærkerr**
sweets	noen godter	**nōōern goterr**
tobacco	tobakk	**toobahk**
wick	en veke	ehn **vāyker**

Miscellaneous   *Forskjellig*

Souvenirs   *Suvenirer*

The most attractive Norwegian souvenirs to look for are products of home craftsmen, like handmade knitwear—pullovers (sweaters), cardigans, mittens, scarves and ski caps—painted wooden figurines, trolls, sealskin slippers and "rose-painted" wooden articles, such as small boxes, egg cups, plates and miniature bellows; the rococo floral designs are typically Norwegian. Other popular souvenirs include miniature Viking ships of wood, pewter, enamel or silver, dolls in native costume, reindeer-skin rugs, woven runners, table cloths and wall hangings.

I'd like a souvenir from ...	**Jeg vil gjerne ha en suvenir fra ...**	yæi vil yǣᵉner haa ehn sewverneer fraa
Something typically Norwegian, please.	**Noe typisk norsk.**	nō̄er tēwpisk noshk
cardigan (with Norwegian design)	**en lusekofte**	ehn lēwsserkofter
doll in native costume	**en dukke med bunad**	ehn dewker meh(d) bēwnahd
drinking horn	**et drikkehorn**	eht drikkerhōōᵉn
hunting knife	**en jaktkniv**	ehn yahktkneev
reindeer skin	**et reinsdyrskinn**	eht ræinsdēwrshin
sealskin slippers	**et par selskinnstøfler**	eht pahr sǣylshinsturflerr
troll	**et troll**	eht trol
Viking ship	**et vikingskip**	eht vēekingsheep
wooden figurine	**en trefigur**	ehn trǣyfiggēwr
woven runner	**en rye**	ehn rēwer
A "rose-painted" ...	**En rosemalt ...**	ehn rōōssermaalt
bowl	**bolle**	boller
candlestick	**lysestake**	lewsserstaaker
plate	**asjett**	ahsheht

Records—Cassettes   *Plater – Kassetter*

I'd like a ...	**Jeg vil gjerne ha ...**	yæi vil yǣᵉner haa
cassette	**en kassett**	ehn kahsseht
video cassette	**en videokassett**	ehn veedyookahsseht
compact disc	**en CD-plate**	ehn sǣy-dǣy-plaater

L.P. (33 rpm)	**LP (33 omdreininger)**	ehl-pāȳ (trehtitrāȳ omdræiningerr)
E.P. (45 rpm)	**EP (45 omdreininger)**	āȳ-pāȳ (fur\`tifehm omdræiningerr)
single	**singel**	singerl

Do you have any records by ...?	**Har du noen plater av ...?**	haar dew nōōern plaaterr ahv
Can I listen to this record?	**Kan jeg få høre på denne platen?**	kahn yæi faw hūrrer paw dehner plaatern
chamber music	**kammermusikk**	kahmerrmewssik
classical music	**klassisk musikk**	klahssisk mewssik
folk music	**folkemusikk**	folkermewssik
folk songs	**folkesanger**	folkersahngerr
instrumental music	**instrumentalmusikk**	instrewmehntaalmewssik
jazz	**jazz**	yahss
light music	**underholdnings-musikk**	ewnerrholdnings-mewssik
orchestral music	**orkestermusikk**	orkehsterrmewssik
pop music	**pop**	pop

Toys and games   *Leker og spill*

I'd like a toy/game.	**Jeg vil gjerne ha en leke/et spill.**	yæi vil yæ\`rner haa ehn lāȳker/eht spil
(beach) ball	**en (bade)ball**	ehn (baader)bahl
board/card game	**et brettspill/kortspill**	eht brehtspil/ko\`tspil
bucket and spade (pail and shovel)	**spann og spade**	spahn o(g) spaader
building blocks (bricks)	**noen byggeklosser**	nōōern bewgerklosserr
building set	**et byggesett**	eht bewgersseht
chess set	**et sjakkspill**	eht shahkspil
doll	**en dukke**	ehn dewker
electronic game	**et elektronisk spill**	eht ehlehktrōōnisk spil
flippers	**et par svømme-føtter**	eht pahr svurmer-furterr
roller skates	**et par rulleskøyter**	eht pahr rewlershoyter
snorkel	**en snorkel**	ehn snorkerl
stuffed animal	**et stoffdyr**	eht stofdēwr
toy car	**en lekebil**	ehn lāȳkerbeel
battery-powered	**batteridrevet**	bahterreedrāȳvert
remote-controlled	**ledningstyrt**	lāȳdningstew\`t

Your money: banks—currency

At most banks there's sure to be someone who speaks English. You'll find small currency exchange offices in most tourist centres, especially during the summer season. Remember to take your passport along with you, as you may need it for identification.

Traveller's cheques and credit cards are widely accepted in tourist-oriented shops, hotels, restaurants, etc. However, if you're exploring way off the beaten track, you'll probably come across stores where they are not taken. The same goes for garages and filling stations—generally, only major agency garages will accept payment in traveller's cheques or by credit card.

Opening hours. Banks are generally open from 8.15 a.m. to 3.30 p.m., Monday to Wednesday and Fridays, until 5 or 6 p.m. on Thursdays. Between June 1 and August 31, however, they close at 3 p.m. (5 or 5.30 p.m. on Thursdays). At Oslo airport and central railway station, the currency exchange offices have longer hours.

Monetary unit. The Norwegian krone (meaning "crown", pronounced **krōō**ner, plural kroner—**krōō**nerr, abbreviated kr/kr.) is divided into 100 øre (**ūr**rer).

Coins: 10 and 50 øre, k. 1, 5 and 10.
Banknotes: kr 50, 100, 500 and 1,000.

Where's the nearest bank?	**Hvor er nærmeste bank?**	voor ær **næ**rmehster bahngk
Where's the nearest currency exchange office?	**Hvor er nærmeste vekslingskontor?**	voor ær **næ**rmehster **vehk**shlingskoontōōr
When is the bank open?	**Når er banken åpen?**	nor ær **bahng**kern **aw**pern
When is the currency exchange office open?	**Når er vekslings-kontoret åpent?**	nor ær **vehk**shlings-koontōōrer **aw**pernt

At the bank   *I banken*

I'd like to change some dollars/pounds.	Jeg vil gjerne veksle noen dollar/pund.	yæi vil yǣᵣner vehkshler nōōern dollahr/pewn
I'd like to cash a traveller's cheque.	Jeg vil gjerne løse inn en reisesjekk.	yæi vil yǣᵣner lūᵣsser in ehn ræissershehk
What's the exchange rate?	Hva er vekslings-kursen?	vaa ær vehkshlings-kēwshern
How much commission do you charge?	Hvor mye tar dere i kommisjon?	voor mēwer taar dāyrer ee koomishōōn
Can you cash this cheque?	Kan du løse inn denne sjekken?	kahn dew lūᵣsser in dehner shehkern
Can you telex my bank in London?	Kan du sende en telex til min bank i London?	kahn dew sehner ehn tāylekss til meen bahngk ee london
I have a/an/some ...	Jeg har ...	yæi haar
credit card	kredittkort	krehditkoᵣt
Eurocheques	eurosjekker	yēwrooshehkerr
letter of credit	et kredittbrev	eht krehditbrāyv
I'm expecting some money from New York. Has it arrived?	Jeg venter penger fra New York. Har de kommet?	yæi vehnterr pehngerr fraa new york. haar dee kommert
Please give me ... in notes (bills) and some small change.	Gi meg ... i sedler og litt småpenger.	yee mæi ... ee sehdlerr o(g) litt smawpehngerr
Give me ... in large notes and the rest in small notes.	Gi meg ... i store sedler og resten i små sedler.	yee mæi ... ee stōōrer sehdlerr o(g) rehstern ee smaw sehdlerr

Deposit—Withdrawal   *Innskudd – Uttak*

I'd like to ...	Jeg vil gjerne ...	yæi vil yǣᵣner
open an account	åpne en konto	awpner ehn kontoo
withdraw ... kroner	ta ut ... kroner	taa ēwt ... krōōnerr
Where should I sign?	Hvor skal jeg undertegne?	voor skahl yæi ewnerrtæiner
I'd like to pay this into my account.	Jeg vil gjerne sette dette inn på kontoen min.	yæi vil yǣᵣner sehter dehter in paw kontooern meen

NUMBERS, see page 147

Business terms *Forretningsuttrykk*

My name is ...	**Mitt navn er ...**	mit nahvn ær
Here's my card.	**Her er mitt kort.**	hǣr ær mit ko'rt
I have an appointment with ...	**Jeg har avtalt et møte med ...**	yǽi haar aavtahlt eht mūrter meh(d)
Can you give me an estimate of the cost?	**Kan du gi meg et overslag over kostnadene?**	kahn dew yee mæi eht awvershlaag awverr kostnahderner
What's the rate of inflation?	**Hvor høy er inflasjonsraten?**	voor hoy ær inflahshōōnsraatern
Can you provide me with a/an ...	**Kan du skaffe meg en ...**	kahn dew skahfer mæi ehn
interpreter	**tolk**	tolk
secretary	**sekretær**	sehkrertǣr
translation	**oversettelse**	awvershehterlser
translator	**oversetter**	awvershehterr
Where can I make photocopies?	**Hvor kan jeg ta fotokopier?**	voor kahn yǽi taa fōōtookoopeeyerr

amount	**et beløp**	eht berlūrp
balance	**en balanse**	ehn bahlahngser
capital	**en kapital**	ehn kahpitaal
contract	**en kontrakt**	ehn koontrahkt
credit	**en kreditt**	ehn krehdit
discount	**en rabatt**	ehn rahbaht
expenses	**utgifter**	ēwtyifterr
interest	**en rente**	ehn rehnter
investment	**en investering**	ehn inverstāyring
invoice	**en faktura**	ehn fahktēwrah
loan	**et lån**	eht lawn
loss	**et tap**	eht taap
mortgage	**et hypotek**	eht hewpootāyk
payment	**en betaling**	ehn bertaaling
percentage	**en prosentsats**	ehn proosehntsahtss
profit	**et utbytte**	eht ēwtbewter
purchase	**et kjøp**	eht khūrp
sale	**et salg**	eht sahlg
share	**en aksje**	ehn ahksher
tax	**en skatt**	ehn skaht
transfer	**en overføring**	ehn awverfūrring
value	**en verdi**	ehn væ'dee

At the post office

The post office only handles mail; for fax, telephone and telegram or telex services you have to go to a *telesenter* office.

Business hours are generally from 8 a.m. to 5 or 5.30 p.m., Monday to Friday (4 or 4.30 p.m. in summer), and from 9 a.m. to 1 p.m. on Saturdays.

Letter (mail) boxes are painted red.

Where's the nearest post office?	**Hvor er nærmeste postkontor?**	voor ær nærmehster postkoontōōr
What time does the post office open/close?	**Når åpner/stenger postkontoret**	nor awpnerr/stehngerr postkoontōōrer
A stamp for this letter/postcard, please.	**Et frimerke til dette brevet/kortet, takk.**	eht freemærker til dehter brāȳver/ko^rter tahk
A ... -kroner stamp, please.	**Et ... -kroners frimerke, takk.**	eht ... -krōōnersh freemærker
What's the postage for a letter to England?	**Hva er portoen for et brev til England?**	vah ær poo^rtooern for eht brāȳv til ehnglahn
What's the postage for a postcard to the U.S.?	**Hva er portoen for et postkort til USA?**	vah ær poo^rtooern for eht postko^rt til ēw-ehss-aa
Where's the letter box (mailbox)?	**Hvor er postkassen?**	voor ær postkahssern
I want to send this parcel.	**Jeg vil gjerne sende denne pakken.**	yæi vil yǣ^rner sehner dehner pahkern
I'd like to register this parcel.	**Jeg vil gjerne rekommandere denne pakken.**	yæi vil yǣ^rner rehkoomahndāȳrer dehner pahkern
I'd like to send this by ...	**Jeg vil gjerne sende dette ...**	yæi vil yǣ^rner sehner dehter
airmail	**med fly**	meh(d) flēw
express mail	**ekspress**	ehksprehss
registered mail	**rekommandert**	rehkoomahndāȳ^rt

I'd like some ..., please.	Jeg vil gjerne ha noen ...	yæi vil yæᶜner haa nōōern
aerogrammes	aerogrammer	ehroograhmerr
airmail labels	luftpostetiketter	lewftpostehtikehterr
At which counter can I cash an international money order?	I hvilken luke kan jeg løse inn en internasjonal postanvisning?	ee vilkern lēwker kahn yæi lūᶜsser in ehn interᶜnahshoonaal postahnveesning
Where's the poste restante (general delivery)?	Hvor er poste-restanteluken?	voor ær post-rehstahngtlēwkern
Is there any post (mail) for me?	Har det kommet noe post til meg?	haar deh kommert nōōer post til mæi
My name is ...	Mitt navn er ...	mit nahvn ær

FRIMERKER	STAMPS
PAKKER	PARCELS
POSTANVISNINGER	MONEY ORDERS

Telegrams—Telex—Fax *Telegrammer – Telex – Telefax*

Where's the nearest telegraph office?	Hvor er nærmeste telesenter?	voor ær nærmehster tāylerssehnterr
I'd like to send a ...	Jeg vil gjerne sende ...	yæi vil yǣᶜner sehner
fax	en telefax	ehn tāylerfahkss
telegram	et telegram	eht tehlergrahm
telex	en telex	ehn tāylehkss
May I have a form, please?	Kan jeg få en blankett?	kahn yæi faw ehn blahngkeht
How much is it per word?	Hva koster det pr. ord?	vaa kosterr deh pær ōōr
How long will a telegram to Boston take?	Hvor lang tid tar et telegram til Boston?	voor lahng teed taar eht tehlergrahm til boston
How much will this telex cost?	Hvor mye vil denne telexen komme på?	voor mēw̄er vil dehner tāylehksern kommer paw

Telephone *Telefon*

International and long-distance calls can be made from phone booths, but if you need help in making a call, go to a telegraph office. Dialling instructions in English are posted inside the booth and can be found at the front of the telephone directory.

For direct calls abroad, dial 095, then the country code (Britain, 44, U.S.A. and Canada, 1), the national dialling (area) code (minus the initial "0") and the local telephone number.

Where's the telephone?	**Hvor er telefonen?**	voor ær tehler**foo**nern
Where's the nearest telephone booth?	**Hvor er nærmeste telefonkiosk?**	voor ær **nærmeh**ster tehler**foo**nkhyosk
May I use your phone?	**Kan jeg få låne telefonen?**	kahn yæi faw **law**ner tehler**foo**nern
Do you have a telephone directory for Bergen?	**Har du en telefonkatalog for Bergen?**	haar dew ehn tehler**foon**kahtahlawg for **bær**gern
I'd like to call someone in England.	**Jeg vil gjerne ringe til England.**	yæi vil y**ǣr**ner ringer til **ehng**lahn
What's the dialling (area) code for ...?	**Hva er retningsnummeret til ...?**	vah ær **reht**ningsnoommerer til
How do I get the international operator?	**På hvilket nummer kan jeg få hjelp med fjernvalg til utlandet?**	paw vilkert **noom**merr kahn yæi faw yehlp meh(d) fy**ǣr**nvahlg til **ewt**lahner

Operator *Telefonist*

Could you give me the number of ...?	**Kan du gi meg nummeret til ...?**	kahn dew yee mæi **noom**merrer til
Can you help me get this number?	**Kan du hjelpe meg å komme til dette nummeret?**	kahn dew **yehl**per mæi aw kommer til **deh**ter **noom**merrer
I'd like to place a personal (person-to-person) call.	**Jeg vil gjerne bestille en personlig samtale.**	yæi vil y**ǣr**ner ber**still**er ehn pæs**hoo**nli **sahm**taaler

NUMBERS, see page 147

| I'd like to reverse the charges (call collect). | **Jeg vil gjerne bestille en note-ringsoverføring.** | yæi vil yǣ'ner berstiller ehn nootāy-ringsawverrfürring |

Telephone alphabet *Bokstavering*

A	**Anna**	ahnah	P	**Petter**	pehterr
B	**Bernhard**	bǣ'nah't	Q	**Quintus**	kvintewss
C	**Cæsar**	sāyssahr	R	**Rikard**	rikah't
D	**David**	daaveed	S	**Sigrid**	sigree
E	**Edith**	āydit	T	**Teodor**	tāyoodōor
F	**Fredrik**	frehdrik	U	**Ulrik**	ewlrik
G	**Gustav**	gewstahv	V	**enkelt-V**	ehngkerlt-vāy
H	**Harald**	hahrahl	W	**dobbelt-V**	dobberlt-vāy
I	**Ivar**	eevahr	X	**Xerxes**	ksærksehss
J	**Johan**	yoohahn	Y	**Yngling**	ewngling
K	**Karin**	kaareen	Z	**Zakarias**	sahkahreeahss
L	**Ludvig**	lewdvik	Æ	**Ærlig**	ǣ'li
M	**Martin**	mah'tin	Ø	**Ørn**	ür'n
N	**Nils**	nilss	Å	**Åse**	awsser
O	**Olivia**	ooleeveeah			

Speaking *Samtale*

Hello. This is ...	**Hallo. Dette er ...**	hahlōō. dehter ær
I'd like to speak to ...	**Kan jeg få snakke med ...?**	kahn yæi faw snahker meh(d)
Is ... there?	**Er ... til stede?**	ær ... til stāyder
Extension ...	**Linje ...**	linyer
Who's speaking?	**Hvem er det jeg snakker med?**	vehm ær deh yæi snahkerr meh(d)
Pardon?	**Unnskyld?**	ewnshewl
Can you speak louder/more slowly, please.	**Kan du snakke litt høyere/litt lang-sommere?**	kahn dew snahker lit hoyerrer/lit lahng-sommerrer

Bad luck *Uheldig*

| Operator, you gave me the wrong number. | **Jeg tror du ga meg feil nummer.** | yæi trōor dew gaa mæi fæil noommerr |
| We were cut off. | **Vi ble avbrutt.** | vee bleh aavbrewt |

Not there   *Ikke til stede*

When will he/she be back?	**Når kommer han/ hun tilbake?**	nor **kommerr** hahn/ hewn tilbaaker
Will you tell him I called?	**Kan du si til ham at jeg har ringt?**	kahn dew see til hahm aht yæi haar ringt
My name is ...	**Mitt navn er ...**	mit nahvn ær
Would you ask her to phone me?	**Kan du be henne om å ringe meg?**	kahn dew bay hehner om aw ringer mæi
My number is ...	**Mitt nummer er ...**	mit **noommerr** ær
Would you take a message?	**Kan du ta imot en beskjed?**	kahn dew taa eemoot ehn bershay
I'll call back later.	**Jeg ringer senere.**	yæi ringerr saynerrer

Charges   *Gebyr*

How much did the call cost?	**Hvor mye kostet samtalen?**	voor mewer kostert sahmtaalern
I'd like to pay for the call.	**Jeg vil gjerne betale samtalen.**	yæi vil yaerner bertaaler sahmtaalern

---

Det er telefon til deg.	There's a telephone call for you.
Hvilket nummer ringer du?	What number are you calling?
Linjen er opptatt.	The line's engaged.
Det svarer ikke.	There's no answer.
Du har ringt feil.	You've got the wrong number.
Telefonen er i uorden.	The phone is out of order.
Et øyeblikk.	Hold on, please/Just a moment.
Han/Hun er ute for øyeblikket.	He's/She's out at the moment.
Han/Hun er tilbake klokken ...	He'll/She'll be back at ...
Kan du prøve igjen litt senere?	Would you try again later?

Doctor

British subjects are covered by a British-Norwegian health insurance agreement. For nationals of other countries it is advisable to take out health insurance covering the cost of illness or accident while on holiday.

General *Allment*

Can you get me a doctor?	**Kan du skaffe meg en lege?**	kahn dew **skah**fer mæi ehn **lay**ger
Is there a doctor here?	**Fins det en lege her?**	finss deh ehn **lay**ger hæær
I need a doctor, quickly.	**Jeg trenger lege øyeblikkelig.**	yæi **treh**ngerr **lay**ger oyerblikkerli
Where can I find a doctor who speaks English?	**Hvor kan jeg få tak i en lege som snakker engelsk?**	voor kahn yæi faw taak ee ehn **lay**ger som **snah**kerr **eh**ngerlsk
Where's the surgery (doctor's office)?	**Hvor er lege-kontoret?**	voor ær **lay**ger-koon**too**rer
What are the surgery (office) hours?	**Når har legen kontortid?**	nor haar **lay**gern koon**too**rteed
Could the doctor come to see me here?	**Kan legen komme hit å undersøke meg?**	kahn **lay**gern **kom**mer heet aw **ew**nershurker mæi
What time can the doctor come?	**Når kan legen komme?**	nor kahn **lay**gern **kom**mer
Can you recommend a/an ...?	**Kan du anbefale en ...?**	kahn dew **ahn**berfaaler ehn
general practitioner	**allmennpraktiker**	**ahl**mehnprahktikkerr
children's doctor	**barnelege**	**baa**^rnerlayger
eye specialist	**øyenlege**	**oy**ernlayger
gynaecologist	**gynekolog**	gewnerkoo**lawg**
Can I have an appointment ...?	**Kan jeg få time ...?**	kahn yæi faw **tee**merr
immediately	**med én gang**	meh(d) **ayn** gahng
tomorrow	**i morgen**	ee **maw**er^rn
as soon as possible	**så snart som mulig**	saw snaa^rt som **mew**li

CHEMIST'S (DRUGSTORE), see page 108

Parts of the body *Kroppsdeler*

appendix	blindtarmen	blintahrmern
arm	armen	ahrmern
artery	pulsåren	pewlsawrern
back	ryggen	rewgern
bladder	urinblæren	ewreenblǣrern
bone	benet (i kroppen)	bāyner (ee kroppern)
bowel	tarmen	tahrmern
breast	brystet	brewster
chest	brystkassen	brewstkahssern
ear	øret	ūrrer
face	ansiktet	ahnsikter
finger	fingeren	fingerrern
foot	foten	fōōtern
genitals	kjønnsorganene	khurnsorgaanerner
gland	kjertelen	khæ^rterlern
hand	hånden	honern
head	hodet	hōōder
heart	hjertet	yæ^rter
jaw	kjeven	khāyvern
joint	leddet	lehder
kidney	nyren	nēwrern
knee	kneet	knāyer
leg	benet	bāyner
lip	leppen	lehpern
liver	leveren	lehverrern
lung	lungen	loongern
mouth	munnen	mewnern
muscle	muskelen	mewskerlern
neck	nakken	nahkern
nerve	nerven	nærvern
nervous system	nervesystemet	nærversewstāymer
nose	nesen	nāyssern
rib	ribbenet	ribbāyner
shoulder	skulderen	skewlderrern
skin	huden	hewdern
spine	ryggraden	rewgraadern
stomach	magen	maagern
tendon	senen	sāynern
thigh	låret	lawrer
throat	halsen	hahlsern
thumb	tommelen	tommerlern
toe	tåen	tawern
tongue	tungen	toongern
tonsils	mandlene	mahndlerner
vein	venen/åren	vāynern/awrern

Accident—Injury   *Ulykke – Skade*

There's been an accident.	**Det har skjedd en ulykke.**	deh haar shehd ehn $\overline{\text{ew}}$lewker
My child has had a fall.	**Barnet mitt har falt og slått seg.**	baa^{r}ner mit haar fahlt o(g) shlot sæi
He/She has hurt his/her head.	**Han/Hun har slått seg i hodet.**	hahn/hewn haar shlot sæi ee h$\overline{\text{oo}}$der
He's/She's unconscious.	**Han/Hun er bevisstløs.**	hahn/hewn ær bervistlürss
He's/She's bleeding (heavily).	**Han/Hun blør (kraftig).**	hahn/hewn blürr (krahfti)
He's/She's (seriously) injured.	**Han/Hun er (alvorlig) skadet.**	hahn/hewn ær (ahlvaw^{r}li) skaadert
His/Her ankle is swollen.	**Han/Hun har en hoven ankel.**	hahn/huhn haar ehn hawvern ahngkerl
I've broken my arm.	**Jeg har brukket armen.**	yæi haar brookkert ahrmern
I've been stung.	**Jeg er blitt bitt.**	yæi ær blit bit
I've got something in my eye.	**Jeg har fått noe i øyet.**	yæi haar fawt n$\overline{\text{oo}}$er ee oyer
I've been bitten by a dog.	**Jeg er blitt bitt av en hund.**	yæi ær blit bit ahv ehn hewn
I've got a/an ...	**Jeg har fått ...**	yæi haar fot
blister	**en blemme**	ehn blehmer
boil	**en byll**	ehn bewl
bruise	**et blått merke**	eht blot mærker
bump	**en kul**	ehn k$\overline{\text{ew}}$l
burn	**et brannsår**	eht brahnsawr
cut	**et kutt**	eht kewt
graze	**et skrubbsår**	eht skrewbsawr
rash	**et utslett**	eht $\overline{\text{ew}}$tshleht
sting	**et stikk**	eht stik
swelling	**en hevelse**	ehn hāyverlser
wound	**et sår**	eht sawr
Could you have a look at it?	**Kan du undersøke det?**	kahn dew ewnershürker deh
I can't move my ...	**Jeg kan ikke bevege ...**	yæi kahn ikker bervāyger
It hurts.	**Det gjør vondt.**	deh yürr voont

Hvor gjør det vondt?	Where does it hurt?
Hva slags smerte er det?	What kind of pain is it?
dump/skarp pulserende/konstant kommer og går	dull/sharp throbbing/constant on and off
Det er ...	It's ...
brukket/vrikket/ute av ledd	broken/sprained/dislocated
Du har et avslitt leddbånd.	You have a torn ligament.
Det bør røntgenfotograferes.	I'd like you to have an X-ray.
Det må gipses.	We'll have to put it in plaster.
Det er infisert.	It's infected.
Er du vaksinert mot stivkrampe?	Have you been vaccinated against tetanus?
Jeg skal gi deg noe smertestillende.	I'll give you a painkiller.
Har du noen allergier?	Do you have any allergies?

Illness *Sykdom*

I'm not feeling well.	**Jeg føler meg ikke bra.**	yæi fūrlerr mæi ikker braa
I'm ill.	**Jeg er syk.**	yæi ær sēwk
I feel ...	**Jeg føler meg ...**	yæi fūrler mæi
dizzy/nauseous/ weak	**svimmel/kvalm/ svak**	svimmerl/kvahlm/ svaak
I feel shivery.	**Jeg har kulde-gysninger.**	yæi haar kewler-yēwsningerr
I have a temperature (fever).	**Jeg har feber.**	yæi haar fāyberr
I've been vomiting.	**Jeg har kastet opp.**	yæi haar kahstert op
I'm constipated.	**Jeg har forstoppelse.**	yæi haar foshtopperlser
I've got diarrhoea.	**Jeg har diarré.**	yæi haar deeahrāy
My ... hurt(s).	**Jeg har vondt i ...**	yæi haar voont ee

I've got (a/an) ...	**Jeg har ...**	yæi haar
asthma	**astma**	ahstmah
backache	**ryggsmerter**	rewgsmæ^{r}terr
cough	**hoste**	hooster
cramps	**krampe**	krahmper
earache	**øreverk**	ūrrerværk
hay fever	**høysnue**	hoysnēwer
headache	**hodepine**	hōōderpeener
indigestion	**fordøyelsesbesvær**	fo^{r}doyelsersbersvǣr
nosebleed	**neseblødning**	nāysserblūrdning
palpitations	**hjerteklapp**	yæ^{r}terklahp
rheumatism	**reumatisme**	rehvmahtismer
sore throat	**sår hals**	sawr hahlss
stiff neck	**stiv nakke**	steev nahker
stomach ache	**magesmerter**	maagersmæ^{r}terr
sunburn	**solforbrenning**	sōōlforbrehning

I've got a cold.	**Jeg er forkjølet.**	yæi ær fo^{r}khūrlert
I have difficulties breathing.	**Jeg har vanskelig-heter med å puste.**	yæi haar vahnskerli-hehter meh(d) aw pewster
I have chest pains.	**Jeg har vondt i brystet.**	yæi haar voont ee brewster
I had a heart attack ... years ago.	**Jeg hadde et hjerteslag for ... år siden.**	yæi hahder eht yæ^{r}tershlaag for ... awr seedern
My blood pressure is too high/too low.	**Jeg har for høyt/ for lavt blodtrykk.**	yæi haar for hoyt/ for laavt blōōtrewk
I'm allergic to ...	**Jeg er allergisk mot ...**	yæi ær ahlærgisk mōōt
I'm diabetic.	**Jeg er diabetiker.**	yæi ær deeahbāytikkerr

At the gynaecologist's *Hos gynekologen*

I have period (menstrual) pains.	**Jeg har menstrua-sjonssmerter.**	yæi haar mehnstrewah-shōōnssmæ^{r}terr
I have a vaginal infection.	**Jeg har underlivs-betennelse.**	yæi haar ewnerrleevs-bertehnerlser
I'm on the pill.	**Jeg tar p-piller.**	yæi taar pāy-pillerr
I haven't had a period for 2 months.	**Jeg har ikke hatt menstruasjon på 2 måneder.**	yæi haar ikkerr haht mehnstrewahshōōn paw 2 mawnerderr
I'm pregnant.	**Jeg er gravid.**	yæi ær grahveed

Hvor lenge har du følt deg slik?	How long have you been feeling like this?
Har du hatt dette før?	Have you had this before?
Jeg skal ta temperaturen/ måle blodtrykket.	I'll take your temperature/ blood pressure.
Vær snill å rulle opp ermet.	Roll up your sleeve, please.
Vær snill å ta av deg ...	Take off your ..., please.
Vær snill å kle av deg (på overkroppen).	Please undress (down to the waist).
Sett/Legg deg ned der borte.	Please sit/lie down over there.
Gap opp.	Open your mouth.
Pust dypt/Host.	Breathe deeply/Cough.
Hvor gjør det vondt?	Where does it hurt?
Du har ...	You've got (a/an) ...

en allergi	allergy
en betennelse i ...	inflammation of ...
blindtarmbetennelse	appendicitis
blærekatarr	cystitis
gulsott	jaundice
influensa	flu
en kjønnssykdom	venereal disease
lungebetennelse	pneumonia
magekatarr	gastritis
en matforgiftning	food poisoning
meslinger	measles

Det er (ikke) smittsomt.	It's (not) contagious.
Jeg skal gi deg en sprøyte.	I'll give you an injection.
Jeg vil ha en blodprøve/ avføringsprøve/urinprøve.	I want a specimen of your blood/stools/urine.
Du bør holde sengen i ... dager.	You must stay in bed for ... days.
Du bør oppsøke en spesialist.	I want you to see a specialist.
Du bør få foretatt en allmenn undersøkelse på sykehuset.	I want you to go to the hospital for a general check-up.

Prescription—Treatment *Resept – Behandling*

This is my usual medicine.	**Dette er min vanlige medisin.**	dehter ær meen vaanleeyer mehdi**seen**
Can you give me a prescription for this?	**Kan du gi meg en resept på dette?**	kahn dew yee mæi ehn rehse**hpt** paw **deh**ter
Can you prescribe a/an/some ...?	**Kan du skrive ut ...?**	kahn dew skreever ēwt
antidepressant	**et middel mot depresjoner**	eht midderl mōōt dehprershōōnerr
sleeping pills	**noen sovetabletter**	nōōern sawvertahblehterr
tranquillizer	**et beroligende middel**	eht berrōōleeyerner midderl
I'm allergic to certain antibiotics/penicillin.	**Jeg er allergisk mot visse antibiotika/penicillin.**	yæi ær ahlærgisk mōōt visser ahntibeeōōtikkah/pehnissileen
I don't want anything too strong.	**Jeg vil ikke ha noe som er for sterkt.**	yæi vil ikker haa nōōer som ær for stærkt
How many times a day should I take it?	**Hvor mange ganger om dagen skal jeg ta det?**	voor **mahng**er **gahng**err om **daag**ern skahl yæi taa deh
Must I swallow the tablets whole?	**Må jeg svelge tablettene hele?**	maw yæi svehlger tahblehterner hāyler

---

Hva slags behandling får du?	What treatment are you having?
Hvilken medisin tar du?	What medicine are you taking?
Tar du noen andre medisiner?	Are you taking any other medicines?
Intravenøst eller oralt?	By injection or orally?
Ta 2 teskjeer/1 tablett ...	Take 2 teaspoons/1 tablet ...
hver ... time	every ... hour(s)
... ganger om dagen	... times a day
før/etter hvert måltid	before/after every meal
om morgenen/om kvelden	in the morning/at night
i ... dager	for ... days
ved smerter	if there is any pain

CHEMIST'S (DRUGSTORE), see page 108

DOCTOR

Fee *Honorar*

How much do I owe you?	**Hvor mye skylder jeg?**	voor mēwer shewlerr yæi
May I have a receipt for my health insurance?	**Kan jeg få en kvittering for syke- forsikringen?**	kahn yæi faw ehn kvittāyring for sēwker- foshikringern
Can I have a medical certificate?	**Kan jeg få en legeattest?**	kahn yæi faw ehn lāygerahtehst
Would you fill in this health insurance form, please?	**Kan du fylle ut dette sykeforsik- ringsskjemaet?**	kahn dew fewler ēwt dehter sēwkerfoshik- ringsshāymaher

Hospital *Sykehus*

Please notify my family.	**Vær snill å under- rette familien min.**	vær snil aw ewnerr- rehter fahmeelyern meen
What are the visiting hours?	**Når er det besøks- tid?**	nor ær deh bersūrks- teed
How long do I have to stay in bed?	**Hvor lenge må jeg ligge til sengs?**	voor lehnger maw yæi ligger til sehngss
When can I get up?	**Når kan jeg stå opp?**	nor kahn yæi staw op
When will the doctor come?	**Når kommer legen?**	nor kommerr lāygern
I am in pain.	**Jeg har smerter.**	yæi haar smæʳterr
I can't eat.	**Jeg kan ikke spise.**	yæi kahn ikker speesser
I can't sleep.	**Jeg får ikke sove.**	yæi fawr ikker sawver
Where is the bell?	**Hvor er ringe- klokken?**	voor ær ringerklokkern

nurse	**en sykepleier**	ehn sēwkerplæierr
patient	**en pasient**	ehn pahsseeyehnt
anaesthetic	**en narkose**	ehn nahrkōōsser
blood transfusion	**en blodoverføring**	ehn bloo(d)awverrfürring
injection	**en sprøyte**	ehn sproyter
operation	**en operasjon**	ehn operrahshōōn
bed	**en seng**	ehn sehng
bedpan	**et stikkbekken**	eht stikbehkern
thermometer	**et termometer**	eht tærmoomāyterr

Lege

Dentist   *Tannlege*

Can you recommend a good dentist?	**Kan du anbefale en god tannlege?**	kahn dew **ahn**berfaaler ehn goo(d) **tahn**lāyger
Can I make an (urgent) appointment to see Dr. ...?	**Kan jeg få time (så snart som mulig) hos dr. ...**	kahn yæi faw **tee**mer (saw snaaᵗ som mēwli) hooss **dok**toor
Couldn't you make it earlier?	**Er det ikke mulig å få time tidligere?**	ær deh **ik**ker mēwli aw faw **tee**mer **tee**leeyerrer
I have a broken tooth.	**Jeg har brukket en tann.**	yæi haar **brook**kert ehn tahn
I have a loose tooth.	**Jeg har en løs tann.**	yæi har ehn lūrss tahn
I have toothache.	**Jeg har tannpine.**	yæi haar **tahn**peener
Is it an abscess?	**Er det en byll?**	ær deh ehn bewl
This tooth hurts.	**Denne tannen verker.**	**dehn**er tahnern **vær**kerr
at the top	**her oppe**	hǣr **op**per
at the bottom	**her nede**	hǣr **nāy**der
at the front	**her foran**	hǣr **for**ahn
at the back	**her bak**	hǣr baak
Can you fix it temporarily?	**Kan du foreta en provisorisk behandling?**	kahn dew **faw**rertah ehn **proo**veess**sōo**risk ber**hahnd**ling
I don't want it taken out.	**Jeg vil ikke ha den trukket.**	yæi vil **ik**ker haa dehn **trook**kert
Could you give me an anaesthetic?	**Kan jeg få bedøvelse?**	kahn yæi faw ber**dūr**verlser
I've lost a filling.	**Jeg har mistet en plombe.**	yæi haar **mis**tert ehn **ploom**ber
My gums are bleeding/sore.	**Tannkjøttet blør/ er sårt.**	**tahnk**hurter blūrr/ ær sawᵗ
I've broken my dentures.	**Jeg har brukket gebisset.**	yæi haar **brook**kert ger**bis**ser
Can you repair my dentures?	**Kan du reparere gebisset?**	kahn dew reh**pah**rāyrer ger**bis**ser
When will they be ready?	**Når blir det ferdig?**	nor bleer deh **fæᵣ**di

Reference section

Where do you come from? *Hvor kommer du fra?*

I'm from ...	Jeg er fra ...	yæi ær fraa
Africa	**Afrika**	aafreekah
Asia	**Asia**	aasseeah
Australia	**Australia**	oustraaleeah
Europe	**Europa**	ourōōpah
North America	**Nord-Amerika**	nōōr-ahmāyreekah
South America	**Sør-Amerika**	sūrr-ahmāyreekah
Austria	**Østerrike**	ursterreeker
Belgium	**Belgia**	behlgeeah
Canada	**Kanada**	kahnahdah
China	**Kina**	kheenah
Croatia	**Kroatia**	krōōahteeah
Denmark	**Danmark**	dahnmahrk
England	**England**	ehnglahn
Finland	**Finland**	finlahn
France	**Frankrike**	frahngkreeker
Germany	**Tyskland**	tewsklahn
Great Britain	**Storbritannia**	stoorbrittahneeah
Greece	**Hellas**	hehlahss
Hungary	**Ungarn**	oonggah'n
Iceland	**Island**	eeslahn
India	**India**	indeeah
Ireland	**Irland**	eerlahn
Israel	**Israel**	eesrahehl
Italy	**Italia**	eetaaleeah
Japan	**Japan**	yaapahn
Luxembourg	**Luxembourg**	lewksermbewrg
Netherlands	**Nederland**	nāyderlahn
New Zealand	**Ny-Zealand**	nēw-sāylahn
Norway	**Norge**	norgger
Poland	**Polen**	pōōlern
Portugal	**Portugal**	poo'tewgahl
Russia	**Russland**	rēwslahn
Scotland	**Skottland**	skotlahn
South Africa	**Sør-Afrika**	sūrr-aafreekah
Spain	**Spania**	spaaneeah
Sweden	**Sverige**	sværyer
Switzerland	**Sveits**	svæitss
Turkey	**Tyrkia**	tewrkeeah
United States	**USA**	ēw-ehss-aa
Wales	**Wales**	væilss

Numbers *Tall*

0	**null**	new
1	**en**	$\overline{a}$yn
2	**to**	t$\overline{oo}$
3	**tre**	tr$\overline{a}$
4	**fire**	fe
5	**fem**	feh
6	**seks**	se
7	**sju**	sh
8	**åtte**	o
9	**ni**	n
10	**ti**	t$\overline{oo}$
11	**elleve**	ehlver
12	**tolv**	tol
13	**tretten**	trehtern
14	**fjorten**	fyoo^{r}tern
15	**femten**	fehmtern
16	**seksten**	sæistern
17	**sytten**	surtern
18	**atten**	ahtern
19	**nitten**	nittern
20	**tjue**	**kh$\overline{e}$wer**
21	**tjueen**	kh$\overline{e}$wer$\overline{a}$yn
22	**tjueto**	kh$\overline{e}$wert$\overline{oo}$
23	**tjuetre**	kh$\overline{e}$wertr$\overline{a}$y
24	**tjuefire**	kh$\overline{e}$werfeerer
25	**tjuefem**	kh$\overline{e}$werfehm
26	**tjueseks**	kh$\overline{e}$wersehkss
27	**tjuesju**	kh$\overline{e}$wersh$\overline{e}$w
28	**tjueåtte**	kh$\overline{e}$werotter
29	**tjueni**	kh$\overline{e}$wernee
30	**tretti**	trehti
31	**trettien**	trehti$\overline{a}$yn
32	**trettito**	trehtit$\overline{oo}$
33	**trettitre**	trehtitr$\overline{a}$y
40	**førti**	fur^{r}ti
50	**femti**	fehmti
60	**seksti**	sehksti
70	**sytti**	surti
80	**åtti**	otti
90	**nitti**	nitti
100	**hundre**	hewndrer
101	**hundreogen**	hewndrero(g)$\overline{a}$yn
102	**hundreogto**	hewndrero(g)t$\overline{oo}$
110	**hundreogti**	hewndrero(g)tee
120	**hundreogtjue**	hewndrero(g)kh$\overline{e}$wer

200
30
148

Allment

	0	to hundre	tōo hewndrer
	0	tre hundre	trāy hewndrer
	400	fire hundre	feerer hewndrer
	500	fem hundre	fehm hewndrer
	600	seks hundre	sehkss hewndrer
	700	sju hundre	shew hewndrer
	800	åtte hundre	otter hewndrer
	900	ni hundre	nee hewndrer
	1,000	tusen	tēwssern
	1,100	et tusen et hundre	eht tēwssern eht hewndrer
	1,200	et tusen to hundre	eht tēwssern tōo hewndrer
	2,000	to tusen	tōo tēwssern
	10,000	ti tusen	tee tēwssern
	50,000	femti tusen	fehmti tēwssern
	100,000	hundre tusen	hewndrer tēwssern
	1,000,000	en million	ehn milyōon
	1,000,000,000	en milliard	ehn milyahrd

first	første	furshter
second	annen/andre	aaern/ahndrer
third	tredje	trāydyer
fourth	fjerde	fyǣrer
fifth	femte	fehmter
sixth	sjette	shehter
seventh	sjuende	shewerner
eighth	åttende	otterner
ninth	niende	neeerner
tenth	tiende	teeerner

once/twice	en gang/to ganger	ehn gahng/tōo gahngerr
three times	tre ganger	trāy gahngerr
a half	en halv	ehn hahl
half a ...	en halv ...	ehn hahl
half of ...	halvparten av ...	hahlpah'tern ahv
half (adj.)	halv	hahl
a quarter	en fjerdedel	ehn fyǣrerdāyl
three quarters	tre fjerdedeler	trāy fyǣrerdāylerr
a third	en tredjedel	ehn trāydyerdāyl
two thirds	to tredjedeler	tōo trāydyerdāylerr
a pair of	et par	eht pahr
a dozen	et dusin	eht dewsseen
3.4%	3,4%	trāy kommah feerer proossehnt

1981	nitten åttien	nittern ottiayn
1992	nitten nittito	nittern nittitōo
2003	to tusen og tre	tōo tēwssern o(g) trāy

Year and age *År og alder*

year	**et år**	eht awr
leap year	**et skuddår**	eht **skew**dawr
decade	**et tiår**	eht **tee**awr
century	**et århundre**	eht **awr**hewndrer
this year	**i år**	ee awr
last year	**i fjor**	ee fy$\overline{oo}$r
next year	**neste år**	**neh**ster awr
each year	**hvert år**	væ^{r}t awr
2 years ago	**for 2 år siden**	for 2 awr **see**dern
in one year	**om et år**	om eht awr
in the eighties	**på 80-tallet/**	paw **otti**tahler/
	i 80-årene	ee **otti**awrerner
the 17th century	**17. århundre/**	**sur**terner **awr**hewndrer/
	1600-tallet	**sæi**stern-hewndrertahler
in the 20th century	**i 20. århundre**	ee kh$\overline{ew}$**werner** **awr**hewndrer
in the 21st century	**i 21. århundre**	ee kh$\overline{ew}$**wer**furshter **awr**hewndrer
old/young	**gammel/ung**	**gah**merl/oong
old/new	**gammel/ny**	**gah**merl/n$\overline{ew}$
How old are you?	**Hvor gammel er du?**	voor **gah**merl ær dew
I'm 30 years old.	**Jeg er 30 år.**	yæi ær 30 awr
At my age ...	**I min alder ...**	ee meen **ah**lderr
He/She was born in 1980.	**Han/Hun ble født i 1980.**	hahn/hewn bleh furt ee **nittern otti**
He/She is under 4.	**Han/Hun er under 4 år.**	hahn/hewn ær **ewn**err **feer**er awr

Seasons *Årstider*

spring	**vår**	vawr
summer	**sommer**	**sommerr**
autumn	**høst**	hurst
winter	**vinter**	**vinterr**
in spring	**om våren**	om **vaw**rern
during the summer	**i løpet av sommeren**	ee **lūr**per(t) ahv **sommerr**ern
in autumn	**om høsten**	om **hurst**ern
during the winter	**i løpet av vinteren**	ee **lūr**per(t) ahv **vinterr**ern
high season	**høysesong**	**hoy**sehssong
low season	**lavsesong**	**laav**sehssong

Months   *Måneder*

January	januar *	yahnewaar
February	februar	fehbrewaar
March	mars	mahsh
April	april	ahpreel
May	mai	maay
June	juni	yēwnee
July	juli	yēwlee
August	august	ougewst
September	september	sehptehmberr
October	oktober	oktawberr
November	november	noovehmberr
December	desember	dehssehmberr

after June	etter juni	ehterr jēwnee
before July	før juli	furr yēwlee
during the month of August	i løpet av august	ee lūrper(t) ahv ougewst
in September	i september	ee sehptehmberr
until October	til oktober	til oktawberr
not until November	ikke før november	ikker fūrr noovehmberr
since December	siden desember	seedern dehssehmberr
last month	forrige måned	foryer mawnerd
next month	neste måned	nehster mawnerd
the month before	måneden før	mawnerdern fūrr
the month after	måneden etter	mawnerdern ehterr
the beginning of January	begynnelsen av januar	beryewnerlsern ahv yahnewaar
the middle of February	midten av februar	mittern ahv fehbrewaar
the end of March	slutten av mars	shlewtern ahv mahsh

Days and date   *Dager og dato*

What day is it today?	Hvilken dag er det i dag?	vilkern daag ær deh ee daag
Monday	mandag *	mahndah(g)
Tuesday	tirsdag	teeshdah(g)
Wednesday	onsdag	oonsdah(g)
Thursday	torsdag	tawshdah(g)
Friday	fredag	frāydah(g)
Saturday	lørdag	lūrʳdah(g)
Sunday	søndag	surndah(g)

* The names of months and days aren't capitalized in Norwegian.

What's the date today?	**Hvilken dato er det i dag?**	vilkern daatoo ær deh ee daag
It's ...	**Det er ...**	deh ær
July 1	**1. juli**	furshter yewlee
March 31	**31. mars**	trehtifurshter mahsh
When's your birthday?	**Når har du fødsels-dag?**	nor haar dew furtserls-daag
May 17th.	**17. mai.**	surterner maay
in the morning	**om morgenen**	om maw^{r}nern
during the day	**om dagen/i løpet av dagen**	om daagern/ee lurper(t) ahv daagern
in the afternoon	**om ettermiddagen**	om ehterrmiddaagern
in the evening	**om kvelden**	om kvehlern
at night	**om natten**	om nahtern
the day before yesterday	**i forgårs**	ee forgosh
yesterday	**i går**	ee gawr
today	**i dag**	ee daag
tomorrow	**i morgen**	ee mawer^{r}n
the day after tomorrow	**i overmorgen**	ee awverrmawer^{r}n
the day before	**dagen før**	daagern furr
the next day	**neste dag**	nehster daag
two days ago	**for to dager siden**	for too daagerr seedern
in a few days	**om et par dager**	om eht pahr daagerr
in three days' time	**om tre dager**	om tray daagerr
the other day	**forleden dag**	fo^{r}laydern daag
all day long	**hele dagen**	hayler daagern
day by day	**dag for dag**	daag for daag
Monday to (through) Friday	**mandag til fredag**	mahndah(g) til fraydah(g)
nowadays	**i våre dager**	ee vawrer daagerr
day off	**fridag**	freedaag
holiday	**helligdag**	hehlidaag
holidays/vacation	**ferie**	fayryer
school holidays	**skoleferie**	skoolerfayryer
week	**uke**	ewker
last week	**forrige uke**	foryer ewker
next week	**neste uke**	nehster ewker
for a fortnight (two weeks)	**i fjorten dager**	ee fyoo^{r}tern daagerr
weekday	**hverdag**	væ^{r}daag
weekend	**weekend**	veekehnd
working day	**arbeidsdag**	ahrbæidsdaag

Greetings and wishes   *Hilsener og gratulasjoner*

Merry Christmas!	**God jul!**	goo(d) yēwl
Happy New Year!	**Godt nytt år!**	got newt awr
Happy Easter!	**God påske!**	goo(d) pawsker
Happy birthday!	**Gratulerer med dagen!**	grahtewlāyrerr meh(d) daagern
Best wishes for a Happy New Year!	**De beste ønsker om et godt nytt år!**	dee behster urnskerr om eht got newt awr
Many happy returns of the day!	**Til lykke med dagen!**	til lewker meh(d) daagern
Congratulations!	**Gratulerer!**	grahtewlāyrerr
Good luck/All the best!	**Lykke til!**	lewker til
Have a good trip!	**God reise!**	goo(d) ræisser
Have a good holiday (vacation)!	**God ferie!**	goo(d) fāyryer
Regards from ...	**Jeg skal hilse fra ...**	yæi skahl hilser fraa
My regards to ...	**Hils til ...**	hilss til

Public (Legal) holidays   *Offentlige høytidsdager*

Offices, banks, post offices and shops close early on Christmas Eve and New Year's Eve.

January 1	**Første nyttårsdag**	New Year's Day
May 1	**Første mai**	May Day (Labor Day)
May 17	**Grunnlovsdagen**	Constitution Day
December 25	**Første juledag**	Christmas Day
December 26	**Annen juledag**	Boxing Day
Movable Dates:	**Skjærtorsdag**	Maundy Thursday
	Langfredag	Good Friday
	Annen påskedag	Easter Monday
	Kristi himmelfarts- dag	Ascension Day
	Annen pinsedag	Whit Monday

What time is it? *Hvor mange er klokken?*

Excuse me. Can you tell me the time?	**Unnskyld, men kan du si meg hvor mange klokken er?**	ewnshewl mehn kahn dew see mæi voor mahnger klokkern ær
It's ...	**Den er ...**	dehn ær
five past one	**fem over ett ***	fehm awverr eht
ten past two	**ti over to**	tee awverr tōō
a quarter past three	**kvart over tre**	kvahᵣt awverr trāy
twenty past four	**tjue over fire/ ti på halv fem**	khēwer awverr feerer/ tee paw hahl fehm
twenty-five past five	**fem på halv seks**	fehm paw hahl sehkss
half past six	**halv sju**	hahl shēw
twenty-five to seven	**fem over halv sju**	fehm awverr hahl shēw
twenty to eight	**ti over halv åtte/ tjue på åtte**	tee awver hahl otter/ khewer paw otter
a quarter to nine	**kvart på ni**	kvahᵣt paw nee
ten to ten	**ti på ti**	tee paw tee
five to eleven	**fem på elleve**	fehm paw ehlver
twelve o'clock	**tolv**	tol
noon	**klokken tolv (om dagen)**	klokkern tol (om daagern)
midnight	**midnatt**	midnaht
in the morning	**om morgenen**	om mawᵣnern
in the afternoon	**om ettermiddagen**	om ehtermiddaagern
in the evening	**om kvelden**	om kvehlern
What time does the train leave?	**Når går toget?**	nor gawr tawger
It leaves at ...	**Det går kl. ...**	deh gawr klokkern
13.04 (1.04 p.m.)	**13.04**	trehtern newl feerer
00.40 (00.40 a.m.)	**00.40**	newl furᵣti
in five minutes	**om fem minutter**	om fehm minnewterr
in a quarter of an hour	**om et kvarter**	om eht kvahᵣtāyr
half an hour ago	**for en halvtime siden**	for ehn hahlteemer seedern
about two hours	**ca. to timer**	sirrkah tōō teemerr
a few seconds	**et par sekunder**	eht pahr sehkewnerr
The clock is fast/ slow.	**Klokken går for fort/sakte.**	klokkern gawr for fooᵣt/sahkter

---

* In everyday conversation, time is expressed as shown here. However, official time uses a 24-hour clock, which means that after noon hours are counted from 13 to 24.

Allment

Common abbreviations   *Vanlige forkortelser*

A/S	aksjeselskap	Ltd./Inc.
ca.	cirka	around
e.Kr.	etter Kristus	A.D.
EM	europamesterskap	European Championship
ent.	entall	singular
et.	etasje	floor
f.Kr.	før Kristus	B.C.
fl.	flertall	plural
f.m.	forrige måned	last month
FN	De forente nasjoner	United Nations
g	gram	gram
gt.	gate	street
hg	hekto(gram)	hectogram
hk	hestekrefter	horsepower
H.M.	Hans Majestet	His Majesty
kg	kilo(gram)	kilogram
kl.	klokken	o'clock
km	kilometer	kilometre
KNA	Kongelig Norsk Auto- mobilklub	Royal Norwegian Automobile Club
kr/kr.	kroner	kroner
l	liter	litre
md.	måned(er)	month(s)
moms	merverdiavgift	VAT/sales tax
NAF	Norges Automobil- Forbund	Norwegian Automobile Association
nr.	nummer	number
NRK	Norsk rikskringkasting	Norwegian Broadcasting System
NSB	Norges Statsbaner	Norwegian State Railways
NTB	Norsk Telegrambyrå	Norwegian News Agency
NTH	Norges tekniske høgskole	Norwegian Technical University
osv.	og så videre	etc.
pk.	pakke	packet, parcel
pr. stk.	per stykk	per item
str.	størrelse	size
s.u.	svar utbes	R.S.V.P.
tlf.	telefon	telephone
t.v.	til venstre	to the left
UD	Utenriksdepartementet	Ministry for Foreign Affairs
veil. pris	veiledende pris	recommended price
VM	verdensmesterskap	World Championship

Signs and notices *Skilt og oppslag*

Adgang forbudt (for uvedkommende)	No trespassing, No entrance
Damer	Ladies
Fare	Danger
Forsiktig	Caution
Forsiktig, trapp	Mind the step
Gangbro/Gangbru	Footbridge
Gratis adgang	Admission free
Gågate	Pedestrian zone
Heis	Lift (Elevator)
Herrer	Gentlemen
Høgspenning	High voltage
Inngang	Entrance
I uorden	Out of order
Kaldt	Cold
Kasse	Cash desk (Cashier)
Ledig	Free/Vacant
Livsfare	Danger of death
Ned	Down
Nymalt	Wet paint
Nødutgang	Emergency exit
Opp	Up
Opptatt	Occupied
Privat	Private
Privat vei/veg	Private road
Reservert	Reserved
Røyking forbudt	No smoking
Røyking (ikke) tillatt	(Non)Smoker
Stengt	Closed
Skyv	Push
Til leie	For hire (rent), To let
Til salgs	For sale
Trekk	Pull
Trykk	Press
Tråkk ikke på gresset	Keep of the grass
Underetasje	Lower ground floor
Utgang	Exit
Utsalg	Sales
Utsolgt	Sold out
Vareheis	Goods lift (Freight elevator)
Varmt	Hot
Vokt deg/Dem for hunden	Beware of the dog
Åpent	Open
Åpningstider	Opening hours

Emergency *Nødsfall*

Call the police	**Ring til politiet**	ring til poolitteeyer
Consulate	**Konsulat**	koonsewlaat
DANGER	**FARE**	faarer
Embassy	**Ambassade**	ahmbahssaader
FIRE	**BRANN**	brahn
Gas	**Gass**	gahss
Get a doctor	**Hent en lege**	hehnt ehn lāyger
Go away	**Gå vekk**	gaw vehk
HELP	**HJELP**	yehlp
Get help quickly	**Hent hjelp øyeblikkelig**	hehnt yehlp oyerblikkerli
I'm ill	**Jeg er syk**	yæi ær sēwk
I'm lost	**Jeg har gått meg bort**	yæi haar got mæi boo'rt
Leave me alone	**La meg være i fred**	lah mæi værer ee frāy(d)
LOOK OUT	**SE OPP**	sāy op
Poison	**Gift**	yift
POLICE	**POLITI**	poolittee
Stop that man/ woman	**Stopp den mannen/ kvinnen**	stop dehn mahnern/ kvinnern
STOP THIEF	**STOPP TYVEN**	stop tēwvern

Emergency telephone numbers *Nødnummere*

In Oslo or Bergen:	Fire	**001**
	Police	**002**
	Ambulance	**003**

Lost property—Theft *Hittegods – Tyveri*

Where's the ...	**Hvor er ...**	voor ær
lost property (lost and found) office	**hittegodskontoret**	hittergoodskoontoorer
police station	**politistasjonen**	poolitteestahshōōnern
I want to report a theft.	**Jeg vil anmelde et tyveri.**	yæi vil ahnmehler eht tewverree
My ... has been stolen.	**... er blitt stjålet.**	... ær blit styawlert
I've lost my ...	**Jeg har mistet ...**	yæi haar mistert
handbag/passport/ wallet	**håndvesken/passet lommeboken**	honvehskern/pahsser/ loommerbōōkern

CAR ACCIDENTS, see page 78

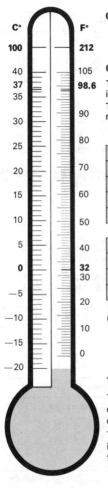

Conversion tables

Centimetres and inches

To change centimetres into inches, multiply by .39.

To change inches into centimetres, multiply by 2.54.

	in.	feet	yards
1 mm.	0.039	0.003	0.001
1 cm.	0.39	0.03	0.01
1 dm.	3.94	0.32	0.10
1 m.	39.40	3.28	1.09

	mm.	cm.	m.
1 in.	25.4	2.54	0.025
1 ft.	304.8	30.48	0.305
1 yd.	914.4	91.44	0.914

(32 metres = 35 yards)

Temperature

To convert centigrade into degrees Fahrenheit, multiply centigrade by 1.8 and add 32.

To convert degrees Fahrenheit into centigrade, subtract 32 from Fahrenheit and divide by 1.8.

Kilometres into miles

1 kilometre (km.) = 0.62 miles

km.	10	20	30	40	50	60	70	80	90	100	110	120	130
miles	6	12	19	25	31	37	44	50	56	62	68	75	81

Miles into kilometres

1 mile = 1.609 kilometres (km.)

miles	10	20	30	40	50	60	70	80	90	100
km.	16	32	48	64	80	97	113	129	145	161

Fluid measures

1 litre (l.) = 0.88 imp. quart or = 1.06 U.S. quart

1 imp. quart = 1.14 l.	1 U.S. quart = 0.95 l.
1 imp. gallon = 4.55 l.	1 U.S. gallon = 3.8 l.

litres	5	10	15	20	25	30	35	40	45	50
imp. gal.	1.1	2.2	3.3	4.4	5.5	6.6	7.7	8.8	9.9	11.0
U.S. gal.	1.3	2.6	3.9	5.2	6.5	7.8	9.1	10.4	11.7	13.0

Weights and measures

1 kilogram or kilo (kg.) = 1000 grams (g.)

100 g. = 3.5 oz.	½ kg. = 1.1 lb.
200 g. = 7.0 oz.	1 kg. = 2.2 lb.

1 oz. = 28.35 g.
1 lb. = 453.60 g.

CLOTHING SIZES, see page 115/YARDS AND INCHES, see page 112

Basic grammar

Norway has two official written, mutually comprehensible languages, *bokmål* and *nynorsk*. A traveller in Norway must expect to see and hear both, but *bokmål*—the most common—is used throughout this book.

Articles

The article shows the gender of Norwegian nouns, that are either common (masculine), feminine or neuter. The majority of feminine* nouns also have a common form, so we have chosen to simplify matters by using only the two most frequently met genders: the common and the neuter.

1. Indefinite article (a/an)

common:	**en bil**	*a* car
neuter:	**et eple**	*an* apple

2. Definite article (the)

Where we, in English say "the house", Norwegians tag the definite article onto the end of the noun and say "house-the". In common nouns "the" is **-(e)n**, in neuter nouns **-(e)t**.

common:	**bilen**	*the* car
neuter:	**eplet**	*the* apple

Nouns

1. There are no easy rules for determining the gender. Learn each new word with its accompanying article.

2. The plural of most nouns is formed by an **-(e)r** ending (indefinite plural) and an **-(e)ne** ending (definite plural).

common:	**biler**	cars	**bilene**	*the* cars
neuter:	**epler**	apples	**eplene**	*the* apples

---

* In the feminine form "a night, the night" would be *ei* natt, natt*a*; the common form is *en* natt, natt*en*.

Many monosyllabic nouns have irregular plurals.

en mann	a man	**menn**	men	**mennene**	the men
en sko	a shoe	**sko**	shoes	**skoene**	the shoes
et hus	a house	**hus**	houses	**husene**	the houses
et barn	a child	**barn**	children	**barna**	the children

3. Possession is shown by adding **-s** (singular and plural). Note that there is no apostrophe.

Johns bror	John's brother
hotellets eier	the owner of the hotel
barnas far	the children's father

Adjectives

1. Adjectives agree with the noun in gender and number. For the indefinite form, the neuter is generally formed by adding **-t**, the plural by adding **-e**.

(en) stor hund	(a) big dog	**store hunder**	big dogs
(et) stort hus	(a) big house	**store hus**	big houses

2. For the definite declension of the adjective, add the ending **-e** (common, neuter and plural). This form is used when the adjective is preceded by **den**, **det**, **de** (the definite article used with adjectives) or by a demonstrative or a possessive adjective.

den store hunden	the big dog
de store hundene	the big dogs
det store huset	the big house
de store husene	the big houses

3. Comparative and superlative

The comparative and superlative are normally formed either by adding the endings **-(e)re** and **-(e)st**, respectively, to the adjective or by putting **mer** (more) and **mest** (most) before the adjective.

stor/større/størst	big/bigger/biggest
lett/lettere/lettest	easy/easier/easiest
imponerende/*mer* **imponerende**/*mest* **imponerende**	impressive/more impressive/ the most impressive

4. Demonstrative adjectives:

	common	neuter	plural
this/these	**denne**	**dette**	**disse**
that/those	**den**	**det**	**de**

5. Possessive adjectives agree in number and gender with the noun they modify, i.e. with the thing possessed and not the possessor.

	common	neuter	plural
my	**min**	**mitt**	**mine**
your	**din**	**ditt**	**dine**
his	**sin, hans**	**sitt, hans**	**sine, hans**
her	**sin, hennes**	**sitt, hennes**	**sine, hennes**
its	**sin, dens/dets***	**sitt, dens/dets**	**sine, dens/dets**
our	**vår**	**vårt**	**våre**
their	**sin, deres**	**sitt, deres**	**sine, deres**

The forms **sin, sitt, sine** always refer back to the subject, but cannot be used to modify a subject.

Han har mistet broken sin.   He has lost his (own) book.
De har mistet bøkene sine.   They have lost their (own) books.

but:

Boken hans er blitt borte.   His book has disappeared.

The forms **hans, hennes, dens/dets, deres** are actually the genitive of the personal pronouns (see page 162). These forms can qualify the subject, as shown above, as well as the object. However, qualifying the latter, they indicate that the subject and the possessor of the object are two different people.

Han har misted boken hans.   He has lost his (John's) book.
De har mistet bøkene deres.   They have lost their (John and Mary's) books.

---

* Use **dens** if ''it'' is of common gender and **dets** if ''it'' is neuter.

Adverbs

Adverbs are often formed by adding **-t** to the corresponding adjective.

rask/raskt	quick/quickly
langsom/langsomt	slow/slowly

Personal pronouns

	subject	object	genitive
I	**jeg**	**meg**	—
you	**du**	**deg**	—
he	**han**	**ham/han**	hans
she	**hun**	**henne**	hennes
it	**den/det**	**den/det**	dens/dets
we	**vi**	**oss**	—
you (plural)	**dere**	**dere**	—
they	**de**	**dem**	deres

Norwegian has two forms for "you", an informal one (**du**) and a formal one (**De**). However, today the use of the formal **De** has practically disappeared from the language.

Verbs

Here we are concerned only with the infinitive, imperative and present tense. The present tense is simple, because it has the same form for all persons. The infinitive of most Norwegian verbs ends in **-e** (some compound and monosyllabic end in other vowels). Here are three useful auxiliary verbs:

	to be	to have	to be able to
Infinitive	**å være**	**å ha**	**å kunne**
Present tense (same form for all persons)	**er**	**har**	**kan**
Imperative	**vær**	**ha**	—

The present tense of most Norwegian verbs ends in **-r**:

	to ask	to buy	to go	to do
Infinitive	**å spørre**	**å kjøpe**	**å gå**	**å gjøre**
Present tense (same form for all persons)	**spør**	**kjøper**	**går**	**gjør**
Imperative	**spør**	**kjøp**	**gå**	**gjør**

There is no equivalent to the English present continuous tense. Thus:

Jeg reiser.	I travel / I am travelling.

Negatives

Negation is expressed by using the adverb **ikke** (not). It is usually placed immediately after the verb in a main clause. In compound tenses, **ikke** appears between the auxiliary and the main verb.

Jeg snakker norsk.	I speak Norwegian.
Jeg snakker ikke norsk.	I do not speak Norwegian.

Questions

Questions are formed by reversing the order of the subject and the verb:

Bussen stanser her.	The bus stops here.
Stanser bussen her?	Does the bus stop here?
Jeg kommer i kveld.	I am coming tonight.
Kommer du i kveld?	Are you coming tonight?

Dictionary
and alphabetical index

English–Norwegian

c common	*nt* neuter	*pl* plural

a en 159; et 159
abbreviation forkortelse *c* 154
able, to be kunne 162
about *(approximately)* ca./cirka 79, 153
above ovenfor 62; over 15
abscess byll *c* 145
absorbent cotton bomull *c* 109
accept, to *(take)* ta 61, 102
accessories tilbehør *nt* 116, 125
accident ulykke *c* 79, 139
accommodation service innkvarteringsservice *c* 22
account konto *c* 130
adaptor adapter *c* 119
address adresse *c* 21, 31, 76, 79, 102
adhesive tape limbånd *nt* 104
admission adgang *c* 82, 155; *(fee)* inngangsbillett *c* 89
adult voksen *c* 82
aerogramme aerogram *nt* 133
Africa Afrika 146
after etter 15, 77, 150
afternoon ettermiddag *c* 151, 153
after-shave lotion etterbarberingsvann *nt* 110
age alder *c* 149
ago for ... siden 149, 153
air bed luftmadrass *c* 106
airmail med fly 132
airmail label luftpostetikett *c* 133
air mattress luftmadrass *c* 106
airplane fly *nt* 65
airport flyplass *c* 16, 21, 65
alarm clock vekkeklokke *c* 121
alcohol alkohol *c* 37, 59
alcoholic alkoholholdig 58
all alt 103
allergic allergisk 141, 143
allergy allergi *c* 140

allowed tillatt 155
almond mandel *c* 54
alphabet alfabet *nt* 9, 135
also også 15
alter, to endre 116
amazing praktfull 84
ambulance sykebil *c* 79, 156
American amerikansk 105
American amerikaner *c* 93
American plan helpensjon *c* 24
amount beløp *nt* 61, 131
amplifier forsterker *c* 119
amusement park fornøyelsespark *c* 81
anaesthetic bedøvelse *c* 145; narkose *c* 144
analgesic analgetikum *nt* 109
analogue analog 122
and og 15
animal dyr *nt* 85
ankle ankel *c* 139
anorak anorakk *c* 116
answer, to svare 136
antibiotic antibiotikum *nt* 143
antidepressant middel mot depresjoner *nt* 143
antique antikvitet *c* 83
antique shop antikvitetsforretning *c* 98
antiseptic antiseptisk 109
any noe 15
anyone noen 12
anything noe 17, 101, 103, 113, 143
anywhere noe sted 89
aperitif aperitiff *c* 58
appendicitis blindtarmbetennelse *c* 142
appendix blindtarm *c* 138
appetizer forrett *c* 43
apple eple *nt* 54, 64
apple juice eplesaft *c* 59

apple pie eplekake c 55, 63
appointment avtalt møte nt 131;
  time c 30, 137, 145
April april (c) 150
aquarium akvarium nt 81
aquavit akevitt c 56
archaeology arkeologi c 83
architect arkitekt c 83
area (of town) strøk nt 81
area code retningsnummer nt 134
arm arm c 138, 139
around (approximately) ca./cirka
  154; (nearby) i nærheten 35
arrival ankomst c 16, 25, 65
arrive, to være fremme 65, 68
art kunst c 83
artery pulsåre c 138
art gallery kunstgalleri nt 98
artificial kunstig 124
artificial sweetener søtningsmiddel nt 37
artist kunstner c 83
art museum kunstmuseum nt 81
ashtray askebeger nt 36
Asia Asia 146
ask, to spørre 76, 163; (beg) be 136
ask for, to be om 25, 60
asparagus asparges c 51
aspirin aspirin c 109
asthma astma c 141
at ved 15
athletics meeting friidrettsstevne
  nt 89
athletic shoe turnsko c 118
at least minst 24
at once med én gang 31
August august (c) 150
aunt tante c 93
Australia Australia 146
automatic automatisk 122, 124;
  (car) med automatgir 20
auto repair shop bilverksted nt 78
autumn høst c 149
average middels(god) 91
awful forferdelig 84, 94

B
baby baby c 24, 111
baby food barnemat c 111
babysitter barnevakt c 27
back rygg c 138
backache ryggsmerte c 141
backpack ryggsekk c 106
bacon bacon nt 38
bacon and eggs egg og bacon 38

bad dårlig 14, 95
bag bag c 17, 18; (carrier)
  bærepose c 103
baggage bagasje c 18, 26, 31, 71
baggage cart bagasjetralle c 18, 71
baggage checking reisegodsekspedisjon c 71
baggage locker oppbevaringsboks
  c 18, 67, 71
baked bakt 52
baker's bakeri c 98
balance (finance) balanse c 131
balcony balkong c 23
ball (inflated) ball c 128
ballet ballett c 88
ball-point pen kulepenn c 104
banana banan c 54, 64
bandage bandasje c 109
Band-Aid plaster nt 109
bangle armring c 121
bank (finance) bank c 98, 129, 130
banknote seddel c 130
bar (room) bar c 33; (chocolate)
  plate c 64
barber's herrefrisør c 30, 98
barrette hårspenne c 111
bath bad nt 23, 25, 27
bathing cap badehette c 116
bathing hut badehus c 91
bathrobe badekåpe c 116
bathroom bad nt 27
bath salts badesalt nt 110
bath towel badehåndkle nt 27
battery batteri nt 75, 78, 119, 125
battery-powered batteridrevet 128
be, to være 162
beach strand c 90
beach ball badeball c 128
bean bønne c 51
beard skjegg nt 31
beautiful pen 14; vakker 84
beauty salon skjønnhetssalong c
  30, 98
bed seng c 24, 144
bed and breakfast rom med
  frokost 24
bedpan stikkbekken nt 144
beef oksekjøtt nt 47; okse- 48
beefsteak biff c 47, 49
beer øl nt 56, 64
before før 15, 143, 150
begin, to begynne 87, 88
beginner begynner c 91
beginning begynnelse c 150
behind bak 15, 77

bell *(electric)* ringeklokke c 144
bell captain portier c 26
bellman bærer c 26
below nedenfor 62; under 15
belt belte nt 117
berth køye c 69, 71
better bedre 14, 25, 101
between mellom 15
bicycle sykkel c 74
bicycle racing sykkelløp nt 89
bidet bidet nt 28
big stor 14, 25, 101, 118
bilberry blåbær nt 54
bill regning c 31, 61, 102;
  (banknote) seddel c 130
billion *(Am.)* milliard c 148
binoculars kikkert c 123
bird fugl c 85
birthday fødselsdag c 151
biscuit *(Br.)* småkake c 63
bite, to bite 139
bitter besk 60
black svart 113
black and white svart-hvitt 124, 125
blackberry bjørnebær nt 54
blackcurrant solbær nt 54
bladder urinblære c 138
blanket ullteppe nt 27
bleed, to blø 139, 145
blind *(window shade)* rullegardin c 29
blister blemme c 139
blood blod nt 141, 142
blood pressure blodtrykk nt 141, 142
blood transfusion blodoverføring c 144
blotting paper trekkpapir nt 104
blouse bluse c 116
blow-dry, to føne 30
blue blå 113
blueberry blåbær nt 54
blusher rouge c 110
boat båt c 73, 74
bobby pin hårklemme c 111
body kropp c 138
boil byll c 139
boiled kokt 49, 51, 52
bone ben nt 138
book bok c 12, 104
booking office billettkontor nt 19, 67
booklet of tickets billetthefte nt 72
bookshop bokhandel c 98, 104

boot støvel c 118
born født 149
botanical gardens botanisk hage c 81
botany botanikk c 83
bottle flaske c 17, 56, 57
bottle-opener flaskeåpner c 106
bowel tarm c 138
bowl *(container)* bolle c 127; skål c 107
bow tie flue c 116
box eske c 120
boy gutt c 112
boyfriend venn c 93
bra behå c 116
bracelet armbånd nt 121
braces *(suspenders)* (bukse)seler c/pl 116
braised braisert 49
brake brems c 78
brake fluid bremsevæske c 75
brandy brandy c 58
brass messing c 122
bread brød nt 36, 38, 64, 120
break, to brekke 139
break down, to få motorstopp 78
breakdown motorstopp c 78
breakdown van kranbil c 78
breakfast frokost c 24, 34, 38
breast bryst c 138
breathe, to puste 141, 142
bridge bro c 81
bring, to gi 13; ta med 95
bring down, to bære ned 31
British brite c 93
broiled *(Am.)* grillstekt 49
broken brukket 140; gått i stykker 29, 119, 123
bronze bronse c 122
brooch brosje c 121
brother bror c 93
brown brun 113
bruise blått merke nt 139
brush børste c 111
Brussels sprouts rosenkål c/pl 51
bubble bath skumbad nt 110
bucket bøtte c 106; spann nt 128
buckle spenne c 117
buffet car kafeteriavogn c 70
build, to bygge 83
building bygning c 81, 83
building blocks/bricks bygge-klosser c/pl 128
bulb *(light)* lyspære c 28, 75, 119
bump *(lump)* kul c 139

bun bolle c 63
burn brannsår nt 139
burned out (bulb) gått 28
bus buss c 18, 19, 65, 66, 72, 80
business forretning c 16, 131
business district forretningskvarter nt 81
business trip forretningsreise c 93
bus stop bussholdeplass c 72
busy opptatt 96
but men 15
butane gas butangass c 32, 106
butcher's slakter c 98
butter smør nt 36, 38, 64
button knapp c 29, 117
buy, to kjøpe 100, 104, 123, 163

C
cabana badehus nt 91
cabbage kål c 51
cabin (camping) hytte c 32; (ship) lugar c 74
cabin luggage håndbagasje c 65
cable car taubane c 74
cable release snorutløser c 125
café kafé c 33
cafeteria kafeteria c 32, 33, 67
cake kake c 55, 63, 64
cake shop konditori nt 98
calculator kalkulator c 105
calendar kalender c 104
call (phone) samtale c 134, 135, 136
call, to (give name) hete 11; (phone) ringe 79, 134, 136, 156
camera case kameraveske c 125
camera shop fotoforretning c 98
camp, to campe 32
camp bed campingseng c 106
camping camping c 32
camping equipment camping-utstyr nt 106
camp site campingplass c 32
can (container) boks c 120
can (be able to) kunne 12, 162
Canada Kanada 146
Canadian kanadier c 93
cancel, to annullere 65
candle stearinlys nt 106
candlestick lysestake c 127
candy godter nt/pl 126
candy store godtebutikk c 98
canoe kano c 74
can opener boksåpner c 106

cap lue c 116
capital (finance) kapital c 131
capsule (medical) kapsel c 109
car bil c 19, 20, 32, 75, 76, 78; (train) vogn c 70, 71
carafe karaffel c 57
carat karat c 121
caravan campingvogn c 32
caraway seed karve c 53
carbon paper blåpapir nt 104
carburettor forgasser c 78
card kort nt 93, 131
cardboard papp c 107
card game kortspill nt 128
cardigan golfjakke c 116; lusekofte c 127
car ferry bilterge c 74
car hire bilutleie c 20
car park parkeringsplass c 77; (multistorey) parkeringshus nt 77
car racing billøp nt 89
car rental bilutleie c 20
carrot gulrot c 51
carry, to bære 21
cart tralle c 18, 71
carton kartong c 17, 126
cartridge (camera) kassett c 124
car wash bilvask c 76
case futteral nt 123; veske c 125; (cigarette) etui nt 121, 126
cash, to løse inn 130, 133
cash desk kasse c 103, 155
cassette kassett c 127
cassette player kassettspiller c 119
cassette recorder kassettopptaker c 119
castle slott nt 81
catalogue katalog c 82
cathedral domkirke c 81
Catholic katolsk 84
cauliflower blomkål c 51
caution forsiktig 155
cave hule c 81
celery selleri c 51
cemetery gravlund c 81
centimetre centimeter c 112
centre sentrum nt 19, 21, 76, 81
century århundre nt 149
ceramics keramikk c 83
cereal frokostblanding c 38
chain (jewellery) kjede nt 121
chain bracelet armlenke c 121
chair stol c 36
chalk kritt nt 104

change *(money)* småpenger *c/pl* 130; vekslepenger *c/pl* 61, 77
change, to endre 65; *(replace)* bytte 60; skifte ut 123; *(money)* veksle 18, 130; *(trains)* bytte 68, 69, 73
changing room prøverom *nt* 115
chapel kapell *nt* 81
charcoal briquet trekullbrikett *c* 106
charcoal tablet kulltablett *c* 109
charge gebyr *nt* 136
charge, to koste 77
charm *(trinket)* berlokk *c* 121
charm bracelet berlokkarmbånd *nt* 121
cheap billig 14; *(inexpensive)* rimelig 24, 25, 101
check sjekk *c* 130; *(restaurant)* regning *c* 61
check, to kontrollere 75
check in, to *(airport)* sjekke inn 65
check out, to reise 31
checkroom *(railway)* bagasje-oppbevaring *c* 67, 71
check-up *(medical)* undersøkelse *c* 142
cheers! skål! 58
cheese ost *c* 38, 53, 62, 64
cheese shop osteforretning *c* 98
chef kjøkkensjef *c* 40
chemist's apotek *nt* 98, 108
cheque sjekk *c* 130
cherry kirsebær *nt* 54
chess sjakk *c* 93
chess set sjakkspill *nt* 128
chest bryst *nt* 141; brystkasse *c* 138
chewing gum tyggegummi *c* 126
chewing tobacco skråtobakk *c* 126
chicken kylling *c* 50
child barn *nt* 24, 60, 82, 90, 93, 139
children's ... barne- 116
children's doctor barnelege *c* 137
chilled avkjølt 58
China Kina 146
china shop glassmagasin *c* 98
chips pommes frites *c/pl* 52, 62; *(Am.)* potetgull *nt* 52, 64
chives gressløk *c* 53
chocolate sjokolade *c* 38, 55, 59, 62
chocolate bar sjokoladeplate *c* 64, 126
cholesterol kolesterol *c* 37
chop *(meat)* kotelett *c* 48

Christmas jul *c* 152
chromium krom *c* 122
church kirke *c* 81, 84
cigar sigar *c* 126
cigarette sigarett *c* 17, 95, 126
cigarette case sigarettetui *nt* 126
cigarette holder sigarett-munnstykke *nt* 126
cigarette lighter lighter *c* 126
cinema kino *c* 86, 96
circle *(theatre)* balkong *c* 87
citadel festning *c* 81
city by *c* 81, 88
city centre sentrum *nt* 81
city hall rådhus *nt* 82
classical klassisk 128
clean ren 61
clean, to vaske 76
cleansing cream rensekrem *c* 110
cliff klippe *c* 85
cloakroom garderobe *c* 87
clock klokke *c* 121, 153
clock-radio klokkeradio *c* 119
close, to stenge 11, 82, 108, 132
closed stengt 155
cloth tøy *nt* 118
clothes klær *pl* 29, 116
clothes peg (pin) klesklype *c* 106
clothing klær *pl* 112
cloud sky *c* 94
coach *(bus)* ekspressbuss *c* 66; rutebil *c* 66
coach station busstasjon *c* 67
coast kyst *c* 85
coat *(man's)* frakk *c* 116; *(woman's)* kåpe *c* 116
coffee kaffe *c* 38, 59, 64
coffee shop konditori *c* 33
cognac konjakk *c* 58
coin mynt *c* 83
cold kald 14, 25, 38, 60, 94, 155
cold *(illness)* forkjølelse *c* 108, 141
collar krage *c* 117
collect call noteringsoverføring *c* 135
colour farge *c* 112, 113, 124, 125
colour chart fargekart *nt* 30
colourfast fargeekte 114
colour rinse fargeskylling *c* 30
colour shampoo fargesjampo *c* 111
comb kam *c* 111
come, to komme 35, 92, 95 137
comedy komedie *c* 86
commission *(fee)* kommisjon *c* 130

compact disc CD-plate c 127
compartment (train) kupé c 71
compass kompass nt 106
complaint klage c 60
concert konsert c 88
concert hall konserthus nt 81, 88
condom kondom nt 109
conductor (orchestra) dirigent c 88
conference room konferanserom nt 23
confirm, to bekrefte 65
confirmation bekreftelse c 23
congratulation gratulasjon c 152
congress hall kongresshall c 81
connection (transport) forbindelse c 65, 68
consommé buljong c 44
constipation forstoppelse c 140
consulate konsulat c 156
contact lens kontaktlinse c 123
contagious smittsom 142
contain, to inneholde 37
contraceptive prevensjonsmiddel nt 109
contract kontrakt c 131
control kontroll c 16
cookie småkake c 63
cool box kjøleboks c 106
cooler ice pack kjøleelement nt 106
copper kopper nt 122
corkscrew korketrekker c 106
corn (Am.) mais c 51; (foot) liktorn c 109
corner hjørne nt 21, 36
corn plaster liktornplaster nt 109
cosmetics kosmetikk c 110
cost kostnad c 131
cost, to koste 11, 24, 80, 136
cot barneseng c 24
cotton bomull c 114
cotton wool bomull c 109
couchette køye c liggevogn c 69
cough hoste c 108, 141
cough, to hoste 142
cough drops halspastiller c/pl 109
cough syrup hostesaft c 109
counter luke c 133
country land nt 92, 146
countryside land nt 85
court house tinghus nt 81
cousin (male) fetter c 93; (female) kusine c 93
crab krabbe c 43, 46
cramp krampe c 141
cranberry tyttebær nt 54

crayfish (river) kreps c 46
crayon fargeblyant c 104
cream fløte c 38, 55, 59; (toiletry) krem c 110; (pharmaceutical) salve c 109
crease resistant krøllfri 114
credit kreditt c 131
credit card kredittkort c 20, 31, 61, 102, 130
crew-neck med rund hals 117
crispbread knekkebrød nt 120
crisps potetgull nt 52, 64
crockery servise c 106, 107
cross kors c 121
cross-country skiing langrenn nt 91
crossing (maritime) overfart c 73
crossroads (vei)kryss nt 77
cruise cruise nt 74
crystal krystall nt 122
cucumber agurk c 51
cuff link mansjettknapp c 121
cuisine kjøkken nt 34
cup kopp c 36, 59, 107
curler hårrull c 111
currant korint c 54
currency valuta c 18, 129
currency exchange office vekslingskontor c 18, 67, 129
current strøm c 90
curry (seasoning) karri c 53
curtain gardin c 28
customs toll c 16, 79, 102
cut (wound) kutt nt 139
cut, to (with scissors) klippe 30
cut off, to avbryte 135
cut glass slepet glass nt 122
cuticle remover neglebåndsfjerner c 110
cutlery (spise)bestikk nt 107
cycling sykling c 90

D
dairy melkebutikk c 98
dance, to danse 88, 96
danger fare c 155, 156
dangerous farlig 90
Danish pastry wienerbrød nt 63
dark mørk 25, 101, 112, 113
date (day) dato c 25, 151; (appointment) stevnemøte nt 95; (fruit) daddel c 54
daughter datter c 93
day dag c 20, 24, 32, 80, 150, 151
daylight dagslys nt 124

day off fridag *c* 151
decade tiår *nt* 149
decaffeinated koffeinfri 38, 59
December desember *(c)* 150
decision avgjørelse *c* 102;
  beslutning *c* 25
deck *(ship)* dekk *nt* 74
deck chair fluktstol *c* 106
declare, to *(customs)* fortolle 17
deep dyp 90, 142
deep fried frityrstekt 46
deer hjort *c* 50
delicatessen delikatesseforretning
  c 98
delicious utsøkt 61
deliver, to levere 102
delivery levering *c* 102
Denmark Danmark 146
dentist tannlege *c* 98, 145
denture gebiss *nt* 145
deodorant deodorant *c* 110
department avdeling *c* 83, 100
department store stormagasin *nt*
  98
departure avgang *c* 65
deposit *(down payment)*
  depositum *nt* 20; *(in bank)*
  innskudd *nt* 130
dessert dessert *c* 37, 55
detour *(traffic)* omkjøring *c* 79
diabetic diabetiker *c* 37, 141
dialling code retningsnummer *nt*
  134
diamond diamant *c* 122
diaper bleie *c* 111
diarrhoea diarré *c* 140
dictionary ordbok *c* 104
diesel diesel *c* 75
diet diett *c* 37
difficult vanskelig 14
difficulty problem *nt* 102;
  vanskelighet *c* 28
dill dill *c* 53
dining car spisevogn *c* 68, 70
dining room spisesal *c* 27
dinner middag *c* 27, 34, 94
direct direkte 65
direct, to vise vei 13
direction retning *c* 76
directory *(phone)* telefonkatalog *c*
  134
disabled bevegelseshemmet *c* 82
disc plate *c* 127
discotheque diskotek *nt* 88, 96
discount rabatt *c* 131

disease sykdom *c* 142
dish asjett *c* 127; fat *nt* 107; *(food)*
  rett *c* 37
dish detergent oppvaskmiddel *nt*
  106
dish of the day dagens rett *c* 39, 40
disinfectant desinfeksjonsmiddel
  nt 109
dislocated ute av ledd 140
display case monter *c* 100
dissatisfied misfornøyd 103
district *(of town)* kvarter *nt* 81
dive, to dykke 90
diversion *(traffic)* omkjøring *c* 79
dizzy svimmel 140
do, to gjøre 163
doctor lege *c* 79, 98. 137, 144, 156;
  (title) dr./doktor 145
doctor's office legekontor *nt* 137
dog hund *c* 139, 155
doll dukke *c* 127, 128
dollar dollar *c* 18, 102, 130
double dobbel 74
double bed dobbeltseng *c* 23
double room dobbeltrom *nt* 19, 23
doughnut smultring *c* 63
down ned 15, 155
downhill skiing utforkjøring *c* 91
downstairs nede 15
downtown area sentrum *nt* 81
dozen dusin *nt* 148
draught beer fatøl *nt* 56
drawing pad tegneblokk *c* 104
drawing pin tegnestift *c* 104
dress kjole *c* 116
dressing gown morgenkåpe *c* 116
drink drikk *c* 58, 59; drikkevare *c*
  56; drink *c* 60, 95
drink, to drikke 35, 36, 59
drinking water drikkevann *nt* 32
drip, to dryppe 28
drive, to kjøre 21, 76, 79
driving licence førerkort *nt* 20, 79
drop *(liquid)* dråpe *c* 109
drugstore apotek *c* 98, 108
dry tørr 30, 58, 111
dry cleaner's rens *c* 29; renseri *nt*
  98
dry shampoo tørrsjampo *c* 111
duck and *c* 50
dummy *(baby's)* narresmokk *c* 111
during i løpet av 15, 149, 151
duty *(customs)* toll *c* 17
duty-free shop tax-free-butikk *c* 19
dye, to farge 30

E

each hver 125, 149
ear øre nt 138
earache øreverk c 141
ear drops øredråper c/pl 109
early tidlig 14, 31
earring ørering c 121
east øst 77
Easter påske c 152
easy lett 14
eat, to spise 36, 37, 62, 144
eel ål c 43, 46
egg egg nt 38, 45, 62, 64
eight åtte 147
eighteen atten 147
eighty åtti 147
elastic elastisk 109
Elastoplast plaster nt 109
electric(al) elektrisk 119
electrical appliance elektrisk utstyr nt 119
electrical goods shop elektrisitetsforretning c 98
electricity elektrisitet c 32
electronic elektronisk 125, 128
elevator heis c 27, 100, 155
eleven elleve 147
elk elg c 50
embarkation point kai c 73
embassy ambassade c 156
emergency nødsfall nt 156
emergency exit nødutgang c 27, 99, 155
emery board sandpapirfil c 110
empty tom 14
enamel emalje c 122
end slutt c 150
engaged (phone) opptatt 136
engagement ring forlovelsesring c 122
engine (car) motor c 78
England England 146
English engelsk 12, 82, 84, 104
English englender c 93
engrave, to gravere 121
enjoyable hyggelig 31
enlarge, to forstørre 125
enough nok 15
enquiry forespørsel c 68
entrance inngang c 67, 99, 155; innkjørsel c 79
entrance fee inngangsbillett c 82
entree (meal) hovedrett c 40
envelope konvolutt c 104
equipment utstyr nt 91, 106

eraser viskelær nt 104
escalator rulletrapp c 100
estimate (cost) overslag nt 131
Europe Europa 146
evening kveld c 87, 95, 96, 151, 153
evening dress (woman's) aftenkjole c 116
event begivenhet c 80; (sport) stevne nt 89
everything alt 61
examine, to undersøke 137
exchange, to bytte 103
exchange rate vekslingskurs c 18, 130
excursion utflukt c 80
excuse, to unnskylde 10
exercise book skrivebok c 104
exhaust pipe eksosrør nt 78
exhibition utstilling c 81
exit utgang c 67, 99, 155; utkjørsel c 79
expect, to vente 130
expenses utgift c 131
expensive dyr 14, 19, 24, 101
exposure (photography) bilde nt 124
exposure counter telleverk nt 125
express ekspress 132
expressway motorvei c 76
extension (phone) linje c 135
extension cord/lead skjøteledning c 119
extra ekstra 27, 36
eye øye nt 139
eyebrow pencil øyenbrynsstift c 110
eye drops øyendråper c/pl 109
eye liner eyeliner c 110
eye shadow øyenskygge c 110
eyesight syn c 123
eye specialist øyenlege c 137

F

fabric (cloth) (tøy)stoff nt 113
face ansikt nt 138
face flannel ansiktsklut c 110
face pack ansiktsmaske c 30
face powder pudder nt 110
facial tissue papirlommetørkle nt 111
factory fabrikk c 81
fair messe c 81
fall (autumn) høst c 149
fall, to falle 139
family familie c 93, 144

fan belt vifterem c 75
fantastic fantastisk 84
far fjern 14; langt 11, 100
fare takst c 69
farm bondegård c 85
fast hurtig 124
fat (meat) fett nt 37
father far c 93
faucet kran c 28
fax telefax c 133
February februar (c) 150
fee (doctor's) honorar nt 144
feeding bottle tåteflaske c 111
feel, to (physical state) føle seg 140, 142
felt filt c 114
felt-tip pen tusjpenn c 104
ferry ferge c 74; ferje c 74
fever feber c 140
few få 14; (a few) noen få 14
field jorde nt 85
fifteen femten 147
fifty femti 147
file (tool) fil c 110
fill in, to fylle ut 26, 144
filling (tooth) plombe c 145
filling station bensinstasjon c 75
film film c 86, 124, 125
film winder fremtrekker c 125
filter filter nt 125
filter-tipped med filter 126
find, to finne 11, 12, 100
fine (OK) bra 11, 25
finger finger c 138
finish, to slutte 87
Finland Finland 146
fire brann c 156
fire lighter tennvæske c 106
first første 68, 69, 148
first-aid kit førstehjelpsskrin nt 109
first class første klasse c 69
first name fornavn nt 25
fish fisk c 45
fish, to fiske 91
fishing fiske nt 90
fishing permit fiskekort nt 90
fishing tackle fiskeutstyr nt 106
fishmonger's fiskebutikk c 98
fit, to passe 115
five fem 147
fix, to reparere 75, 145
fizzy (mineral water) med kullsyre 59
fjord fjord c 85
flash (photography) blitz c 125

flashlight lommelykt c 106
flat (shoe) lavhælt 118
flat (apartment) leilighet c 19
flat tyre punktering c 75, 78
flatware (spise)bestikk nt 107
flea market loppemarked nt 81, 98
flight fly nt 65
flippers svømmeføtter c/pl 128
floor etasje c 23, 27, 154
floor show show nt 88
florist's blomsterbutikk c 98
flounder flyndre c 45
flour mel nt 37
flower blomst c 85
flu influensa c 142
fluid væske c 75, 123
foam rubber skumgummi c 106
fog tåke c 94
folding chair klappstol c 106
folding table klappbord nt 106
folk art folkekunst c 83
folk music folkemusikk c 128
follow, to følge 77
food mat c 37, 60, 111
food poisoning matforgiftning c 142
foot fot c 138
football fotball c 89
footbridge gangbro c 155
foot cream fotkrem c 110
footpath sti c 85
for for 15; (time) i 143, 151
forbid, to forby 155
forest skog c 85
forget, to glemme 60
fork gaffel c 36, 60, 107
form (document) blankett c 133; skjema nt 25, 26, 144
fortnight fjorten dager c/pl 151
fortress borg c 81
forty førti 147
foundation cream underlagskrem c 110
fountain fontene c 81
fountain pen fyllepenn c 104
four fire 147
fourteen fjorten 147
fowl fugl c 50
frame (for glasses) innfatning c 123
France Frankrike 146
free (of charge) gratis 155; (vacant) ledig 14, 71, 96, 155
French bean brekkbønne c 51
French fries pommes frites c/pl 52

fresh fersk 60; frisk 54
Friday fredag c 150
fried stekt 46, 49
fried egg speilegg nt 38, 45
friend venn c 93, 95
from fra 15
frost frost c 94
fruit frukt c 54, 55
fruit juice (frukt)juice c 37, 38
fruit salad fruktsalat c 54
frying pan stekepanne c 106
full full 14
full board helpensjon c 24
full insurance full forsikring c 20
fur coat pels c 116
furniture møbler nt/pl 83
furrier's pelsforretning c 98

G

gallery galleri nt 98
game spill nt 128; (food) vilt nt 50
gangway landgang c 74
garage (parking) garasje c 26;
    (repairs) bilverksted nt 78
garden(s) hage c 81, 85
garlic hvitløk c 52, 53
gas gass c 126, 156
gasoline bensin c 75
gastritis magekatarr c 142
gauze gasbind nt 109
gem edelsten c 121
general allmenn 27; vanlig 100
general delivery poste restante 133
general practitioner allmenn-
    praktiker c 137
genitals kjønnsorgan nt 138
gentleman herre c 155
genuine (real) ekte 118, 121
geology geologi c 83
Germany Tyskland 146
get, to (obtain) få 108; (fetch)
    skaffe 21, 31, 137; (find) få tak i
    11, 19, 21, 32
get off, to gå av 72
get to, to komme til 11, 19, 70, 76
get up, to stå opp 144
gherkin sylteagurk c 51, 64
gift gave c 17
gin and tonic gin tonic c 58
girdle hofteholder c 116
girl pike c 112
girlfriend venninne c 93
give, to gi 13, 131, 135
gland kjertel c 138
glass glass nt 36, 57, 59, 60

glasses briller c/pl 123
glasses case brillefutteral nt 123
gloomy dyster 84
glove hanske c 116
glue lim nt 105
go, to gå 96, 163
go away! gå vekk! 156
gold gull nt 121, 122
golden gullfarget 113
gold plated gullbelagt 122
golf golf c 89
golf course golfbane c 89
good bra 14, 101; god 10
good afternoon god dag 10
goodbye adjø 10
good evening god aften 10
Good Friday langfredag c 152
good morning god morgen 10
good night god natt 10
goods vare c 16
goose gås c 50
gooseberry stikkelsbær nt 54
go, to gå 163
go out, to gå ut 96
gram gram nt 120
grammar book grammatikk c 105
grape drue c 54, 64
grapefruit grapefrukt c 54
grapefruit juice grapefruktjuice c
    38, 59
gravel grus c 79
gravy brun saus c 52
gray grå 113
graze skrubbsår nt 139
greasy fet 30, 111
Great Britain Storbritannia 146
green grønn 113
green bean brekkbønne c 51
greengrocer's grønnsakhandel c
    98
greeting hilsen c 152
grey grå 113
grilled grillstekt 46, 49
grocer's matvarehandel c 98, 120
grotto grotte c 81
groundsheet teltunderlag nt 106
group gruppe c 82
guesthouse pensjonat nt 19, 22
guide guide c 80
guidebook guidebok c 82; reise-
    håndbok c 104, 105
gum (teeth) tannkjøtt nt 145
gymnasium trimrom nt 23
gynaecologist gynekolog c 137,
    141

DICTIONARY

H

habit vane *c* 34
hail hagl *nt* 94
hair hår *nt* 30, 111
hairbrush hårbørste *c* 111
haircut klipp *c* 30
hairdresser frisør *c* 98; frisørsalong *c* 27, 30
hair dryer hårføner *c* 119
hair dye hårfargingsmiddel *nt* 111
hair styling gel hårgelé *c* 111
hairgrip hårklemme *c* 111
hair lotion hårvann *nt* 111
hair mousse hårskum *nt* 111
hairpin hårnål *c* 111
hair slide hårspenne *c* 111
hair spray hårlakk *c* 30, 111
half halv 148
half halvpart *c* 148
half an hour halvtime *c* 153
half board halvpensjon *c* 24
half price halv pris *c* 69
hall porter portier *c* 26
ham skinke *c* 38, 48, 62, 64
ham and eggs egg og skinke 38
hamburger hamburger *c* 48
hammer hammer *c* 106
hammock hengekøye *c* 106
hand hånd *c* 138
handbag håndveske *c* 116, 156
hand cream håndkrem *c* 110
handicrafts kunsthåndverk *nt* 83, 127
handkerchief lommetørkle *nt* 116
handmade håndlaget 113
hanger (kles)henger *c* 27
happy god 152
harbour havn *c* 74, 81
hard hard 123
hard-boiled *(egg)* hardkokt 38
hardware store jernvarehandel *c* 98
hare hare *c* 50
hat hatt *c* 116
have, to ha 141, 162
hay fever høysnue *c* 108, 141
hazelnut hasselnøtt *c* 54
he han 162
head hode *nt* 138, 139
headache hodepine *c* 108, 141
headphones høretelefoner *c/pl* 119
head waiter hovmester *c* 61
health food shop helsekost-forretning *c* 99

health insurance sykeforsikring *c* 144
heart hjerte *nt* 138
heart attack hjerteslag *nt* 141
heated oppvarmet 90
heating varme *c* 23, 28
heavy tung 14, 101
heel hæl *c* 118
helicopter helikopter *nt* 74
hello hallo 10, 135
help hjelp *c* 156
help, to hjelpe 13, 21, 71, 100, 134; *(oneself)* ta selv 120
hen høne *c* 50
her hennes, sin, sitt *(pl* sine) 161
herb urt *c* 53
here her 14
herring sild *c* 41, 43, 46, 47
hi hei 10
high høy 85, 141
high season høysesong *c* 149
hike, to vandre 74
hill høyde *c* 85
hire utleie *c* 20
hire, to leie 19, 20, 74, 90, 91, 155
his hans, sin, sitt *(pl* sine) 161
history historie *c* 83
hitchhike, to haike 74
hold on! *(phone)* et øyeblikk! 136
hole hull *nt* 29
holiday helligdag *c* 151
holidays ferie *c* 16, 151, 152; *(school)* skoleferie *c* 151
home address hjemstedsadresse *c* 31
home town hjemsted *nt* 25
honey honning *c* 38
hope, to håpe 96
horseback riding ridning *c* 90
horse racing hesteveddeløp *nt* 89
horseradish pepperrot *c* 52
hospital sykehus *nt* 99, 144
hot varm 14, 25, 38, 59, 94, 155
hotel hotell *nt* 19, 21, 22
hotel directory/guide hotell-fortegnelse *c* 19
hotel reservation værelses-bestilling *c* 19
hot water varmt vann *nt* 23, 28
hot-water bottle varmeflaske *c* 27
hour time *c* 80, 90, 143, 153
house hus *nt* 83, 85
how hvordan 11
how far hvor langt 11, 76, 85
how long hvor lenge 11, 24

Ordliste

how many hvor mange 11
how much hvor mye 11, 24, 102
hundred hundre 147
hungry sulten 13, 35
hunting knife jaktkniv c 127
hurry *(to be in a)* ha det travelt 21
hurt, to gjøre vondt 140; ha vondt 140; verke 145; *(oneself)* slå seg 139
husband mann c 93
hydrofoil hydrofoil c 74

I
I jeg 162
ice is c 94
ice chest kjøleboks c 106
ice cream is(krem) c 55, 62
ice cube isbit c 27
iced tea iste c 59
ice hockey ishockey c 89
Iceland Island 146
ice pack kjøleelement nt 106
ignition tenning c 78
ill syk 140, 156
illness sykdom c 140
important viktig 13
imported importert 113
impressive imponerende 84
in i 15
include, to inkludere 24
included inkludert 20, 31, 40, 61, 80
India India 146
indicator *(car)* blinklys nt 78
indigestion fordøyelsesbesvær nt 141
indoor innendørs 90
inexpensive rimelig 35, 124
infected infisert 140
infection betennelse c 141
inflammation betennelse c 142
inflation inflasjon c 131
influenza influensa c 142
information informasjon c 67
information desk informasjons-skranke c 18
initial *(letter)* initial c 121
injection sprøyte c 142, 144
injure, to skade 139
injured skadet 79, 139
injury skade c 139
ink blekk nt 105
inlet vik c 85
inquiry forespørsel c 68
insect bite innsektstikk nt 108
insect killer insektgift c 106

insect repellent insektmiddel nt 109
insect spray insektgift c 106
inside inne 15
insole innleggssåle c 118
instant coffee pulverkaffe c 64
instead i stedet 37
insurance forsikring c 20, 71, 144
insurance company forsikrings-selskap nt 79
interest *(finance)* rente c 131
interested, to be være interessert 83
interesting interessant 84
international internasjonal 133
interpreter tolk c 131
intersection *(vei)*kryss nt 77
introduce, to presentere 92
introduction *(social)* presentasjon c 92
investment investering c 131
invitation innbydelse c 94
invite to, to by på 94
invoice faktura c 131
iodine jod c 109
Ireland Irland 146
Irish irlender c 93
iron *(for laundry)* strykejern nt 119
iron, to stryke 29
ironmonger's jernvarehandel c 99
island øy c 85
Israel Israel 146
its dens/dets, sin, sitt *(pl* sine) 161

J
jack *(tool)* jekk c 78
jacket jakke c 116
jam *(preserves)* syltetøy nt 38, 63
jam, to sitte fast 28, 125
January januar *(c)* 150
Japan Japan 146
jar *(container)* glass nt 120
jaundice gulsott c 142
jaw kjeve c 138
jeans jeans c/pl 116
jerry can bensinkanne c 78
jetty brygge c 74
jewel box smykkeskrin nt 121
jeweller's gullsmed c 99, 121
jewellery smykke nt 121
joint ledd nt 138
juice juice c 37, 38, 59
July juli *(c)* 150
June juni *(c)* 150
just *(only)* bare 16, 37, 100

K

kayak kajakk *c* 74
keep, to beholde 61
kerosene parafin *c* 106
key nøkkel *c* 27
kidney nyre *c* 48, 138
kilo(gram) kilo *nt* 120
kilometre kilometer *c* 20, 79
kind snill 96
kind *(type)* slags *nt/pl* 47, 140
knee kne *nt* 138
kneesocks knestrømper *c/pl* 116
knife kniv *c* 36, 60, 107
know, to kjenne 114; vite 16, 24, 96
krone *(money)* krone *c* 18, 101, 129

L

label etikett *c* 105, 133
lace knipling *c* 114
lady dame *c* 155
lake (inn)sjø *c* 81, 90
lamb *(meat)* lammekjøtt *nt* 47; lamme- 48
lamp lampe *c* 29, 106, 119
landmark landemerke *nt* 85
language språk *nt* 104, 159
lantern lykt *c* 106
large stor 20, 101, 118, 130
last forrige 150, 151; siste 14, 68
last, to vare 87
late forsinket 69, 70; sen 14
later senere 136
laugh, to le 95
launderette selvbetjeningsvaskeri *nt* 99
laundry *(place)* vaskeri *nt* 99; *(clothes)* vask *c* 29
laundry service vaskeri-service *c* 23
laxative laksermiddel *nt* 109
lead *(metal)* bly *nt* 75
leap year skuddår *nt* 149
leather lær *nt* 114, 118
leave, to *(depart)* gå 68, 69, 74, 95; reise 31; *(deposit)* deponere 26; *(hand in)* levere inn 71; *(return)* levere tilbake 20
leave alone, to la være i fred 156
leek purre *c* 51
left venstre 21, 62, 69, 77
left-luggage office bagasje-oppbevaring *c* 67, 71
leg ben *nt* 138
legal holiday offentlig høytidsdag *c* 152

lemon sitron *c* 38, 54, 59
lemonade sitronbrus *c* 59
lend, to låne 78
lens *(for glasses)* glass *nt* 123; *(for camera)* objektiv *nt* 125
lens cap linsebeskytter *c* 125
lentil linse *c* 51
less mindre 14
lesson time *c* 90
let, to *(hire out)* til leie 155
letter brev *nt* 28, 132
letter box postkasse *c* 132
letter of credit kredittbrev *nt* 130
lettuce hodesalat *c* 51
library bibliotek *nt* 81, 99
licence *(driving)* førerkort *nt* 20, 79
lie down, to legge seg ned 142
life belt livbelte *nt* 74
life boat livbåt *c* 74
life jacket flytevest *c* 74
lift *(elevator)* heis *c* 27, 100, 155
ligament leddbånd *nt* 140
light *(weight)* lett 14, 55, 101; *(colour)* lys 101, 112, 113
light lys *nt* 28, 124; *(for cigarette)* fyr *c* 95
light bulb lyspære *c* 28, 75, 119
lighter lighter *c* 126
lighter fluid lighterbensin *c* 126
lighter gas lightergass *c* 126
light meter lysmåler *c* 125
lightning lyn *nt* 94
like, to like 25, 92, 102, 112; ha lyst på 96; *(want)* ville 20
line linje *c* 73
linen *(cloth)* lin *nt* 114
lip leppe *c* 138
lipsalve leppepomade *c* 110
lipstick leppestift *c* 110
liqueur likør *c* 58
liquid *(fluid)* væske *c* 123
liquor store vinmonopol *nt* 99
listen to, to høre på 128
litre liter *c* 75, 120
little *(a little)* lite 14
live, to leve 83; *(reside)* bo 83
liver lever *c* 48, 64, 138
loan lån *nt* 131
lobster hummer *c* 43, 45
local lokal 36
local train lokaltog *nt* 66, 69
long lang 116
long time lang tid 60, 76, 116; lenge 77, 92, 144
long-sighted langsynt 123

look, to se 100, 123
look for, to se etter 13
look out! se opp! 156
loose løs 145; *(clothes)* vid 116
lose, to miste 123, 156
loss tap *nt* 131
lost, to be gå seg bort 13, 156
lost and found office hittegods-
   kontor *nt* 67, 156
lost property office hittegods-
   kontor *nt* 67, 156
lot *(a lot)* mye 14
loud *(voice)* høy 135
lovely herlig 94
low lav 141
lower under- 69, 71
low season lavsesong *c* 149
luggage bagasje *c* 18, 26, 31, 71;
   (registered) reisegods *nt/pl* 71
luggage insurance reisegods-
   forsikring *c* 71
luggage locker oppbevaringsboks
   c 18, 67, 71
luggage trolley bagasjetralle *c* 18,
   71
lunch lunsj *c* 27, 34, 80, 94
lung lunge *c* 138

M

machine maskin *c* 114
magazine ukeblad *nt* 105
magnificent storslagen 84
maid værelsespike *c* 26
mail post *c* 28, 132, 133
mail, to poste 28
mailbox postkasse *c* 132
main hoved- 80; størst 100
main course hovedrett *c* 40
make, to lage 113, 114
make up, to *(prepare)* gjøre i stand
   71, 108
make-up bag sminkepung *c* 110
man mann *c* 115, 156; herre *c* 155
manager bestyrer *c* 61; direktør *c*
   26
manicure manikyr *c* 30
man's ... herre- 116
many mange 11, 14
map kart *nt* 76, 105
March mars *(c)* 150
marinated marinert 46
maritime history sjøfartshistorie *c*
   83
market torghandel *c* 81, 99

marmalade appelsinmarmelade *c*
   38
married gift 93
marzipan marsipan *c* 63
mascara øyensverte *c* 110
mashed potatoes potetstappe *c*
   52, 62
mass *(church)* messe *c* 84
match *(matchstick)* fyrstikk *c* 106,
   126; *(sport)* kamp/match *c* 89
matinée matiné *c* 87
mattress madrass *c* 106
May mai *(c)* 150
may *(can)* kunne 12, 162
meadow eng *c* 85
meal måltid *nt* 24, 143
mean, to bety 11, 26
measles meslinger *c/pl* 142
measure, to ta mål av 114
meat kjøtt *nt* 47, 60
meatball frikadelle *c* 47; kjøttbolle
   c 48
mechanic mekaniker *c* 78
mechanical pencil skrublyant *c*
   105, 121
medical certificate legeattest *c*
   144
medicine medisin *c* 83, 143
medium *(meat)* medium stekt 49
medium-sized mellomstor 20
meet, to møtes 96; treffes 92; ses
   96
melon melon *c* 54
memorial minnesmerke *nt* 81
mend, to lappe 29; reparere 75
menstrual pains menstruasjonssmerter *c/pl* 141
menthol mentol *c* 126
menu meny *c* 36, 37, 39; *(printed)*
   spisekart *nt* 36, 39, 40
message beskjed *c* 28, 136
metre meter *c* 112
mezzanine *(theatre)* balkong *c*
   87
middle midten 69, 87, 150
midnight midnatt *c* 153
midnight sun midnattssol *c* 94
mild mild 126
mileage kjørelengde *c* 20
milk melk *c* 38, 59, 64
milkshake milkshake *c* 59
milliard milliard *c* 148
million million *c* 148
mineral water naturlig mineral
   vann *nt* 59

minister *(religion)* protestantisk prest *c* 84
minute minutt *nt* 21, 153
mirror speil *nt* 115, 123
miscellaneous forskjellig 127
Miss frøken *c* 92
miss, to mangle 18, 29, 60
mistake feil *c* 31, 61, 102; *(misunderstanding)* misforståelse *c* 60
modern moderne 83
modified American plan halvpensjon *c* 24
moisturizing cream fuktighetskrem *c* 110
moment øyeblikk *nt* 12, 136
monastery kloster *c* 81
Monday mandag *c* 150
money penger *c/pl* 129, 130
money order postanvisning *c* 133
month måned *c* 16, 150
monument monument *nt* 81
moon måne *c* 94
moped moped *c* 74
more mer 14
morning morgen *c* 31, 151, 153
mortgage hypotek *nt* 131
mosque moské *c* 84
mosquito net myggnett *nt* 106
mother mor *c* 93
motorbike motorsykkel *c* 74
motorboat motorbåt *c* 74
motorway motorvei *c* 76
mountain fjell *nt* 85
moustache bart *c* 31
mouth munn *c* 138
mouthwash munnvann *nt* 109
move, to bevege 139
movie film *c* 86
movies kino *c* 86, 96
Mr. herr *c* 92
Mrs. fru *c* 92
much mye 11, 14
mug krus *nt* 107
muscle muskel *c* 138
museum museum *nt* 81
mushroom sopp *c* 51
music musikk *c* 83, 128
musical musikal *c* 86
music box spilledåse *c* 121
mussel blåskjell *nt* 43, 45
must *(have to)* måtte 23, 31, 95
mustard sennep *c* 64
mutton fårekjøtt *nt* 42, 47, 49
my min, mitt *(pl* mine) 161

N

nail *(human)* negl *c* 110
nail brush neglebørste *c* 110
nail clippers negleklipper *c* 110
nail file neglefil *c* 110
nail polish neglelakk *c* 110
nail polish remover neglelakkfjerner *c* 110
nail scissors neglesaks *c* 110
name navn *nt* 23, 79, 133; *(surname)* etternavn *nt* 25
napkin serviett *c* 36, 105, 106
nappy bleie *c* 111
narrow trang 118
nationality nasjonalitet *c* 25, 92
natural history naturhistorie *c* 83
nauseous kvalm 140
near i nærheten av 19; nær 14
nearby i nærheten 77
nearest nærmeste 73, 75, 78, 132
neat *(drink)* bar 58
neck nakke *c* 30, 138
necklace halskjede *nt* 121
need, to trenge 29, 118, 137
needle nål *c* 27
negative negativ *nt* 124, 125
nephew nevø *c* 93
nerve nerve *c* 138
nervous system nervesystem *nt* 138
never aldri 15
new ny 14, 118, 149
newspaper avis *c* 104, 105
newsstand aviskiosk *c* 19, 67, 104
New Year nyttår *nt* 152
New Zealand Ny-Zealand 146
next neste 14, 65, 68, 73, 76, 149
next time neste gang 95
next to ved siden av 15, 77
nice *(beautiful)* pen 94
niece niese *c* 93
night natt *c* 10, 24, 151
nightclub nattklubb *c* 88
night cream nattkrem *c* 110
nightdress/-gown nattkjole *c* 116
nine ni 147
nineteen nitten 147
ninety nitti 147
no nei 10
noisy støyende 25
nonalcoholic alkoholfri 56, 57, 59
none ingen 15
nonsmoker ikke-røyker *c* 36
noodle nudel *c* 52
noon klokken tolv (om dagen) 153

normal normal 30
north nord 77
North America Nord-Amerika 146
Norway Norge 113, 146
Norwegian norsk 11, 12, 18, 95, 114, 127
nose nese c 138
nosebleed neseblødning c 141
nose drops nesedråper c/pl 109
not ikke 15, 163
note (banknote) seddel c 130
notebook notisbok c 105
note paper brevpapir nt 105
nothing ikke noe 15, 17; ingenting 15, 16
notice (sign) oppslag nt 155
notify, to underrette 144
November november (c) 150
now nå 15
number nummer nt 25, 134, 135, 136; tall nt 147
nurse sykepleier c 144

O

observatory observatorium nt 81
occupation (profession) yrke nt 25
occupied opptatt 14, 155
ocean hav nt 85
o'clock kl./klokken c 154
October oktober (c) 150
office kontor nt 22, 67, 80, 132
oil olje c 37, 75, 111
oily (greasy) fet 30, 111
ointment salve c 109
old gammel 14, 149
old town gamleby c 81
omelet omelett c 38, 45
on på 15
once en gang 148
one en 147
one-way ticket enkeltbillett c 65, 69
on foot til fots 76
onion løk c 51, 62
only bare 15, 24
on time i rute 68
open åpen 14, 82, 129, 155
open, to åpne 11, 17, 82, 108, 130
open-air utendørs 90
opening hours åpningstider c/pl 155
opera opera c 88
opera house operahus nt 81, 88
operation operasjon c 144

operator telefonist c 134
operetta operette c 88
opposite midt imot 77
opposite motsetning c 14
optician optiker c 99, 123
or eller 15
orange oransje 113
orange appelsin c 54, 64
orange juice appelsinjuice c 38, 59
orchestra orkester nt 88; (seats) parkett c 87
order, to (goods, meal) bestille 36, 60, 102, 103
ornithology ornitologi c 83
other andre 58, 74, 101
our vår, vårt (pl våre) 161
out of order i uorden 136
out of stock utsolgt 103
outlet (electric) stikkontakt c 27
outside ute 15, 36
oval oval 101
overalls overall c 116
overdone for mye stekt 60
overheat, to (engine) gå varm 78
overnight (stay) natten over 24
overtake, to kjøre forbi 79
owe, to skylde 144
oyster østers c 43, 46

P

pacifier (baby's) narresmokk c 111
packet pakke c 120, 126
pail spann nt 128
pain smerte c 140, 141, 143, 144
painkiller smertestillende middel nt 109
paint, to male 83
paintbox malerskrin nt 105
painter maler c 83
pair par nt 116, 118, 148
pajamas pyjamas c 117
palace slott nt 81
palpitation hjerteklapp c 141
pancake pannekake c 45
panties truser c/pl 116
pants (trousers) langbukser c/pl 117
panty hose strømpebukse c 117
paper papir nt 105
paperback pocketbok c 105
paperclip binders c 105
paper napkin papirserviett c 105
paper towel husholdningspapir nt 106
paraffin (fuel) parafin c 106

parcel pakke *c* 132
pardon unnskyld 10
parents foreldre *c/pl* 93
park park *c* 81
park, to parkere 26, 77
parka anorakk *c* 117
parking parkering *c* 77, 79
parking garage parkeringshus *nt* 77
parking lot parkeringsplass *c* 77
parking meter parkometer *nt* 77
parliament building storting *nt* 81
parsley persille *c* 53
part del *c* 138
partridge rapphøne *c* 50
party *(social gathering)* fest *c* 95
pass, to *(driving)* kjøre forbi 79
passport pass *nt* 16, 17, 25, 26, 156
passport photo passfoto *nt* 124
pass through, to være på gjennomreise 16
pastry bakverk *nt* 63
pastry shop konditori *nt* 99
path sti *c* 85
patient pasient *c* 144
pattern mønster *nt* 112
pay, to betale 31, 61, 100, 102
payment betaling *c* 131
pea ert *c* 51
peach fersken *c* 54
peak topp *c* 85
pear pære *c* 54
pearl perle *c* 122
pearl strand perlekjede *nt* 121
peg *(tent)* plugg *c* 107
pen penn *c* 105
pencil blyant *c* 105
pendant hengesmykke *nt* 121
penicillin penicillin *nt* 143
penknife lommekniv *c* 106
pensioner pensjonist *c* 82
people folk *nt/pl* 92
pepper pepper *c* 37, 38, 53, 64
per cent prosent *c* 148
percentage prosentsats *c* 131
per day pr. dag 20, 32, 90
perfume parfyme *c* 110
perfumery parfymeri *nt* 99
perhaps kanskje 15
per hour pr. time 77, 90
period *(monthly)* menstruasjon *c* 141
period pains menstruasjonssmerter *c/pl* 141
permanent wave permanent *c* 30

per night pr. natt 24
per person pr. person 32
person person *c* 32
personal personlig 17
personal call personlig samtale *c* 134
person-to-person call personlig samtale *c* 134
per week pr. uke 20, 24
petrol bensin *c* 75, 78
pewter tinn *c* 122
pharmacy apotek *nt* 99, 108
pheasant fasan *c* 50
photo bilde *nt* 125; foto *nt* 124
photocopy fotokopi *c* 131
photograph, to fotografere 82
photographer fotograf *c* 99
photography fotografering *c* 124
phrase uttrykk *nt* 12
phrase book parlør *c* 105
pick up, to *(person)* hente 80, 96
pickled gherkin sylteagurk *c* 51, 64
picnic picnic *c* 64
picture bilde *nt* 83
picture-book billedbok *c* 105
piece stykke *nt* 63, 120
pier pir *c* 74
pill pille *c* 109; *(contraceptive)* p-pille *c* 141
pillow pute *c* 27
pin nål *c* 110, 111, 122
pineapple ananas *c* 54
pink rosa 113
pipe pipe *c* 126
pipe cleaner piperenser *c* 126
place sted *nt* 25, 76
place of birth fødested *nt* 25
plane fly *nt* 65
plaster, to put in gipse 140
plastic plast *c* 107
plastic bag plastpose *c* 107
plate asjett *c* 127; tallerken *c* 36, 60, 107
platform *(station)* perrong *c* 67, 68, 69, 70
play *(theatre)* stykke *nt* 86, 87
play, to spille 86, 88, 89, 93
playground lekeplass *c* 32
playing card spillkort *nt* 105
please vær (så) snill å ... 10; ... takk 10
pliers tang *c* 78, 107
plimsoll turnsko *c* 118
plug *(electric)* støpsel *nt* 29
plum plomme *c* 54

pneumonia lungebetennelse *c* 142
poached pochert 46; *(egg)*
  forlorent 45
pocket lomme *c* 117
pocket calculator lommekalkulator
  c 105
pocket dictionary lommeordbok *c*
  104
pocketknife lommekniv *c* 107
pocket radio lommeradio *c* 119
pocket watch lommeur *nt* 121
point, to peke 12
poison gift *c* 109, 156
poisoning forgiftning *c* 142
pole *(ski)* stav *c* 91; *(tent)* stang *c*
  107
police politi *nt* 79, 156
police station politistasjon *c* 99,
  156
polo-neck høyhalset 117
pond dam *c* 85
pork svinekjøtt *nt* 47; svine- 48
porridge grøt *c* 38
port havn *c* 74; *(wine)* portvin *c* 58
portable bærbar 119
porter bærer *c* 18, 26, 71
portion porsjon *c* 37, 60
possible mulig 137
post *(mail)* post *c* 28, 133
post, to poste 28
postage porto *c* 132
postage stamp frimerke *nt* 28, 126,
  132, 133
postcard postkort *nt* 105, 126, 132
poste restante poste restante 133
post office postkontor *nt* 99, 132
pot kanne *c* 59
potato potet *c* 52
pottery pottemakerkunst *c* 83
poultry fugl *c* 50
pound pund *nt (money)* 18, 102,
  130, *(weight)* 120
powder pudder *nt* 110
powder compact pudderdåse *c*
  121
prawn reke *c* 43, 46
prefer, to foretrekke 101
pregnant gravid 141
premium *(gasoline)* super 75
prescribe, to skrive ut 143
prescription resept *c* 108, 143
present presang *c* 121
press, to *(iron)* presse 29
press stud trykknapp *c* 117
pressure trykk *nt* 75, 141

pretty søt 84
price pris *c* 69, 124
priest katolsk prest *c* 84
primus stove primus *c* 107
print *(photo)* kopi *c* 125
private privat 80, 155
processing *(photo)* fremkalling *c*
  124
profit utbytte *nt* 131
programme program *nt* 87
pronounce, to uttale 12
pronunciation uttale *c* 6
propelling pencil skrublyant *c* 105
propose, to anbefale 40
Protestant protestantisk 84
provide, to skaffe 131
prune sviske *c* 54
ptarmigan rype *c* 50
public holiday offentlig høytidsdag
  c 152
pull, to trekke 155
pullover genser *c* 117
pump pumpe *c* 107
puncture punktering *c* 75
purchase kjøp *nt* 131
pure ren 114
purple fiolett 113
push, to *(open)* skyve 155
put, to sette 24
pyjamas pyjamas *c* 117

Q
quail vaktel *c* 50
quality kvalitet *c* 113
quantity mengde *c* 14
quarter fjerdedel *c* 148; *(district of
  town)* kvarter *nt* 81
quarter of an hour kvarter *nt* 153
question spørsmål *nt* 11
quick rask 14
quickly øyeblikkelig 137, 156
quiet rolig 23, 25
quilt dyne *c* 27

R
rabbi rabbiner *c* 84
rabbit kanin *c* 50
race (vedde)løp *nt* 89
race course/track heste-
  veddeløpsbane *c* 89
racket *(sport)* racket *c* 90
radiator *(car)* kjøler *c* 78
radio radio *c* 23, 28, 119

radio cassette recorder radio-
kassettopptaker *c* 119
railway jernbane *c* 67, 154
railway station jernbanestasjon *c*
19, 21, 67
rain regn *nt* 94
rain, to regne 94
rainbow trout regnbueørret *c* 46
raincoat regnfrakk *c* 117
rainy regnfull 94
raisin rosin *c* 54, 63
rangefinder avstandsmåler *c* 125
rare *(meat)* blodig 60; råstekt 49
rash utslett *nt* 139
raspberry bringebær *nt* 54
rate *(of exchange)* kurs *c* 18, 130
razor barberhøvel *c* 110
razor blade barberblad *nt* 110
read, to lese 27
reading lamp leselampe *c* 27
ready ferdig 118, 123, 125, 145;
klar 29, 31
real *(genuine)* ekte 118, 121
rear bak 69, 75
reason *(purpose)* hensikt *c* 25
receipt kvittering *c* 102, 103, 144
reception resepsjon *c* 23
receptionist resepsjonist *c* 26
recommend, to anbefale 35, 36,
80, 145; *(suggest)* foreslå 44
record *(disc)* plate *c* 127, 128
record player platespiller *c* 119
rectangular rektangulær 101
red rød 113
redcurrant rips *c* 54
reduction rabatt *c* 82; reduksjon *c*
24
refill *(pen)* refill *c* 105
refrigerator kjøleskap *nt* 28
refund, to get a få pengene tilbake
103
regards hilsen *c* 152
register, to *(luggage)* ekspedere
71; *(mail)* rekommandere 132
registered mail rekommandert 132
registration innskriving *c* 25
registration form meldeskjema *nt*
25
regular *(petrol)* normal 75
reindeer reinsdyr *nt* 50
reindeer skin reinsdyrskinn *nt* 127
religion religion *c* 83
religious service gudstjeneste *c* 84
rent, to leie 19, 20, 74, 90, 91, 155
rental utleie *c* 20

repair reparasjon *c* 125
repair, to reparere 29, 118, 119,
121, 123, 125, 145
repeat gjenta 12
report, to *(a theft)* anmelde 156
reservation bestilling *c* 19, 69;
reservasjon *c* 65
reserve, to bestille 19, 23, 35, 87;
reservere 69, 155
restaurant restaurant *c* 33, 35, 67
return ticket tur-returbillett *c* 65,
69
return, to *(come back)* være tilbake
21, 80; *(give back)* levere tilbake
103
reverse-charge call noteringsoverføring *c* 135
revue revy *c* 86
rheumatism reumatisme *c* 141
rib ribben *nt* 138
ribbon bånd *nt* 105
rice ris *c* 52
ridge ås *c* 85
right *(correct)* 14; *(direction)* høyre
21, 62, 69, 77
ring *(jewellery)* ring *c* 122
river elv *c* 85, 90
road vei *c* 76, 77
road assistance hjelp på veien *c* 78
road map veikart *nt* 105
road sign trafikkskilt *nt* 79
roast ovnsstekt 49
roast stek *c* 47, 48
roast beef oksestek *c* 48; roastbiff *c*
48
roll rull *c* 109; *(bread)* rundstykke
nt 38, 64
roller skates rulleskøyter *c/pl* 128
roll film rullefilm *c* 124
romantic romantisk 84
room rom *nt* 19, 23, 24, 25; *(space)*
plass *c* 32
room number romnummer *nt* 26
rope tau *nt* 107
rosé rosévin *c* 58
round rund 101
round *(golf)* runde *c* 90
round-trip ticket tur-returbillett *c*
65, 69
route vei *c* 85
rowing boat robåt *c* 74
royal kongelig 81
rubber *(eraser)* viskelær *nt* 105;
(material) gummi *c* 118
rubber band gummistrikk *c* 105

rucksack ryggsekk *c* 107
ruin ruin *c* 82
ruler *(for measuring)* linjal *c* 105
rum rom *c* 58
running water rennende vann *nt* 23

S

safe *(free from danger)* trygg 90
safe safe *c* 26
safety pin sikkerhetsnål *c* 110
sailing boat seilbåt *c* 74
salad salat *c* 44, 51
sale salg *nt* 131; *(bargains)* (ut)salg 100, 155
sales tax moms *c* 24, 102, 154
salmon laks *c* 43, 46, 47
salt salt *nt* 37, 38, 53, 64
salty salt 60
same samme 118
sand sand *c* 90
sandal sandal *c* 118
sandwich smørbrød *nt* 41, 62
sanitary napkin/towel sanitetsbind *nt* 109
Saturday lørdag *c* 150
sauce saus *c* 52
saucepan kasserolle *c* 107
saucer skål (til kopp) *c* 107
sauna badstue *c* / sauna *c* 23, 32
sausage pølse *c* 48, 62, 64
Scandinavia Skandinavia 25
scarf skjerf *nt* 117
scenery *(landscape)* natur *c* 92
scenic naturskjønn 85
school skole *c* 151
school holidays skoleferie *c* 151
scissors saks *c* 107, 110
scooter scooter *c* 74
Scotland Skottland 146
scrambled egg eggerøre *c* 38
screwdriver skrutrekker *c* 107
sculptor billedhugger *c* 83
sculpture skulptur *c* 83
sea sjø *c* 85, 90
seafood sjømat *nt/pl* 45
sealskin selskinn *nt* 127
search for, to lete etter 13
season årstid *c* 149
seasoning krydder *nt* 37
seat plass *c* 69, 70, 87
seat belt bilbelte *nt* 75
second andre 148; annen 148
second sekund *nt* 153

second class andre klasse *c* 69; annen klasse *c* 69
second hand sekundviser *c* 122
second-hand shop marsjandiseforretning *c* 99
secretary sekretær *c* 27, 131
see, to se 12, 80; *(examine)* undersøke 137
self-adhesive selvklebende 105
sell, to selge 100
send, to sende 78, 102, 132, 133
send up, to bringe opp 26
senior citizen pensjonist *c* 82
sentence setning *c* 12
September september *(c)* 150
serve, to servere 27, 40
service *(church)* gudstjeneste *c* 84
service charge service *c* 61
serviette serviett *c* 36
set menu meny *c* 36
setting lotion leggevann *nt* 30, 111
seven sju 147
seventeen sytten 147
seventy sytti 147
sew, to sy 29
shade *(colour)* nyanse *c* 112
shallow langgrunt 91
shampoo sjampo *c* 30, 111
shampoo and set vask og legg *c* 30
shape form *c* 103
share *(finance)* aksje *c* 131
shave barbering *c* 31
shaver barbermaskin *c* 27, 119
shaving cream barberkrem *c* 111
she hun 162
shellfish skalldyr *nt/pl* 45
sherbet sorbett *c* 55
ship skip *nt* 74
shirt skjorte *c* 117
shoe sko *c* 118
shoelace skolisse *c* 118
shoemaker's skomaker *c* 99
shoe polish skokrem *c* 118
shoe shop skoforretning *c* 99
shop butikk *c* / forretning *c* 98, 99
shopping shopping *c* 97
shopping area handlestrøk *nt* 82, 100
shopping centre butikksenter *nt* 99
shop window (utstillings)vindu *nt* 100, 112
short kort 30, 116
shorts shorts *c/pl* 117
short-sighted nærsynt 123

shoulder skulder *c* 138
shovel spade *c* 128
show nt 88; *(theatre)* forestilling *c* 87
show, to vise 13, 76, 100, 101, 119
shower dusj *c* 23, 32
shrimp reke *c* 43, 46
shrink, to krympe 114
shut stengt 14
shutter *(camera)* lukker *c* 125
sick *(ill)* syk 140, 156
sickness *(illness)* sykdom *c* 140
side side *c* 31
sideboards/-burns kinnskjegg *nt* 31
side dish tilbehør *nt* 40
sightseeing sightseeing *c* 80
sightseeing tour sightseeingtur *c* 80
sign *(notice)* skilt *nt* 79, 155
sign, to undertegne 26, 130
signature underskrift *c* 25
signet ring signetring *c* 122
silk silke *c* 114
silver *(colour)* sølvfarget 113
silver sølv *nt* 121, 122
silver plate sølvplett *c* 122
silverware sølvtøy *nt* 122
simple enkel 124
since siden 15, 150
sing, to synge 88
single *(unmarried)* ugift 93
single enkel 74; *(unmarried)* ugift 93
single room enkeltrom *nt* 19, 23
single ticket enkeltbillett *c* 65, 69
sink vask *c* 28
sister søster *c* 93
sit down, to sette seg 95, 142
six seks 147
sixteen seksten 147
sixty seksti 147
size *(clothes)* størrelse *c* 114, 115; *(film)* format *nt* 124; *(shoes)* nummer *nt* 118
skate skøyte *c* 91
skating rink skøytebane *c* 91
ski ski *c* 91
ski, to gå på ski 91
ski boot skistøvel *c* 91
ski jumping skihopping *c* 89
ski lift skiheis *c* 91
skin hud *c* 138
ski race skirenn *nt* 89
skirt skjørt *nt* 117
ski run skibakke *c* 91

ski track/trail skiløype *c* 91
sky himmel *c* 94
sleep, to sove 144
sleeping bag sovepose *c* 107
sleeping car sovevogn *c* 68, 71
sleeping pill sovetablett *c* 143
sleeve erme *nt* 116
slice skive *c* 62, 120
sliced oppskåret 120
slide *(photo)* lysbilde *nt* 124
slide film film for lysbilder *nt/p*124
slide projector lysbildeapparat *nt* 125
slip *(underwear)* underkjole *c* 117
slipper tøffel *c* 118, 127
slow sakte 14
slowly langsom 12, 135; sakte 21
small liten 14, 20, 25, 101, 118, 130
smoke, to røyke 95
smoked røkt 42, 43, 46, 49
smoker røyker *c* 36
smorgasbord koldtbord *nt* 41
snack småretter *c/pl* 62
snack bar snackbar *c* 67
snail snegle *c* 43
snap fastener trykknapp *c* 117
snorkel snorkel *c* 128
snow snø *c* 94
snow, to snø 94
snuff snus *c* 126
soap såpe *c* 27, 111
soccer fotball *c* 89
sock sokk *c* 117
socket *(electric)* stikkontakt *c* 27
soda water sodavann *nt* 58
soft myk 123
soft-boiled *(egg)* bløtkokt 38
soft drink leskedrikk 40, 59, 64
soft ice cream softis *c* 62
sold out utsolgt 87, 155
sole *(fish)* sjøtunge *c* 46; *(shoe)* såle *c* 118
soloist solist *c* 88
some litt15; noe 15
someone noen 95
something noe 29, 36, 55, 108
son sønn *c* 93
song sang *c* 128
soon snart 15, 137
sorbet sorbett *c* 55
sore *(painful)* sår 141, 145
sorry, to be beklage 10, 16, 103
sort *(kind)* slags *nt/pl* 86, 120
soup suppe *c* 44
south sør 77

South Africa Sør-Afrika 146
South America Sør-Amerika 146
souvenir suvenir c 127
souvenir shop suvenirbutikk c 99
spade spade c 128
spanner skrunøkkel c 78
sparerib svineribbe c 48
spare tyre reservedekk nt 75
spark(ing) plug tennstift c 75
sparkling (spring water) med kull-
    syre 59; (wine) musserende 58
speak, to snakke 12, 135
speaker (loudspeaker) høyttaler c
    119
special spesial- 20, 37; spesiell 80
specialist spesialist c 142
speciality spesialitet c 36, 40, 42
specimen (medical) prøve c 142
spell, to bokstavere 12
spend, to gi 101
spice krydder nt 53
spinach spinat c 51
spine ryggrad c 138
sponge svamp c 111
sponge bag toalettmappe c 111
spoon skje c 36, 60, 107
sport sport c 89
sporting event sportsstevne nt
    89
sporting goods shop sports-
    forretning c 99
sportswear sportsklær pl 117
sprain, to vrikke 140
spring (season) vår c 149; (water)
    kilde c 85
spring water naturlig mineralvann
    nt 59
square firkantet 101
square plass c 82; torg nt 82
stadium stadion nt 82
staff (personnel) personale nt 26
stain flekk c 29
stainless steel rustfritt stål nt 107
stalls (theatre) parkett c 87
stamp (postage) frimerke nt 28,
    126, 132, 133
staple heftestift c 105
stapler heftemaskin c 105
star stjerne c 94
start, to starte 78, 80
starter (meal) forrett c 43
station stasjon c; (railway)
    jernbanestasjon 19, 21, 67, 70;
    (underground/subway)
    T-banestasjon 73

stationer's papirhandel c 99, 104
statue statue c 82
stave church stavkirke c 82
stay opphold nt 31
stay, to bli 16, 24; (reside) bo 93
steak biff c 47
steal, to stjele 156
steamed dampkokt 46
steamer dampbåt c 74
steering (car) styring c 78
stew pot gryte c 107
stiff stiv 141
still (mineral water) uten kullsyre
    59
sting stikk nt 139
sting, to bite 139
stitch, to sy sammen 29, 118
stock exchange børs c 82
stocking strømpe c 117
stomach mage c 138
stomach ache magesmerte c 141
stools avføring c 142
stop (place) holdeplass c, 72
stop, to stanse 21, 68, 72; stå 70
stop thief! stopp tyven! 156
store (shop) butikk c 98, 99;
    forretning c 98, 99
straight (drink) bar 58
straight ahead rett frem 21, 77
strange underlig 84
strawberry jordbær nt 54, 55
stream bekk c 85
street gate c 77
streetcar trikk c 72
street map kart nt 19, 105
string hyssing c 105; (of pearls)
    perlekjede nt 121
strong sterk 126, 143
student student c 82, 93
study, to studere 93
stuffed fylt 49, 51
sturdy robust 101; solid 101
styling gel hårgelé c 111
subway (railway) T-bane c 73
suede semsket skinn nt 114, 118
sugar sukker nt 37, 64
suit (man's) dress c 117;
    (woman's) drakt c 117
suitcase koffert c 18
summer sommer c 149
sun sol c 94
sunburn solforbrenning c 108, 141
Sunday søndag c 150
sunglasses solbriller c/pl 123
sunshade (beach) parasoll c 91

sun-tan cream solkrem *c* 110
sun-tan oil sololje *c* 111
super *(petrol)* super 75
superb ypperlig 84
supermarket supermarked *nt* 99
suppository stikkpille *c* 109
surgery *(consulting room)* legekontor *nt* 137
surname etternavn *nt* 25
suspenders *(Am.)* (bukse)seler *c/pl*
117
swallow, to svelge 143
sweater genser *c* 117
sweat suit treningsdrakt *c* 117
Sweden Sverige 146
sweet søt 58, 60
sweet *(confectionery)* godter *nt/pl*
126
sweet corn mais *c* 51
sweetener søtningsmiddel *nt* 37
sweet pepper paprika *c* 51
sweet shop godtebutikk *c* 99
swelling hevelse *c* 139
swim, to bade 90; svømme 90
swimming svømming *c* 90
swimming pool badebasseng *nt*
32; svømmebasseng *nt* 23, 90
swimming trunks badebukse *c* 117
swimsuit badedrakt *c* 117
switch *(electric)* bryter *c* 29
switch on, to sette i gang 119
switchboard operator sentralbord-
betjent *c* 26
swollen hoven 139
synagogue synagoge *c* 84
synthetic syntetisk 114
system system *nt* 138

T

table bord *nt* 36; *(list)* tabell *c* 157
tablet *(medical)* tablett *c* 109, 143
tailor's skredder *c* 99
tail pipe eksosrør *nt* 78
take, to ta 18, 25, 60, 73, 76, 102
take away, to *(carry)* ta med seg
62
talcum powder talkum *c* 111
tampon tampong *c* 109
tap *(water)* kran *c* 28
tap beer fatøl *nt* 56
taste, to smake 60
tax skatt *c* 131
tax-free shop tax-free-butikk *c* 19
taxi drosje *c* 18, 19, 21, 31, 67

taxi rank/stand drosjeholdeplass *c*
21
tea te *c* 38, 59, 64
team lag *nt* 89
teashop konditori *nt* 33
teaspoon teskje *c* 107, 143
telegram telegram *nt* 133
telegraph office telesenter *nt* 99,
133
telephone telefon *c* 27, 28, 79, 134
telephone, to *(call)* ringe 134, 136
telephone booth telefonkiosk *c* 134
telephone call (telefon)samtale *c*
136; telefon *c* 136
telephone directory telefonkatalog
c 134
telephone number (telefon-
nummer *nt* 134, 135, 136
telephoto lens teleobjektiv *nt* 125
television TV *c* 23, 28, 119
telex telex *c* 133
telex, to sende telex 130
tell, to si 13, 76, 153
temperature temperatur *c* 142;
(fever) feber *c* 140
temporary provisorisk 145
ten ti 147
tendon sene *c* 138
tennis tennis *c* 89
tennis court tennisbane *c* 89
tennis match tenniskamp *c* 89
tennis racket (tennis)racket *c* 90
tent telt *nt* 32, 107
tent peg teltplugg *c* 107
tent pole teltstang *c* 107
terrible forferdelig 84
tetanus stivkrampe *c* 140
than enn 14
thank, to takke 10, 95, 96
that den 161; det 11, 100, 161
theatre teater *nt* 82, 86
theft tyveri *nt* 156
their deres 161
then da 15
there der 14
thermometer termometer *nt* 109
these disse 62, 161
they de 162; dem 162
thief tyv *c* 156
thigh lår *nt* 138
thin tynn 113
think, to *(believe)* tro 31, 94
thirsty tørst 13, 35
thirteen tretten 147
thirty tretti 147

this denne 161; dette 11, 100, 161
those dem 62, 120; de 161
thousand tusen 148
thread tråd *c* 27
three tre 147
throat hals *c* 138, 141
throat lozenge halstablett *c* 109
through gjennom 15; til 151
through train gjennomgående tog *nt* 68, 69
thumb tommel *c* 138
thumbtack tegnestift *c* 105
thunder torden *c* 94
thunderstorm tordenvær *nt* 94
Thursday torsdag *c* 150
ticket billett *c* 65, 69, 72, 87, 89
ticket office billettluke *c* 67
tie slips *nt* 117
tie clip slipsklype *c* 122
tie pin slipsnål *c* 122
tight *(close-fitting)* trang 116
tights strømpebukse *c* 117
time tid *c* 80; *(occasion)* gang *c* 95, 148; *(clock)* klokken 153
timetable rutetabell *c* 68
tin *(container)* boks *c* 120
tin opener boksåpner *c* 107
tint hårtoningsmiddel *nt* 111
tinted farget 123
tire dekk *nt* 75
tired trett 13
tissue *(handkerchief)* papir-lommetørkle *nt* 111
tissue paper silkepapir *nt* 105
to til 15; å 162
toast ristet brød *nt* 38
tobacco tobakk *c* 126
tobacconist's tobakkshandel *c* 99, 126
today i dag 29, 150, 151
toe tå *c* 138
toilet paper toalettpapir *nt* 111
toiletries bag toalettmappe *c* 111
toiletry toalettartikkel *c* 110
toilets toalett *nt* 27, 32, 67
toilet water eau de toilette *c* 111
tomato tomat *c* 51
tomato juice tomatjuice *c* 43
tomb grav *c* 82
tomorrow i morgen 29, 94, 96, 151
tongue tunge *c* 48, 138
tonic tonic *c* 58
tonight i kveld 29, 86, 87, 88, 96
tonsils mandler *c/pl* 138
too for 15, 19; *(also)* også 15, 75

tool verktøy *nt* 78
too much for mye 15
tooth tann *c* 145
toothache tannpine *c* 145
toothbrush tannbørste *c* 111, 119
toothpaste tannpasta *c* 111
torch *(flashlight)* lommelykt *c* 107
torn avslitt 140
tough *(meat)* seig 60
tour tur *c* 74, 80
tourist office turistkontor *nt* 22, 80
towards mot 15
towel håndkle *nt* 111
tower tårn *nt* 82
town by *c* 19, 88
town hall rådhus *nt* 82
towrope slepetau *nt* 78
tow truck kranbil *c* 78
toy leke *c* 128
toy shop leketøysbutikk *c* 99
track *(railway)* spor *nt* 67, 68, 69
track-and-field meeting friidretts-stevne *nt* 89
tracksuit treningsdrakt *c* 117
traffic trafikk *c* 76
traffic light trafikklys *nt* 77
trailer campingvogn *c* 32
train tog *nt* 66, 67, 68, 69, 70
tram trikk *c* 72
tranquillizer beroligende middel *nt* 143
transfer *(finance)* overføring *c* 131
transformer transformator *c* 119
translate, to oversette 12
translation oversettelse *c* 131
translator oversetter *c* 131
transport transport *c* 74
travel, to reise 93
travel agency reisebyrå *nt* 99
travel guide reisehåndbok *c* 105
traveller's cheque reisesjekk *c* 18, 61, 102, 130
travel sickness reisesyke *c* 108
treatment behandling *c* 143
tree tre *nt* 85
tremendous forskrekkelig 84
trim, to *(a beard)* stusse 31
trip reise *c* 93, 152; tur *c* 74
troll troll *nt* 127
trolley tralle *c* 18, 71
trousers langbukser *c/pl* 117
trout ørret *c* 46; aure *c* 45
try, to forsøke 136; *(sample)* prøve 42, 57

try on, to prøve 115

T-shirt T-skjorte *c* 117
tube tube *c* 120
Tuesday tirsdag *c* 150
tumbler drikkeglass *nt* 107
turkey kalkun *c* 50
turn, to *(change direction)* svinge 21
turtleneck høyhalset 117
tweezers pinsett *c* 111
twelve tolv 147
twenty tjue 147
twice to ganger 148
twin beds to senger *c/pl* 23
two to 147
typewriter skrivemaskin *c* 27
typically typisk 127
typing paper skrivemaskinpapir *nt* 105
tyre dekk *nt* 75

U

ugly stygg 14, 84
umbrella paraply *c* 117
uncle onkel *c* 93
unconscious bevisstløs 139
under under 15
underdone *(meat)* råstekt 49; for lite stekt 60
underground *(railway)* T-bane *c* 73
underpants underbukse *c* 117
undershirt trøye *c* 117
understand, to forstå 12, 16
undress, to kle av seg 142
United States USA 146
university universitet *nt* 82
unleaded blyfri 75
until til 15, 150
up opp 15, 155
upper over- 69
upset stomach urolig mage *c* 108
upstairs oppe 15; opp trappen 69
urgent, to be haste 13
urine urin *c* 142
use bruk *c* 17, 109
useful nyttig 15
usual vanlig 143

V

vacancy ledig rom *nt* 23
vacant ledig 14
vacation ferie *c* 16, 151, 152
vaccinate, to vaksinere 140
vacuum flask termosflaske *c* 107
vaginal infection underlivs-betennelse *c* 141

valid gyldig 65
valley dal *c* 85
value verdi *c* 131
value-added tax moms *c* 24, 102
vanilla vanilje *c* 55
VAT *(sales tax)* moms *c* 154
veal kalvekjøtt *nt* 47; kalve- 48
vegetable grønnsak *c* 40, 51
vegetable store grønnsakhandel *c* 99
vegetarian vegetar(isk) 37, 40
vein vene *c* 138; åre *c* 138
venereal disease kjønnssykdom *c* 142
venetian blind persienne *c* 29
venison rådyr *nt* 50
very meget 15
vest trøye *c* 117; *(Am.)* vest *c* 117
veterinarian dyrlege *c* 99
video camera videokamera *nt* 124
video cassette videokassett *c* 119, 124, 127
video recorder videokassett-opptaker *c* 119
view *(panorama)* utsikt *c* 23, 25
viking ship vikingskip *nt* 127
village tettsted *nt* 76
vinegar eddik *c* 37
visit besøk *nt* 92; *(stay)* opphold *nt* 25
visiting hours besøkstid *c* 144
visit, to *(a person)* besøke 95; *(a place)* se 84
vitamin pill vitaminpille *c* 109
voltage strømstyrke *c* 119
vomit, to kaste opp 140

W

waffle vaffel *c* 55
waistcoat vest *c* 117
wait, to vente 108
wait for, to vente på 21, 95
waiter kelner *c* 26; servitør *c* 26
waiting room ventesal *c* 67
waitress serveringsdame *c* 26; servitør *c* 26
wake, to vekke 27, 71
Wales Wales 146
walk, to spasere 74, 85
wall mur *c* 85
wallet lommebok *c* 156
walnut valnøtt *c* 54
want, to *(wish)* ønske 13
warm varm 94
wash, to vaske 29

washbasin vask *c* 28
washcloth ansiktsklut *c* 111
washing powder vaskepulver *nt* 107
watch klokke *c* 121, 122
watchmaker's urmaker *c* 99, 121
watchstrap klokkerem *c* 122
water vann *nt* 23, 28, 32, 38, 75, 91
watercolors *(box of)* malerskrin *nt* 105
waterfall foss *c* 85
water flask feltflaske *c* 107
watermelon vannmelon *c* 54
waterproof vanntett 122
water-ski vannski *c* 91
way vei *c* 76, 77
we vi 162
weak svak 140
weather vær *nt* 94
weather forecast værutsikter *c/pl* 94
wedding ring giftering *c* 122
Wednesday onsdag *c* 150
week uke *c* 16, 20, 24, 80, 151
weekday hverdag *c* 151
weekend helg *c* 24; weekend *c* 20, 151
well bra 10
well brønn *c* 85
well-done *(meat)* godt stekt 49
west vest 77
what hva 11
wheel hjul *nt* 78
when når 11
where hvor 11
which hvilken 11
whipped cream pisket krem *c* 55
white hvit 113
Whit Monday 2. pinsedag *c* 152
who hvem 11
whole hel 49
why hvorfor 11
wick veke *c* 126
wide vid 118
wide-angle lens vidvinkelobjektiv *nt* 125
wife kone *c* 93
wig parykk *c* 111
wild duck villand *c* 50
wind vind *c* 94
window vindu *nt* 28, 36, 100, 112
window seat vindusplass *c* 65, 69
windscreen/shield frontrute *c* 76
windsurfer seilbrett *nt* 91
wine vin *c* 57, 60, 64

wine list vinkart *nt* 57
wine merchant's vinmonopol *nt* 99
winter vinter *c* 149
winter sports vintersport *c* 91
wiper *(car)* vindusvisker *c* 75
wish gratulasjon *c*/ønske *nt* 152
with med 15
withdraw, to *(from account)* ta ut 130
without uten 15
woman kvinne *c* 115, 156
woman's ... dame- 117
wood *(material)* tre *nt* 127
woodcock rugde *c* 50
woodgrouse tiur *c* 50
wool ull *c* 114
word ord *nt* 12, 15, 133
work arbeid *nt* 79
work, to *(function)* fungere 119; virke 28
working day arbeidsdag *c* 151
worse verre 14
wound sår *nt* 139
wrap up, to pakke inn 103
wrapping paper innpakningspapir *nt* 105
wrinkle-free krøllfri 114
wristwatch armbåndsur *nt* 122
write, to skrive 12, 101
writing pad skriveblokk *c* 105
writing paper skrivepapir *nt* 105
wrong feil 14, 135

X
X-ray, to røntgenfotografere 140

Y
year år *nt* 149
yellow gul 113
yes ja 10
yesterday i går 151
yet ennå 15, 16
yoghurt yoghurt *c* 38
you du 162
young ung 14, 149
your din, ditt *(pl* dine) 161
youth hostel vandrerhjem *nt* 22, 32

Z
zero null 147
zip(per) glidelås *c* 117
zoo dyrehage *c* 82
zoology zoologi *c* 83

Norsk register